THE ART PERFECTED

PORTRAITURE FROM THE CRONISE STUDIO

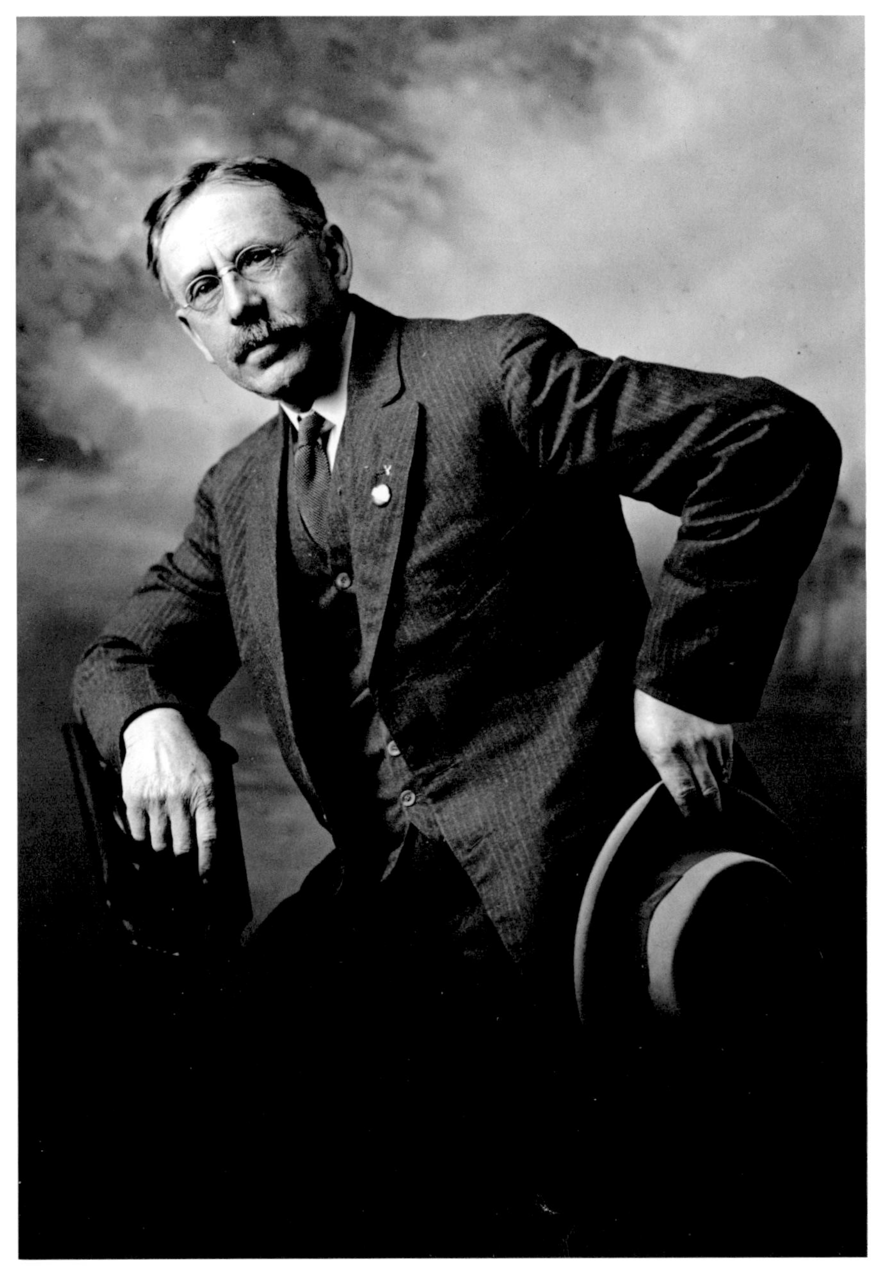

Thomas Jefferson Cronise

THE ART PERFECTED

PORTRAITURE FROM THE CRONISE STUDIO

INTRODUCTION BY

SUSAN K. SEYL

in association with

GEORGE CHAMPLIN

OREGON HISTORICAL SOCIETY

1980

Funding from the National Endowment for the Arts (NEA) supported the major portion of this project. Additional support was provided by the Weyerhaeuser Foundation, the S. S. Johnson Foundation and the Oregon Historical Society.

All photographs in this volume were printed from original glass plates by George Champlin.

Published in conjunction with a traveling exhibition which opened December 18, 1980, at the Oregon Historical Society.

Library of Congress Catalog Card Number: 80-83177

ISBN 0-87595-070-1

Printed in the United States of America

CONTENTS

PREFACE

The Cronise Photograph Collection was bequeathed to the Oregon Historical Society by Harry Wilmot Cronise, the final proprietor of the Cronise Studio, located in Salem, Oregon. The entire collection of glass and film negatives, prints, studio registers, photographic literature and equipment arrived at the Society in October, 1974. The 30,000 negatives were arranged in numbered glass plate boxes and packed in wooden crates. Some glass plates had been broken or damaged, but, aside from a few decades of dirt, most were in satisfactory condition. Regrettably, a sizeable portion of the early, dangerous nitrocellulose negatives were badly decomposed and had to be disposed of promptly.

The Cronise family of photographers (Tom, his wife, Nellie, and their son, Harry) was responsible for saving this collection of negatives, which spans nearly a century of portrait and scenic photography in Oregon's state capital. The studio's entire collection of negatives, dating back to 1880, was acquired by Tom Cronise when he purchased the business in 1902. The business's first owner, William P. Johnson, photographed the major events that took place in Salem, in addition to operating the portrait studio. His successor, Miss Myra "Sperry the Artist," ran a fashionable gallery which was patronized by many of Salem's prominent families during the Gay Nineties. Preston M. Hart and Martha F. McLennon also successfully operated the studio for a short time before Cronise bought the business. Cronise maintained the studio's reputation for fine work that had been established by his predecessors. The business remained in his family until 1972.

During the nineteenth and early twentieth centuries, it was common practice for a photographer's negatives to be passed on to a successor or new studio owner. However, relatively few of these negative collections have survived. Often the image-carrying emulsion was removed from the glass plates so the plates could be re-used. Some collections became glass windows in greenhouses, while others were simply disposed of for lack of storage space—victims of housecleaning.

Tom Cronise was aware of the importance of the old negatives. The studio's records indicate that he made prints from them upon request and for exhibitions. More importantly, he offered albums for sale, entitled "Early Days in Salem," which consisted entirely of prints made from the old plates. However, Harry Cronise (Tom Cronise's son) should receive the ultimate credit for saving these negatives, for during the nearly half century that he operated the business he kept them in a separate "Historic Negatives" file and occasionally made prints, for customers, exhibits, and newspapers. The fact that he also kept each photographer's studio registers is of paramount importance. These listings of patrons indicate, by negative number, the date each negative was made, the style of the prints that were ordered, the name of the person who purchased the photographs, and often their address. Helpful notes sometimes appear in the margin to indicate whether the subjects photographed were a family group, a school debating team, or members of the legislature.

To the staff of the Oregon Historical Society the historical significance of such an extensive photograph collection was evident, but the aesthetic value was not discovered until the collection was cataloged, cleaned and printed. Then the artistic achievements of the portraitists were revealed. They had captured the spirit of a thriving, ethnically diverse community in their images of its citizens: farmers, students, legislators, society matrons, craftsmen, mothers and their children.

The group of photographs shown in this volume represents the first five decades of the studio's existence, the years 1880-1927, the latter date the year of Tom Cronise's death. Although the collection contains a number of significant views of early Salem, the strength of the collection lies in its portraits—a powerful and unique visual account of a special time and place. The images appear chronologically and are, therefore, grouped by photographer. Annotation about each of the plates follows the photograph portfolio.

This album is intended to serve a number of functions: foremost among these is to reproduce selected examples from a photograph collection that is worthy of recognition for its aesthetic qualities; secondly, to make known the Cronise Collection's value to the expanding knowledge about a particular local and regional history; finally, to provide information about a previously obscure photographer, whose work's historical significance (as with many of his compatriots') has recently become apparent. Hopefully this volume will encourage others to seek similar collections, make them accessible in institutions with proven skills and commitments to insure their preservation.

ACKNOWLEDGMENTS

Many persons have been associated with the organization and presentation of the Cronise Collection and the production of this book. The success of this project is a direct result of their efforts.

Thanks must go to the staff of the Oregon Historical Society, under the direction of Thomas Vaughan, especially to E.A.P. Crownhart-Vaughan. George Champlin deserves special recognition for his discovery of special values in the collection, his technical expertise, and his unflagging enthusiasm for this project.

Staff members of the OHS Library contributed significantly: Louis Flannery, Chief Librarian; members of the Photograph Department, Paul Ewing, Janice Worden, and John Purcell; Elizabeth Winroth, Maps Librarian. Special appreciation is extended to Sandra Moore, Project Cataloger, who directed much of the organization of the collection.

Members of the OHS Volunteer Corps, under the able direction of Mrs. Leonard Shaver, Jr., provided invaluable service to the Society, many specifically to this project. While a great many volunteers worked with this collection a few gave especially outstanding service: Mrs. John Alberthal, Mrs. Ben Anderson, Mrs. Sidney Brewster, Mrs. William Clancy, Mrs. Doris Duval, Mrs. Chad Karr, Mrs. Adele Knerr, Mrs. Delbert Mannan, Mrs. Gwen Miller, and Mrs. James Morrison.

The staff of a CETA Special Project should be recognized for their efforts on this project: Samuel Bryant, Rebecca Farver, Cory Metcalf, Deborah Miller, and John Mouser.

Persons in Salem who assisted with the research of the Cronise Collection include Glen Hartwell and Betty Book, both of the Oregon State Library. Others in Salem who have shown a continuing generous interest in the collection and this project are Hugh Morrow, former Head Librarian, Salem Public Library and Executor of the Harry W. Cronise Estate, and David Duniway, former State Archivist.

Sincere thanks to Idamay Benjamin, granddaughter of Tom Cronise, and Minnie Aline, granddaughter of Martha F. McLennan, for their invaluable insight and assistance.

Bruce T. Hamilton edited the manuscript, offered suggestions, supervised the design and handled the production of the book. He was assisted with the production by Colleen R. Campbell. Contributions to the aesthetics of this publication were made by Messrs. Champlin, Hamilton and Vaughan.

Funding from the National Endowment for the Arts supported the major portion of this project.

INTRODUCTION

One hundred years ago the price of silver was $1.15 an ounce and a dozen photographs could be purchased for less than $2.00. Studio portraits were desired by all segments of a community, giving the professional photographer an endless variety of subjects on which to practice his art. The Cronise Collection reveals the art perfected; its images capture a people as they saw themselves, allowing us glimpses at life in another time.

The photographs are remarkable, not only for their style and technical excellence, but for their presence. There is an elusive quality that forces the viewer to examine the images more closely and to discover their strength. The best seem to penetrate the mantle of formalized studio sittings and allow entry, momentarily, into the inner being of the subject. The eyes are often the most direct route to the mind, but a smile, a wrinkle, a posture, or a tilt to the hat also speak a language we instinctively understand. Clothing is rendered in detail and commands nearly tactile examination of laces, velvets and silks, stiff collars, tweeds and straw hats. This sharpness and texture may partially explain the immediacy one feels when looking at these photographs. The subjects often posed with what was important to them, their family, their favorite object (such as a bicycle or a musical instrument), in their team uniform, or a special friend. Through these images we sense the true character of these persons, the town and the times.

A. D. Coleman, noted photograph critic and writer, has stressed the need to revise the history of photography. This involves not only a reassessment of the works of known photographers, but the examination of images produced by previously unknown photographers and in newly discovered collections. The recent acceptance of photography as an art form, and historical photographs as a primary resource, has facilitated this reevaluation. A visual revolution still in progress is nurturing the discovery of new masters and challenging previously established thought. A collection like the Cronise contributes to the revision process and furthers our knowledge of the art and craft as practiced by portraitists of another time.

The photographers represented in the Cronise Collection mastered the changes portrait photography had undergone since its beginnings, when it imitated the styles of portrait painting; evolving from rigidly posed subjects toward a more informal, although sometimes dramatic, style. Around the turn of the century they began to experiment with a variety of new posing styles and illumination techniques. A subject was sensitively portrayed in an effort to convey an attitude or personality instead of simply recording a likeness. However, while portraiture was pursuing an independent path, a correlation still existed between photography and the prevailing art influences of the day.

The images produced by Tom Cronise exemplify this artistic progression. His style was influenced by Carl Nordstrom, a young artist from Portland whom he hired as an assistant shortly after Cronise opened his studio. Nordstrom had been a photographer and a retoucher for various studios in Portland for at least three years before joining the Cronises. He possessed a great deal of knowledge about photographic techniques, especially the newly popular carbon process of printing with pigments and methods of hand coloring prints. During his short stay with the Cronises, Nordstrom instilled in them a sense of artistry and style that made their work distinctive. Nordstrom also taught Nellie the art of retouching negatives.

As an artist and a technician Tom Cronise excelled. His greatest gift was his ability to capture and hold the fleeting expressions that subtly flow across the faces in waves of whimsy, concentration, or even melancholy. His work exhibits stylistic progressions, particularly evident in the posing of groups, in firelight scenes, and the use of backgrounds and props. His friendly nature and outgoing personality allowed him to establish rapport with his subjects, enabling them to pose in a self-assured manner. A number of staged sittings and amusing poses reveal a visual sense of humor as well as a dramatic flair. His sensitive portrayal of women was noteworthy as was his ability to capture the spontaneity of expression in children in an age of slow exposures.

Technically he kept his formula for success simple: natural light, modulated and controlled by reflectors and diffusers; generally plain backgrounds, with the occasional painted drape or window; a basic studio camera, which produced 5″×7″ negatives—all glass until 1918. These same basic elements were the tools used by nearly every portrait photographer of the time, and their purity has inspired many recent photographers to their best work.

During his 25-year career Cronise produced thousands of images of persons and places. His success was determined by his talent, his determination to excel, his enterprising nature and his position as an integral member of the community. But the key to his success lies with one crucial element—he knew many of his subjects well enough to pose them to advantage. His resultant insight allowed him to create the compelling, intimate characterizations so essential to fine portraiture. Because of this, his work merits recognition as that of a superb photographic craftsman.

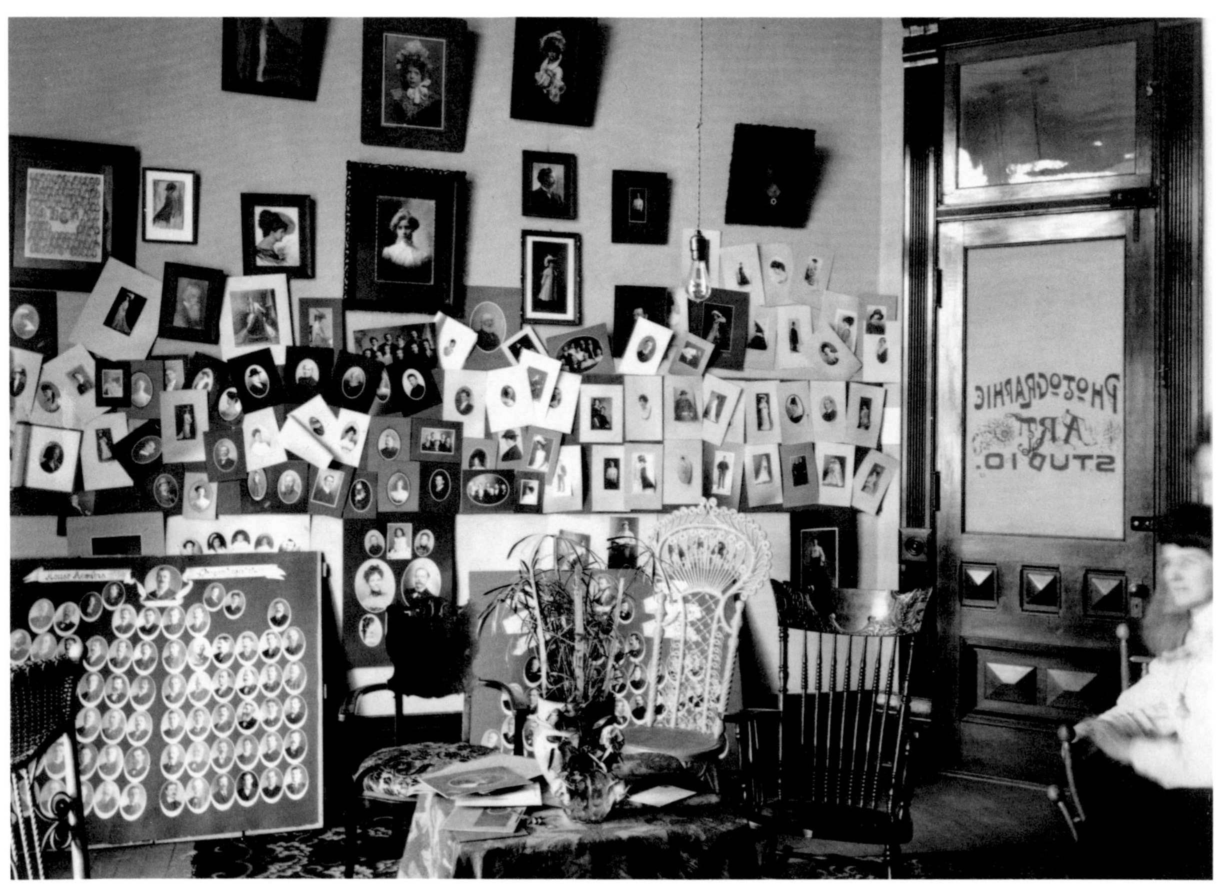

Interior view of Tom Cronise's Photographic Art Studio in the Bush-Brey Building, about 1910. Nellie Cronise can be seen seated at the far right.

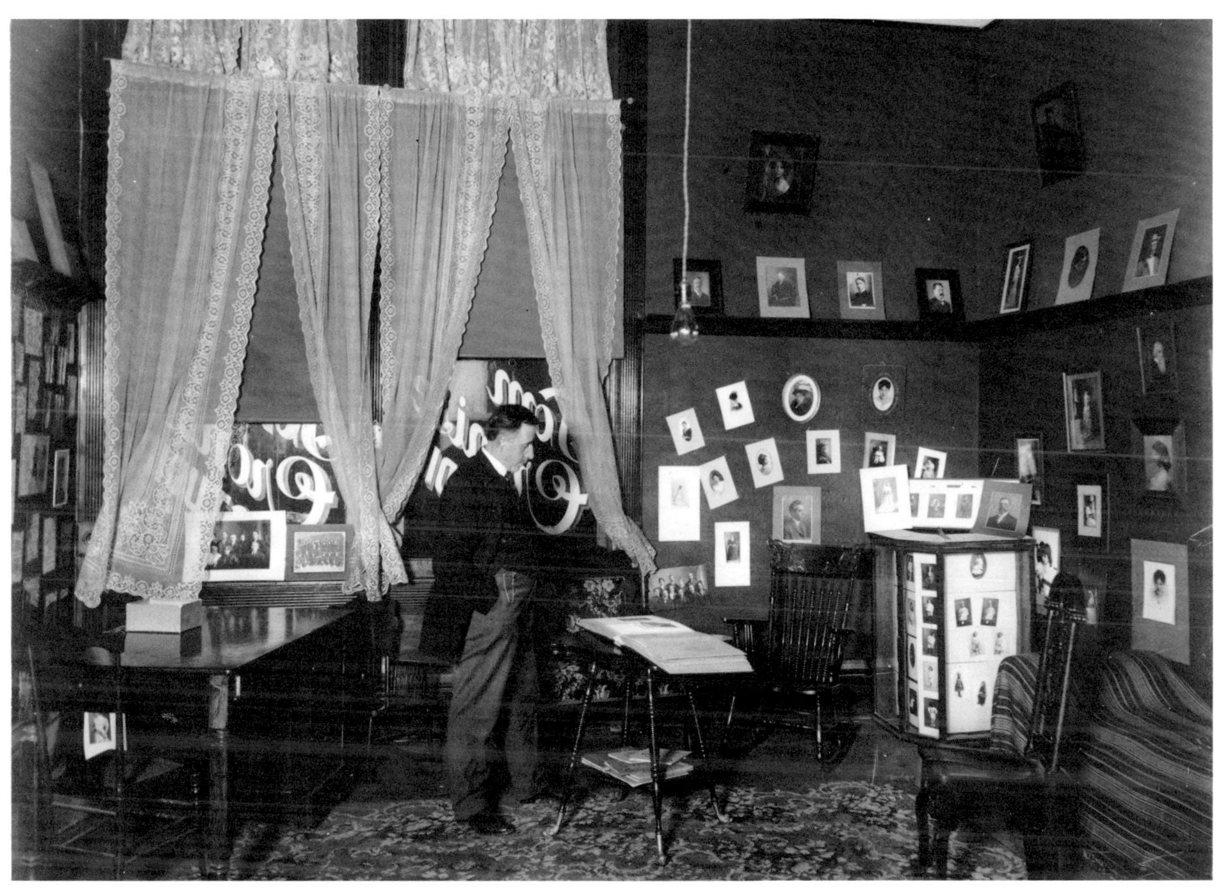

Tom Cronise proudly admires one of his photograph albums in the studio's reception salon, about 1910.

THE STUDIO AND THE PHOTOGRAPHERS

Thomas Jefferson Cronise was born on October 11, 1853, in Peru, Illinois, one of four children of Henry and Louise Hosmer Cronise. The family later moved to Tiffin, Ohio, where Henry Cronise was a successful merchant with Tom's grandfather, also named Henry. His mother was the daughter of Henry Hosmer; the Hosmers were a prominent Connecticut family.

While the children were still young, Tom Cronise's father left for California and his mother moved the family to Seville, Ohio, where she worked as a newspaper woman. When Tom was 14 his formal education ended and he was sent to nearby Wadsworth, Ohio, to serve an apprenticeship under an experienced printer and newspaper owner, John Clark. After learning the printer's trade, Cronise returned to Seville to work with his mother, who had become the editor of the *Seville Times*. He also worked for an undetermined time as a printer in York, Ohio.

In 1875, his older brother, Harry H. Cronise, had come to Oregon. Harry's enthusiasm for the West influenced Tom to make the same journey. In 1880 the latter moved to Spokane, Washington—he was 27 years old. Two years later he came to Oregon, settling in Salem.

One of the earliest settlements in the state, Salem was just beginning to flourish during the 1880s. Attractive homes were constructed, but the quiet, rural appearance remained. The new state house was a particular source of pride. The town's population of 4,100 in 1880 grew to nearly 15,000 by 1893, yet a strong sense of community prevailed. By the turn of the century Salem was experiencing its most rapid period of growth. It was a city proud of its handsome residences, wide tree-lined streets and substantial business district. The state's major institutions, including the capitol, were located here, as were some of the finest educational facilities in Oregon. Its proximity to rail and river transportation, its prosperous business climate and its cultural offerings made it a regional center of activity for the mid-Willamette Valley.

These factors, no doubt, attracted Tom Cronise to Salem, and influenced his decision to remain there, pursue a career, and raise a family. After his arrival in 1882, he first worked for Mrs. A. L. Stinson, the owner of an established printing business on Commercial Street, and later for R. J. Hendricks, of the *Oregon Statesman*; he eventually became foreman of the newspaper's technical department.

In August, 1884, Cronise married Nellie Riggs, the daughter of Rufus and Evelyn Nicklin Riggs, both Oregon pioneers. Nellie worked as a milliner in Charles Calvert's shop, another Commercial Street business. By 1891 the couple had purchased a house at the corner of Front and Academy; there they remained until 1921 when they moved to an apartment behind their studio.

By 1886 Cronise was operating his own print shop in the State Insurance Building on Commercial Street and was a respected member of the business community. He was recognized as one of the most artistic printers in the state, and his advertisements in the city directory proclaimed his superior workmanship. From 1891 to 1893 he was in partnership with Gaylord W. Cooke in a commercial printing firm. However, an allergy to printer's ink eventually forced Cronise to quit the business and pursue a different trade. This malady proved to have a positive effect on his life, because, through his sister, it led him into the field of photography.

Around 1892, Cronise's sister, Anna Louise, moved from Ohio to Salem to be with her brother. She was introduced to the photography business, receiving her training in a well-known Salem photography studio founded by W. H. Catterlin and continued by Francis J. "Jud" Catterlin. Less than a year later Anna purchased this studio, located at the corner of State and High streets. At this point, Tom developed an interest in the profession, often assisting Anna in her studio. In 1893 he advertised himself as both a printer and a photographer; the *Salem City Directory* for that year lists Anna's studio as "CRONISE & CRONISE, The Photographers."

ARISTO

CRONISE & CRONISE, The Photographers

ARISTO means the Latest known Process in Photography.

With the Largest and Best Instruments and Scenery in the State, we are enabled to give entire Satisfaction to all our Customers.

SPECIAL ATTENTION GIVEN TO LARGE WORK. BRING YOUR BABIES.

PRICES ALWAYS REASONABLE.

160 State Street, - SALEM, OREGON.

In 1893 the Cronises hired a young photographer, Howard D. Trover, to work in the studio, replacing a Miss Cravens who had worked with Anna for a short time. Howard and Anna were married in December of that same year. After 1893 Cronise was not officially associated with Anna's studio. However, during the next few years he apparently spent a good deal of time working with the Trovers, learning photography while Nellie operated a dress-cutting school, first on Commercial Street and later at their home.

In May of 1902, Cronise bought Hart & McLennon's "Elite Studio," having finally decided to enter the profession on his own. The studio was located in the Bush-Brey Building at Commercial and Court and was named the Tom Cronise Photo Studio. Anna and Howard's Cronise Photo Studio, located in the Eldridge Building at Commercial and Chemeketa, was renamed the Trover-Cronise Photo Studio after 1907 to avoid confusion. The two studios existed as friendly competitors for over 40 years.

The studio purchased by Tom Cronise had been in existence for 25 years and had always been one of the major photographic galleries in Salem. William P. Johnson founded the studio around 1877 (Johnson apparently had been active in Salem as early as 1873, when he photographed the laying of the cornerstone for the new Capitol). The initial location of the Johnson studio is uncertain; no address is given for Johnson in any Salem directory until 1880. However, the entry in the *Salem City Directory* for that year describes Mr. Johnson's new studio on Commercial between State and Court Streets:

> We call especial attention to this gallery, now being fitted up in splendid style on Commercial Street, opposite the Statesman Office. Mr. Johnson's gallery was recently

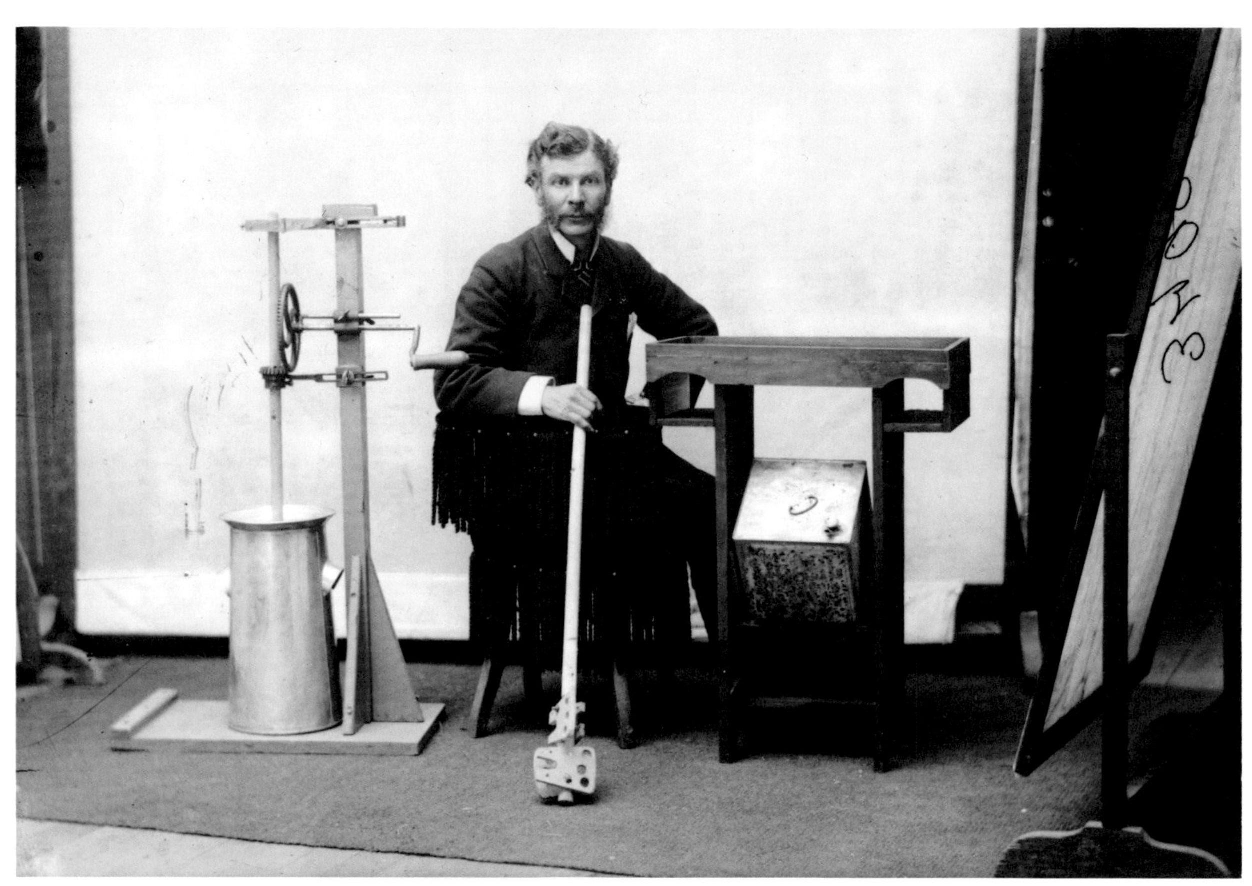

Frank Smith, inventive state mute school employee, with his butter churn. Number on reflecting screen matches one in a studio register. Photographed by William Johnson, April 15, 1887.

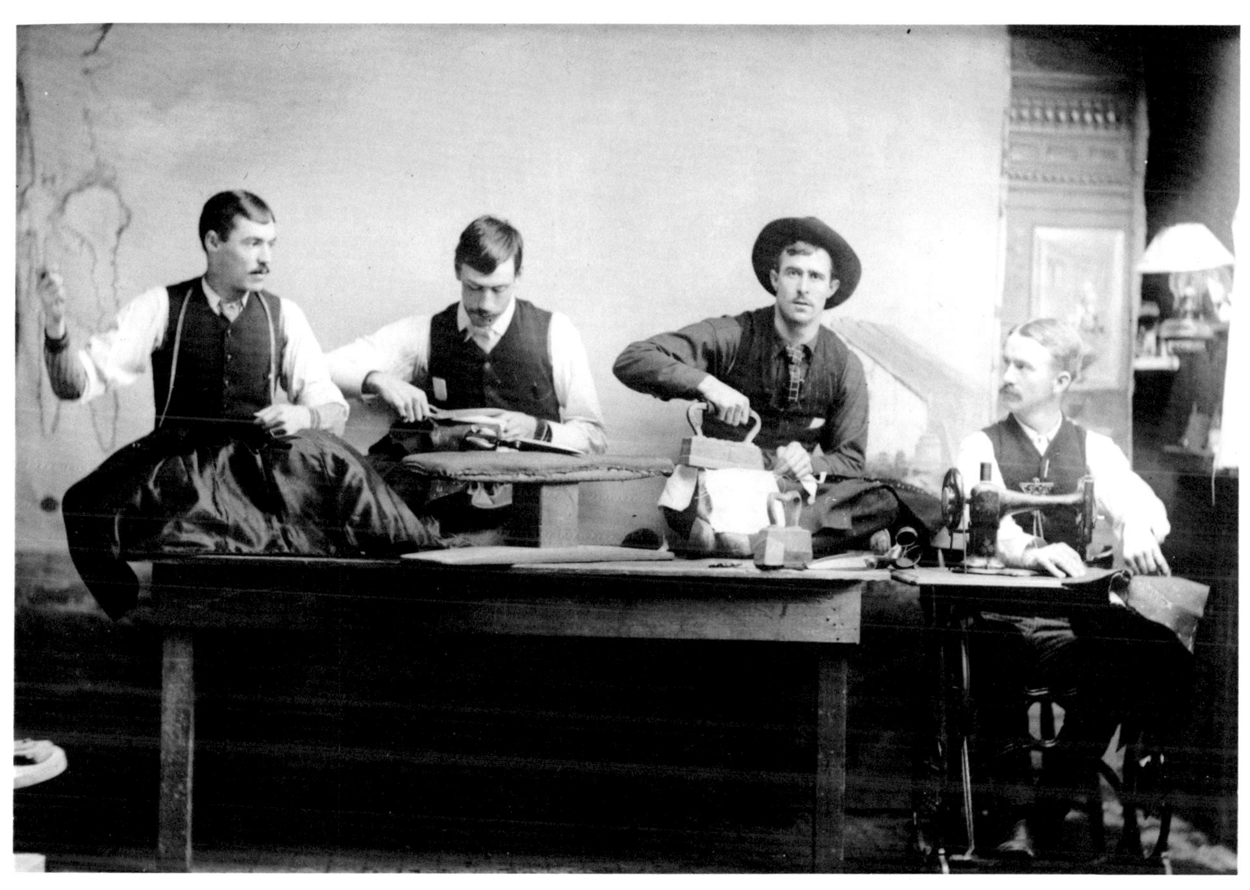

Workers in Williams and Hibb's tailor shop, McMinnville, Oregon, demonstrate their skills for William P. Johnson's camera, December, 1887.

George Anderson, a drayman from Salem, was photographed with his dog by William P. Johnson on October 2, 1885.

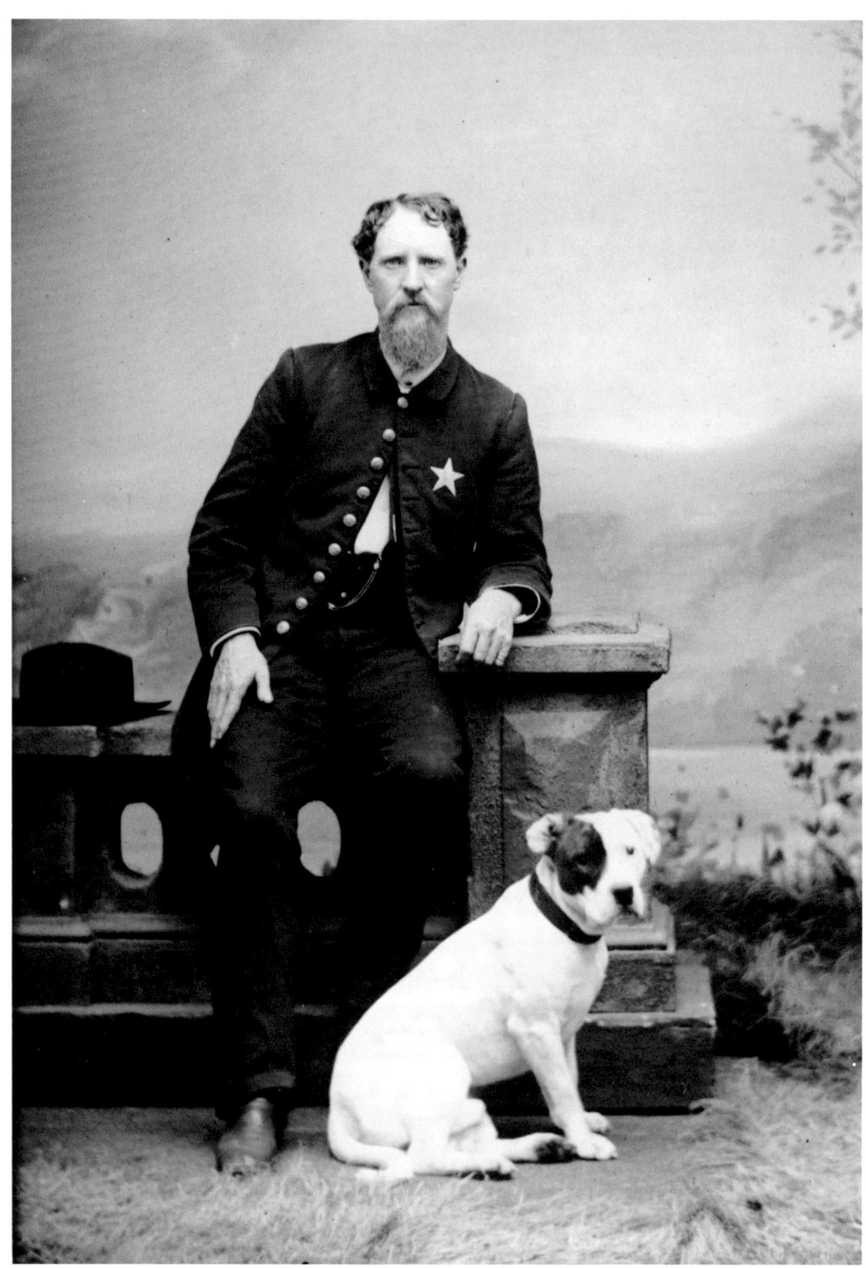

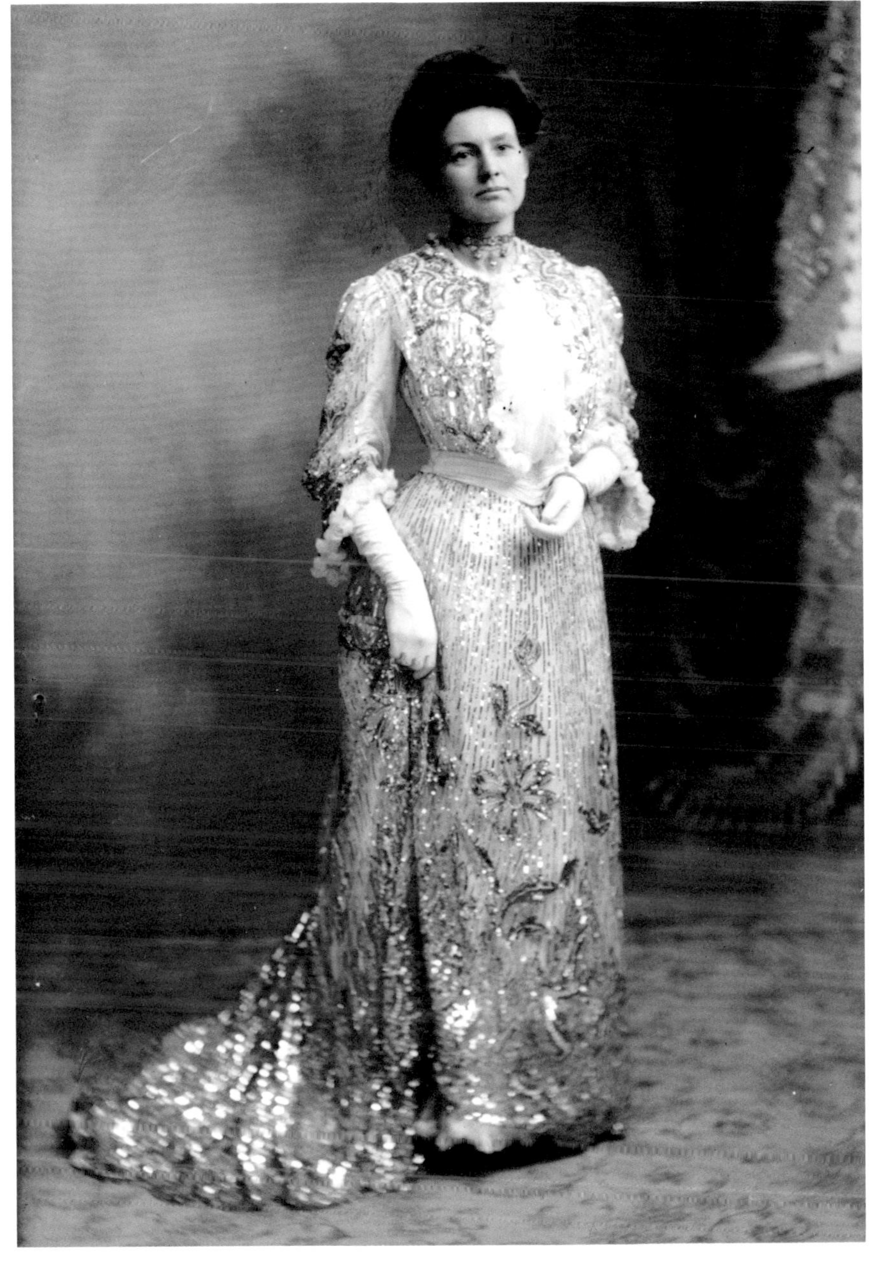

In 1886 William P. Johnson captured the play of light on this woman's gown.

burned out, and all his apparatus and stock became a total loss. Consequently his new gallery will contain an entirely new outfit, embracing the newest and most improved instruments, and as Mr. Johnson has just returned from a tour of inspection, and improvement is his art, we may expect the very finest styles of pictures, and all the novelties in his line.

Although Johnson had done much portrait work, he spent a considerable amount of time outside the studio photographing specific occasions, buildings and street scenes in and around Salem. His images record such events as the Stallion Show, Independence Day parade, Cherry Fair, and the annual Fireman's Tournament. Views of local residences, schools and public buildings were common subjects. Of particular note is his panorama of Salem, in sectional views, taken in 1885.

Miss Myra E. Sperry bought the studio from Johnson in September, 1888, after working with him to learn photography. Soon after acquiring the gallery she moved it to the Bush-Brey Building at Commercial and Court, where it remained throughout its existence. The studio was located at 277 Commercial Street, which became 197 North Commercial Street in 1907 when the street numbers were changed to their present form. Known as "Sperry the Artist," she had a fine reputation for style and creativity in the way she posed subjects. Her portraits include those of important business and political figures as well as individuals and family groups. Her work was not limited to formal studio portraiture, however, as her camera recorded weddings, club gatherings, picnics, farms scenes, municipal improvements and holiday celebrations.

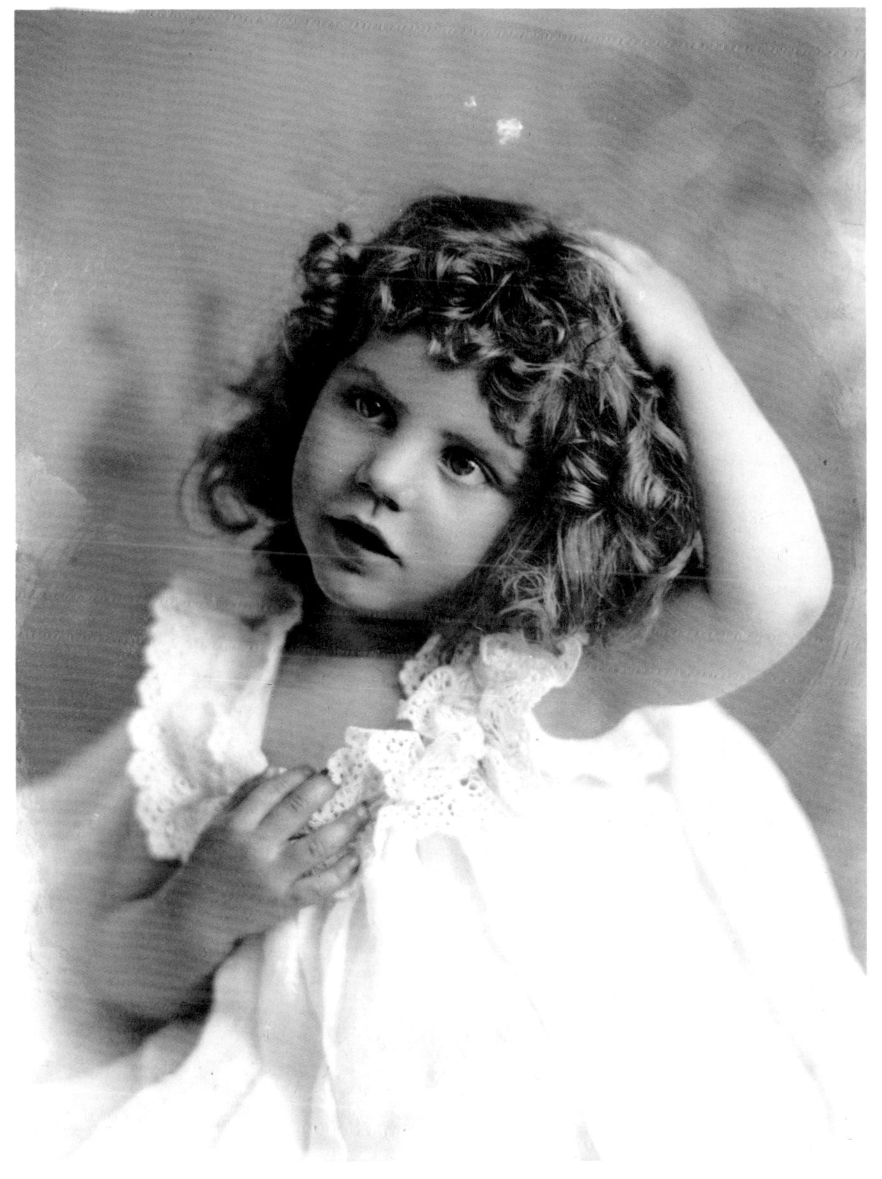

The young daughter of Mrs. Buchart poses playfully for Miss Myra E. Sperry. Photograph was taken in 1894.

With a name befitting his apparent character, Bill Bridle and his dog posed for Miss Sperry in July, 1890.

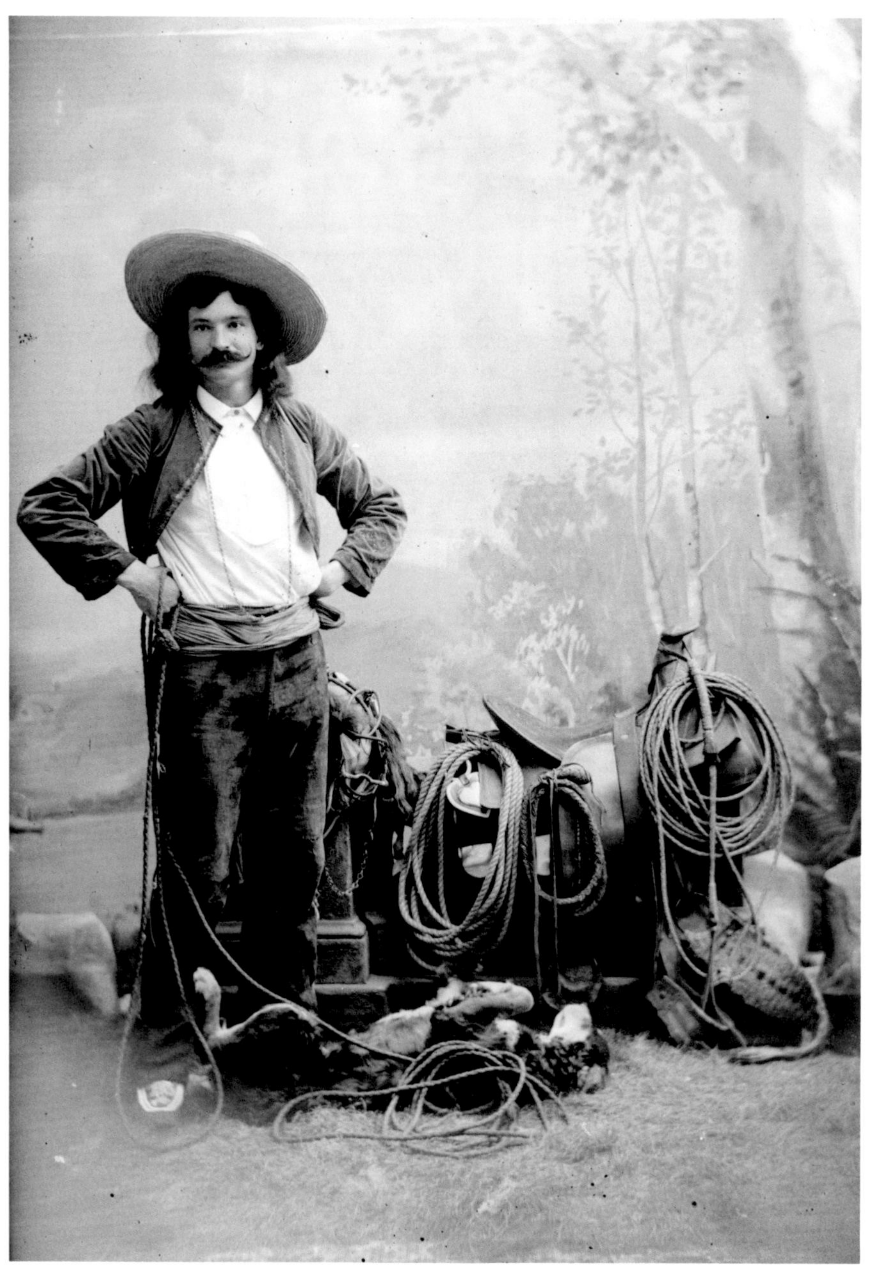

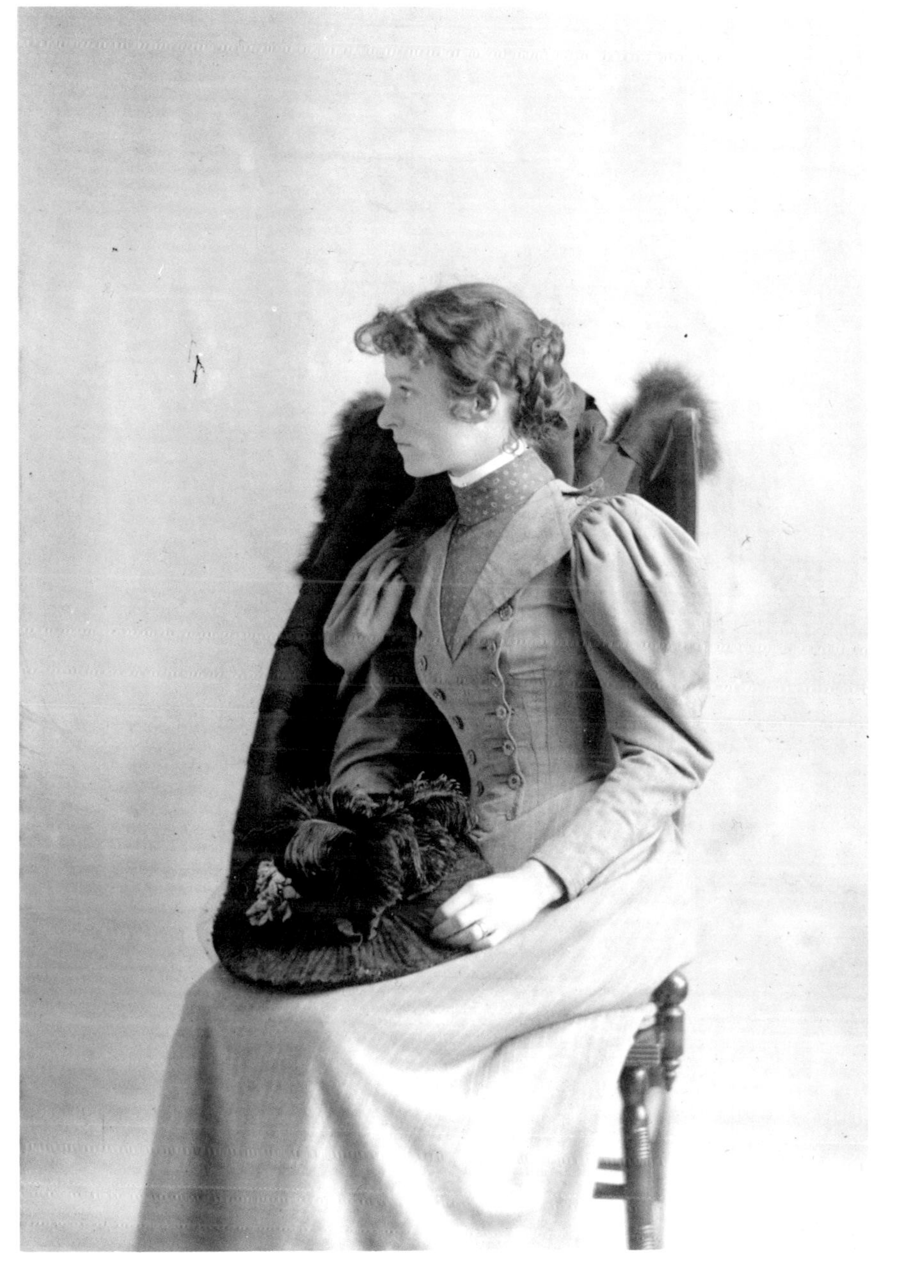

Edith Farrar, with feathers and fur, photographed by "Sperry the Artist" in 1894.

The shy son of a clerk, Charles G. Boothby, of Salem, peers at the camera of Myra E. Sperry, August 12, 1892.

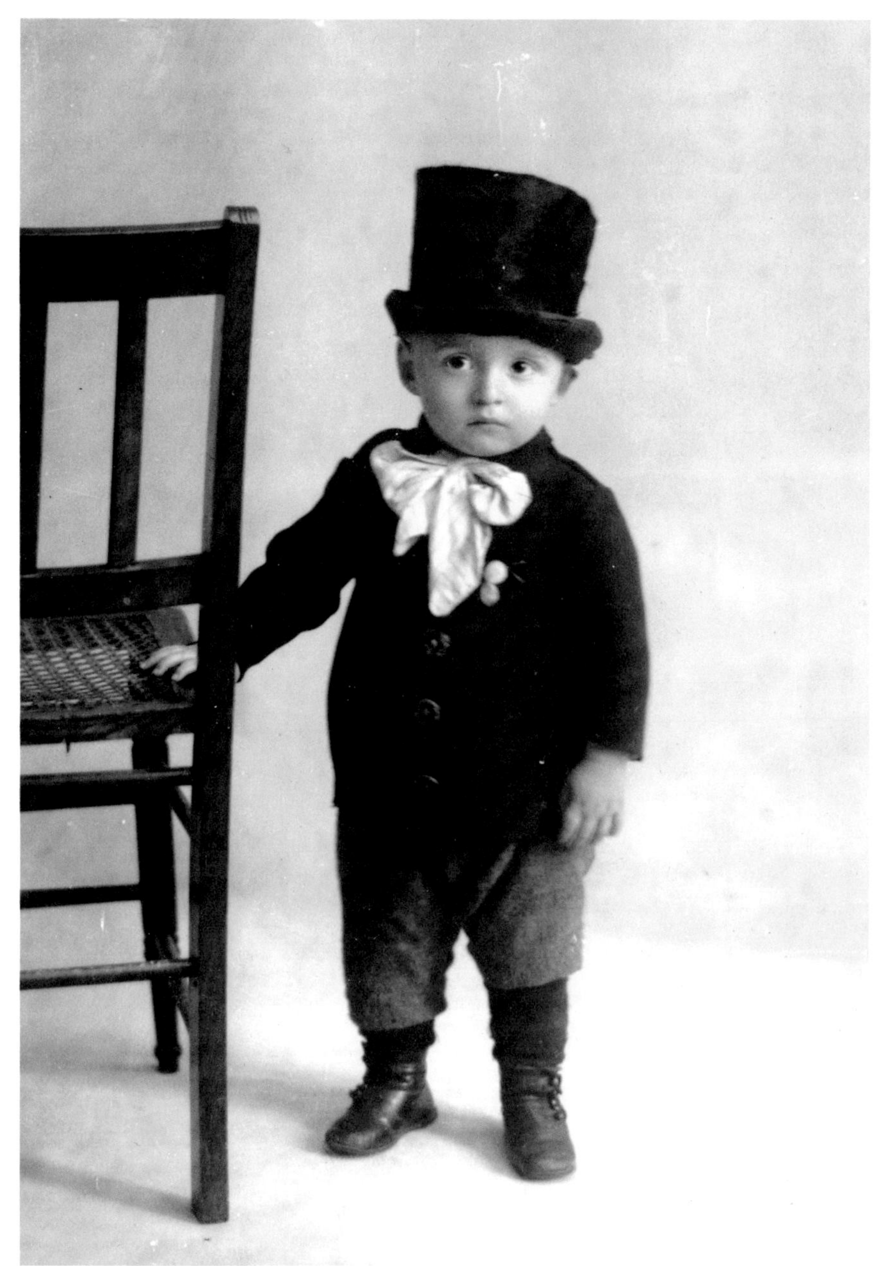

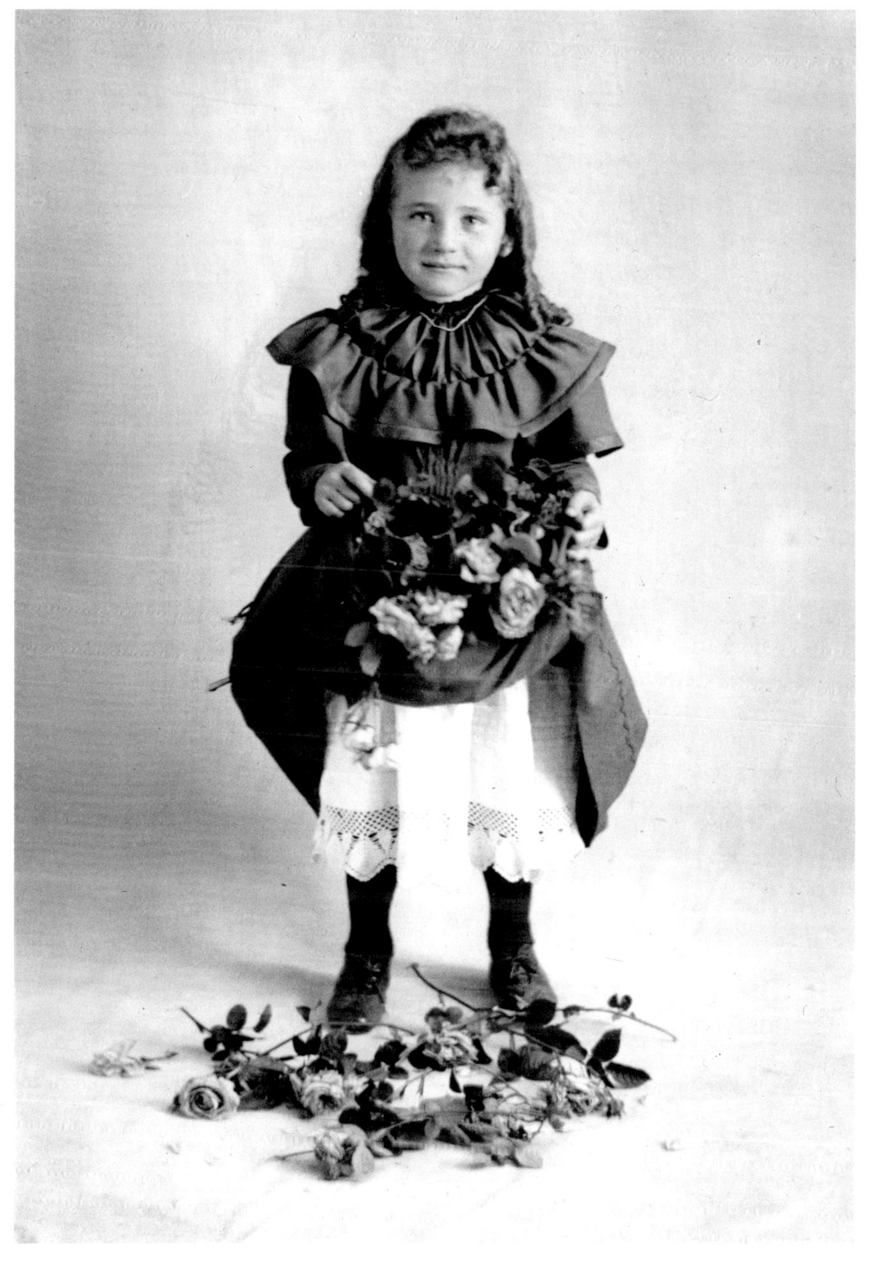

Minnie Feichtinger, daughter of Matthew, a peddler in Salem, poses coyly with a cascading bouquet of roses. Photographed in 1894 by Miss Sperry.

An unidentified Chinese man was photographed holding book and fan by Sperry the Artist in 1891, with typical accessories of the Victorian era.

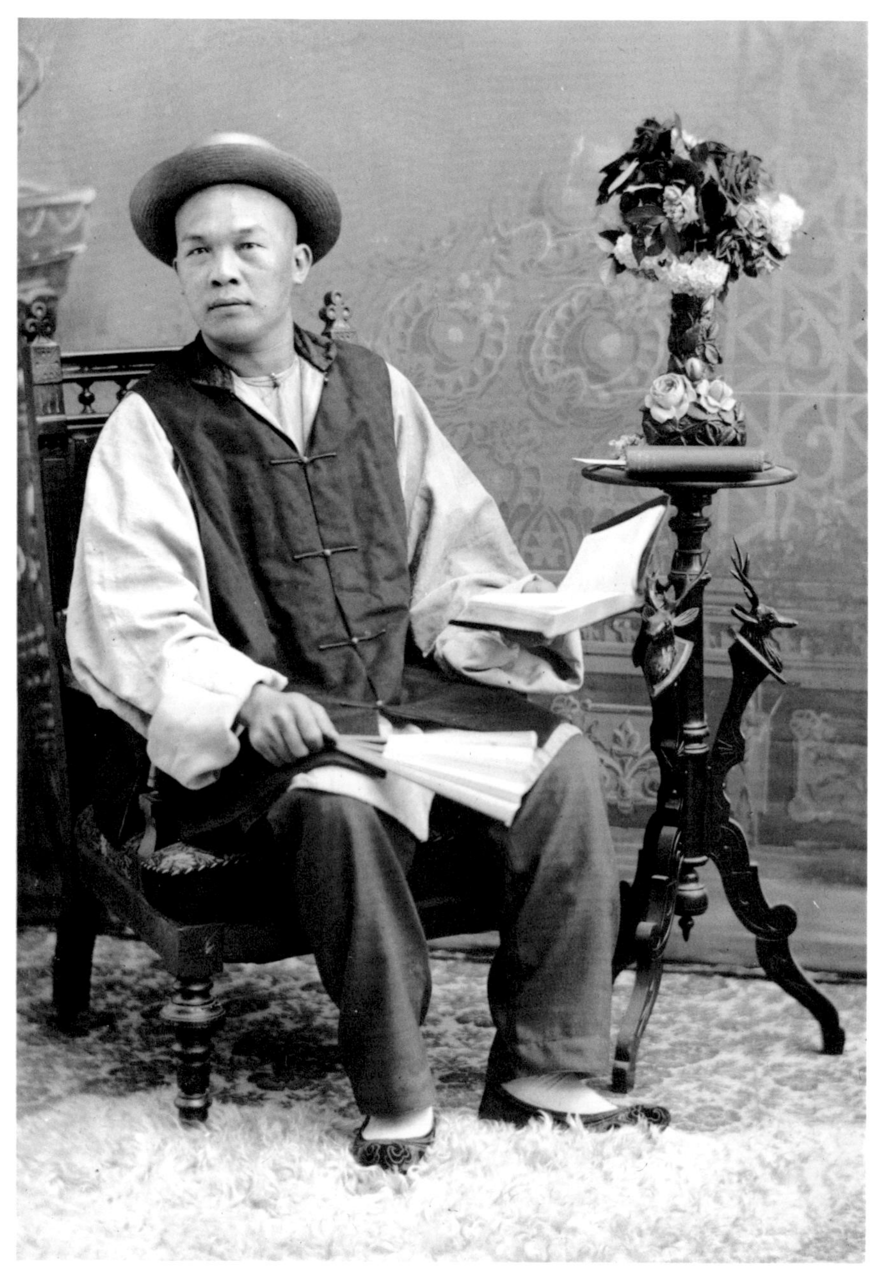

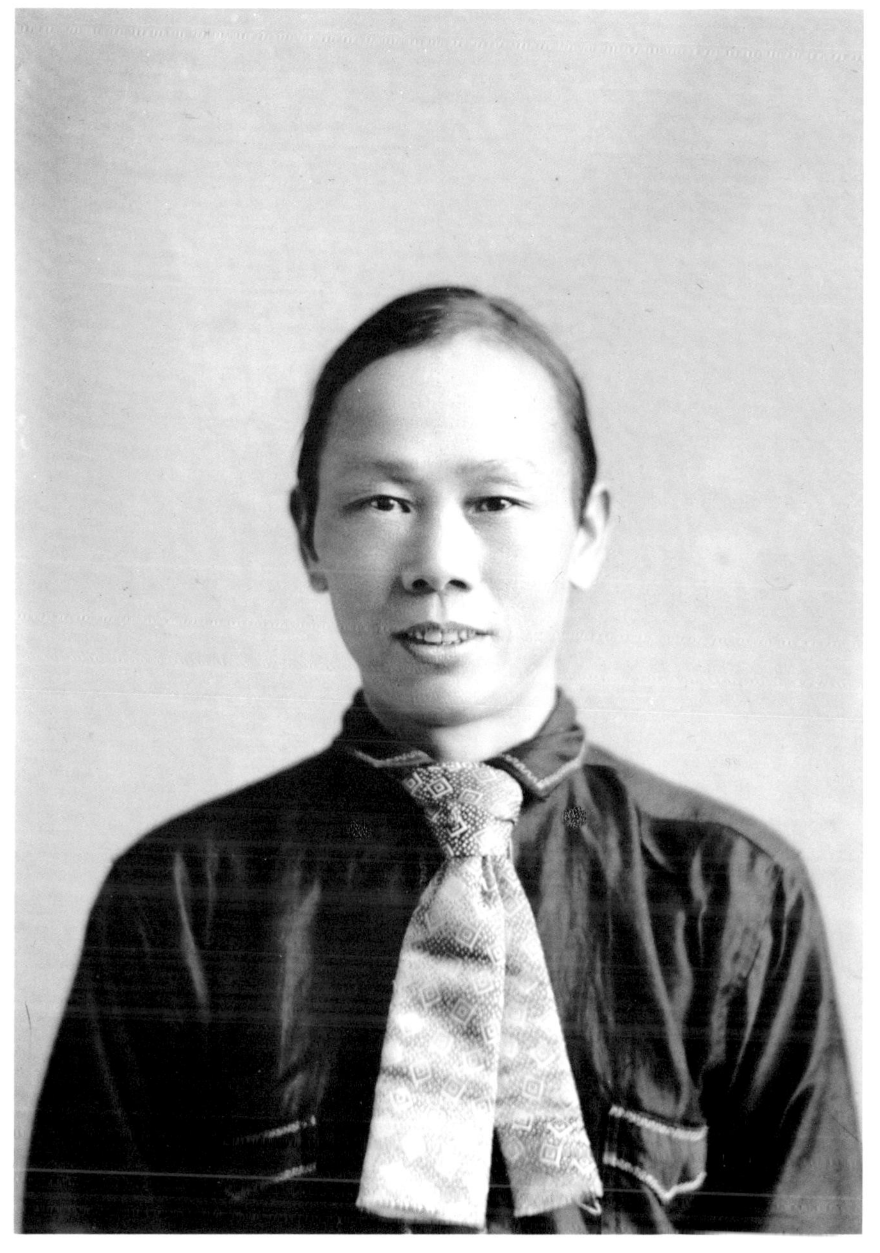

Mr. Sing wears a silk shirt and tie for this 1893 portrait by Miss Sperry.

In 1899 Miss Sperry sold the studio to Preston M. Hart and Martha F. McLennon who named it the "Elite Studio." Portraiture was their mainstay, although a few views of events and places are to be found in their negative files. Cronise later used a number of portraits done by Hart and McLennon in 1901 and 1902 in his album series "Early Days in Salem."

Salem's prosperous business climate and community spirit certainly contributed to the success of many commercial establishments located there, including photograph galleries. The studio registers of the different photographers represented in the Cronise Collection indicate that many patrons came from Salem's environs. While persons from other parts of Oregon, the state of Washington, and even San Francisco are often listed, the majority of patrons were residents of Salem. The growing population, the abundance of schools, and the presence of persons and events associated with state government, provided Salem with a wealth of subjects to be photographed. In this vigorous community Cronise used his extensive business and social contacts and outgoing personality to create a successful enterprise. His fine artistry and reputation for quality work and fairness won for him a large following, which led to his recognition as one of Salem's finest photographers.

The Tom Cronise Photo Studio, located on the second floor of the Bush-Brey Building, was reached by stairway from the street. As was typical of the time, display cases or windows were provided at the street level for advertising business establishments on the upper floors of the building. In his glass case Cronise was fond of displaying carefully arranged photographs depicting the latest styles of portraiture. The reception salon of the studio was also haphazardly decorated with photographs, including portraits of prominent persons and particular favorites of the photographer

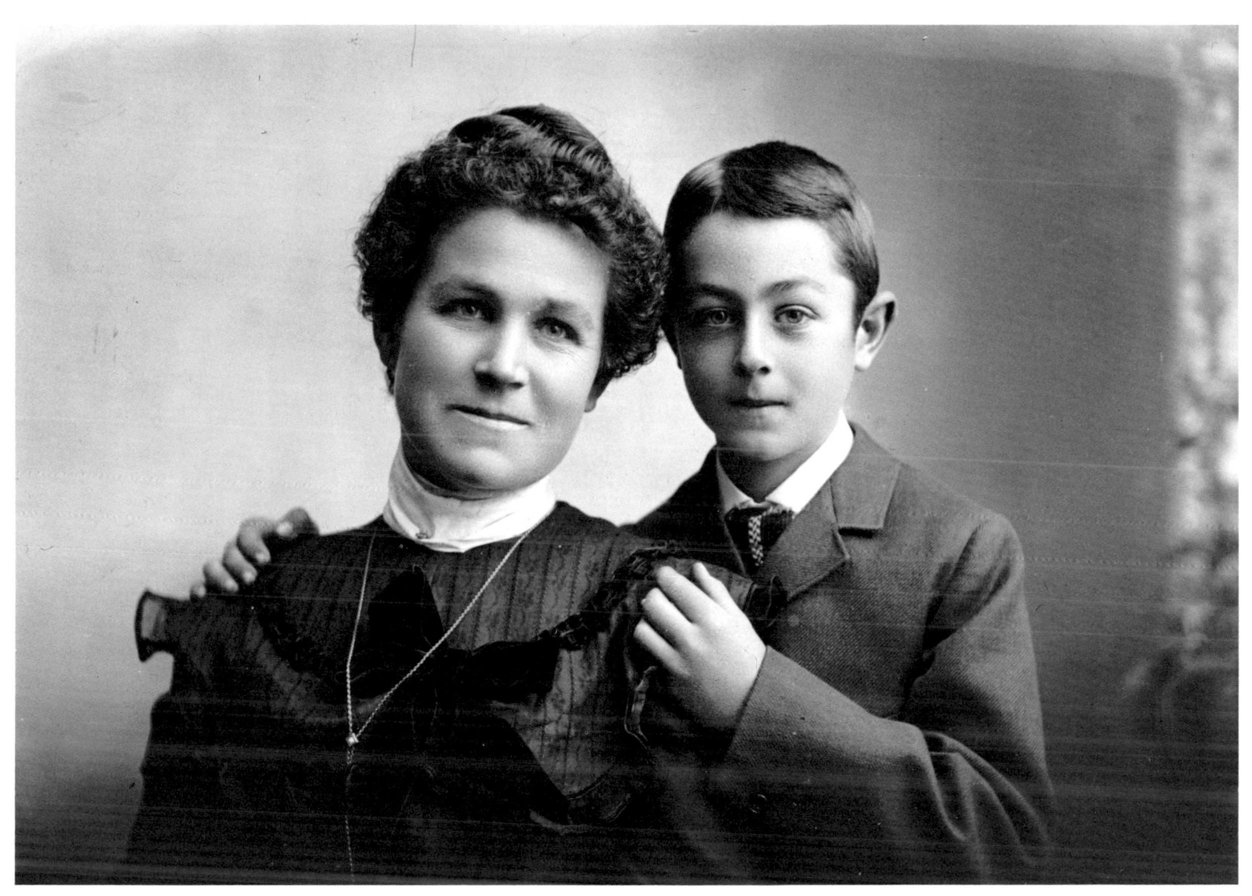

Subtle smiles emanate from the faces of Mrs. Bernardi and her son in this portrait taken by Preston M. Hart and Martha F. McLennan, about 1901.

Miss Alice Hastings of Salem, an attendant at the Oregon State Insane Asylum and later a waitress, is sensitively portrayed by Hart and McLennan, about 1900.

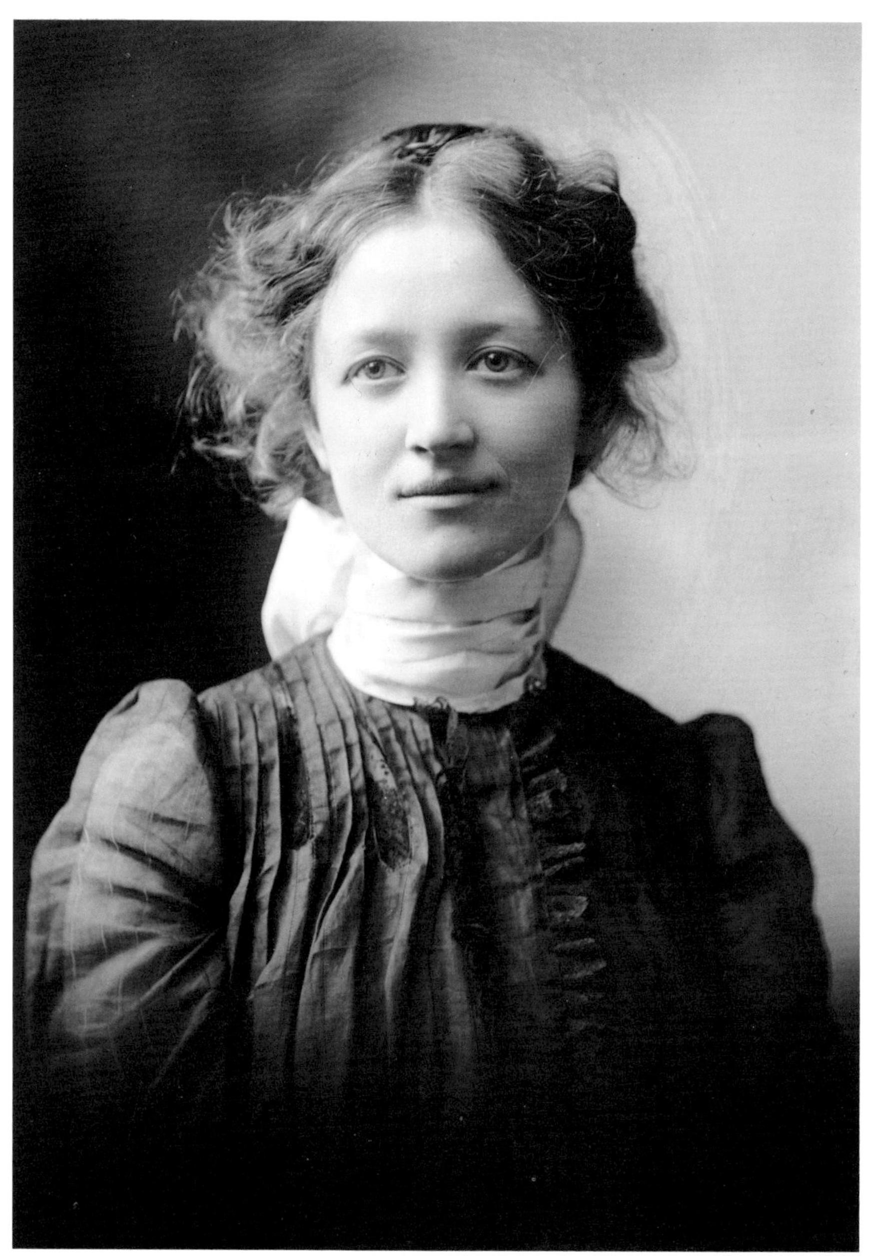

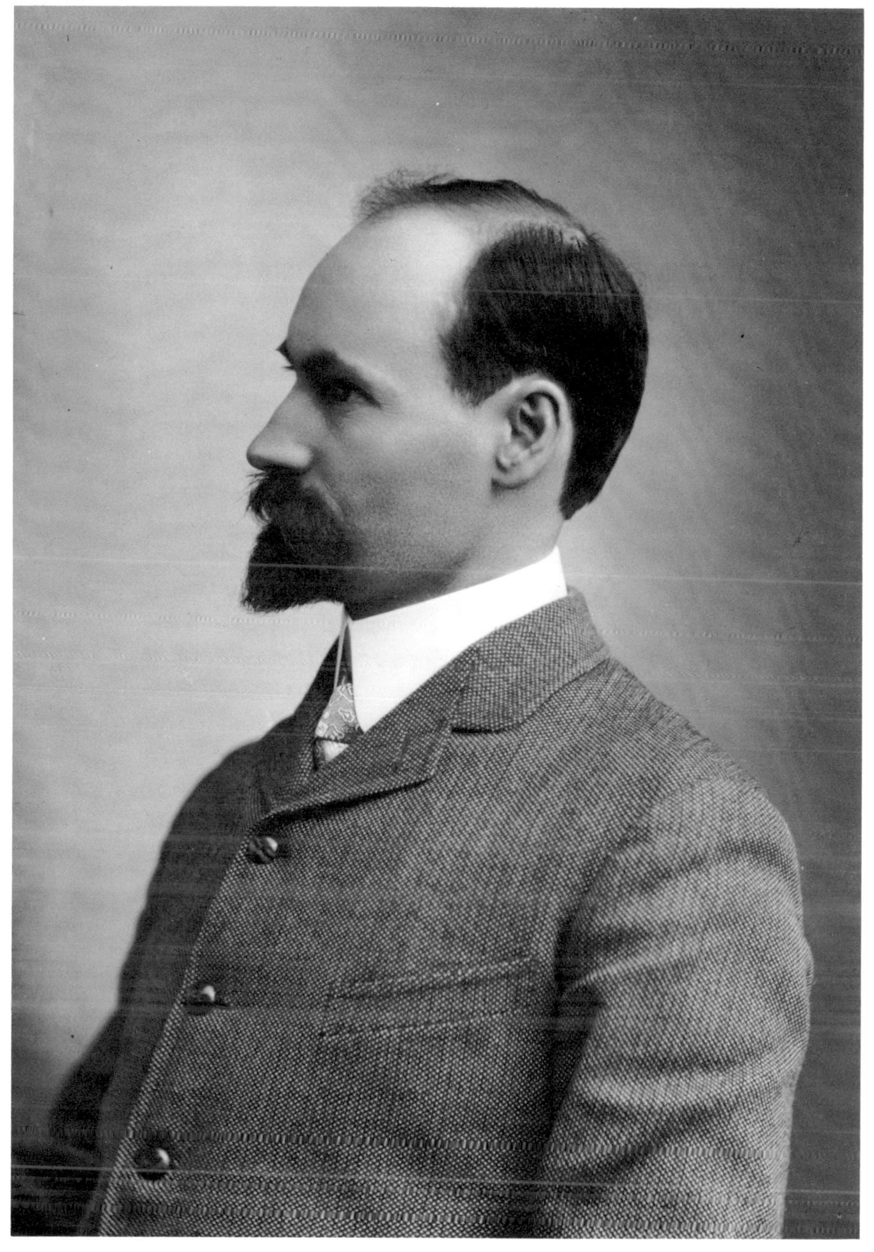

The interplay of angles is striking in this formal portrait of Charles H. Cusick taken by Hart and McLennan in 1901. "Doctor" Cusick was a druggist and agent for Wells, Fargo & Co. Express in Jefferson, Oregon.

In the rear of the studio was the camera room where the usual array of photographic equipment, backdrops and props was located. A skylight allowed diffused north light to enter the camera room providing the soft, natural illumination so essential to fine portraiture.

The darkroom was not unlike a chemist's lab because of the tremendous number of chemicals, solutions and compounds required by turn-of-the-century photography. Cronise kept notebooks full of formulas for processing negatives and prints, correcting problems and creating desired effects. Some of these formulas he received through correspondence with fellow members of the Photographers Association of the Pacific Northwest, but most were clipped from articles found in the many photography journals he received including *Photographic Digest*, *Portrait*, and *Studio Light*.

Cronise used an 11″ × 14″ studio portrait camera made by the E. & H. T. Anthony Company of New York, the oldest manufacturer of photographic equipment in the United States. (The company is now part of the GAF Corp.) The camera, made of mahogany with brass fittings, sat on a table specifically designed for raising and lowering the outfit. A variety of plate sizes were used, both horizontally and vertically, and a number of removable masks on the camera back allowed a wide range of image sizes to be produced. The lens, a fourteen-inch Goertz, had an iris diaphragm and a Packard air-operated mechanical shutter. A velvet curtain on an expandable gate could be attached to the front of the camera to act as a shield against glare. A brass birdie, affixed to the top of the camera, moved its beak and tail when an air bulb was squeezed. The birdie was supplemented by a "Jocko" hand puppet for holding the attention of children. Both gimmicks elicited amused expressions from subjects of all ages.

By 1902 dry plates were the standard negative format; although they were a great improvement over wet plates, the process involved was primitive by today's standards. Printing-out papers such as "Solio" and "Aristo" were used to make proofs from which the customer selected the desired image. Cronise made his proofs on the roof of the building where ample light was available to activate the printing-out paper. After World War I, flexible film sheets were readily available and Cronise, along with most other professional photographers, made the transition from glass to film negatives. At this time he began using artificial lighting in the studio by employing rather primitive flood lights made from tin can reflectors.

The studio was frequented by patrons, friends and family. Tom and Nellie's granddaughter, Idamay Benjamin, recalls spending a great deal of time there. She describes her grandfather as "kind and mild-mannered with twinkling blue eyes and a wonderful sense of humor." She remembers him as being well-read and particularly interested in political events, though he had little formal education. Cronise was most sociable and loved to visit with customers at the studio, people he met on the street and members of his lodge. He was a member of the Elks and the Knights of Pythias. His friendly and industrious nature was closely akin to the personality of the town and this, no doubt, contributed to his success.

Throughout their marriage Tom and Nellie supported each other in their pursuits and enjoyed a close and lasting relationship. They were family-oriented, as evidenced by numerous pictures of relatives, clan gatherings and the children. The oldest son, Ralph, married Greta Fortmiller and worked as a newspaperman, eventually becoming editor and publisher of the *Albany Democrat-Herald*. Their daughter, Louise, taught dance in Salem and was later a telephone operator in Rockaway. She was married to attorney James Benjamin and had three children: Idamay, Marie and Joe. Harry, the youngest child, studied architecture but did not practice; his mother needed his help to operate the studio after Tom's death. Harry assumed sole ownership of the business upon her passing in 1930.

These observations are an indication of the kind of man Tom Cronise was, but perhaps his character is best described in his obituary from the April 24, 1927 *Oregon Statesman:*

> "Tommy" Cronise, as he was known to his familiars . . . was always interested in all community activities. He was a companionable man, generous, sympathetic and honest. He was a sterling citizen and a good neighbor, and a faithful and loving husband and father. He filled a place from which he will be missed.

The Cronise Collection captures the spirit of a town, a time and a people. Through its images we truly see the art perfected.

THE ART PERFECTED

PLATE 1

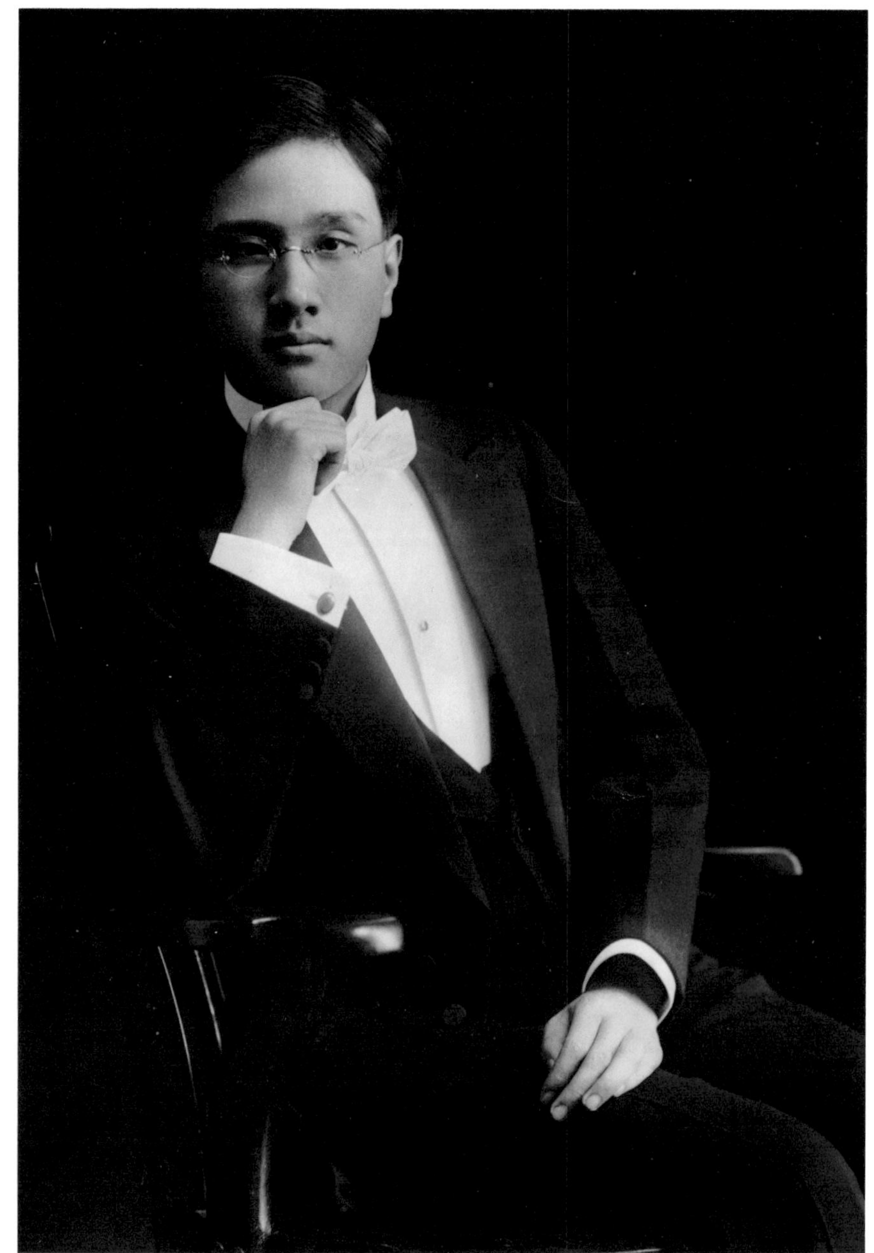

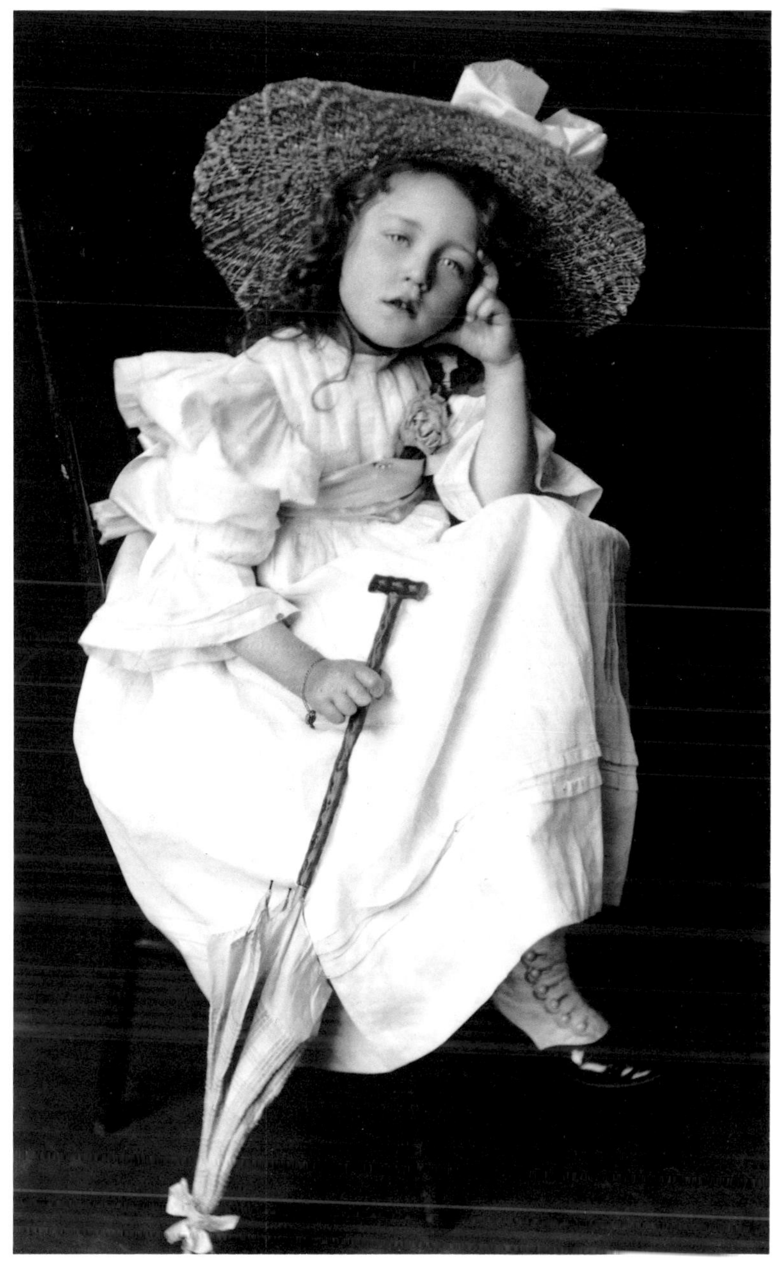

PLATE 3

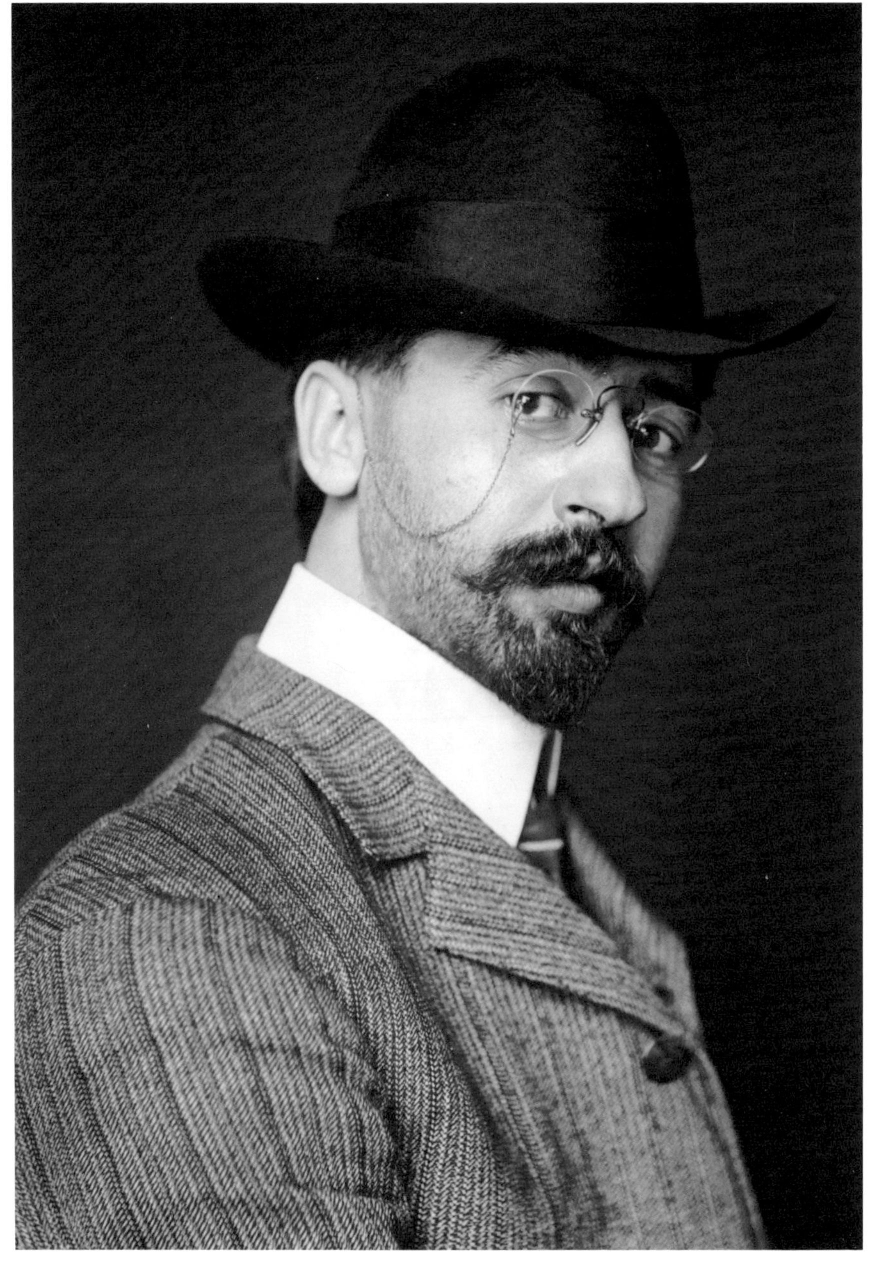

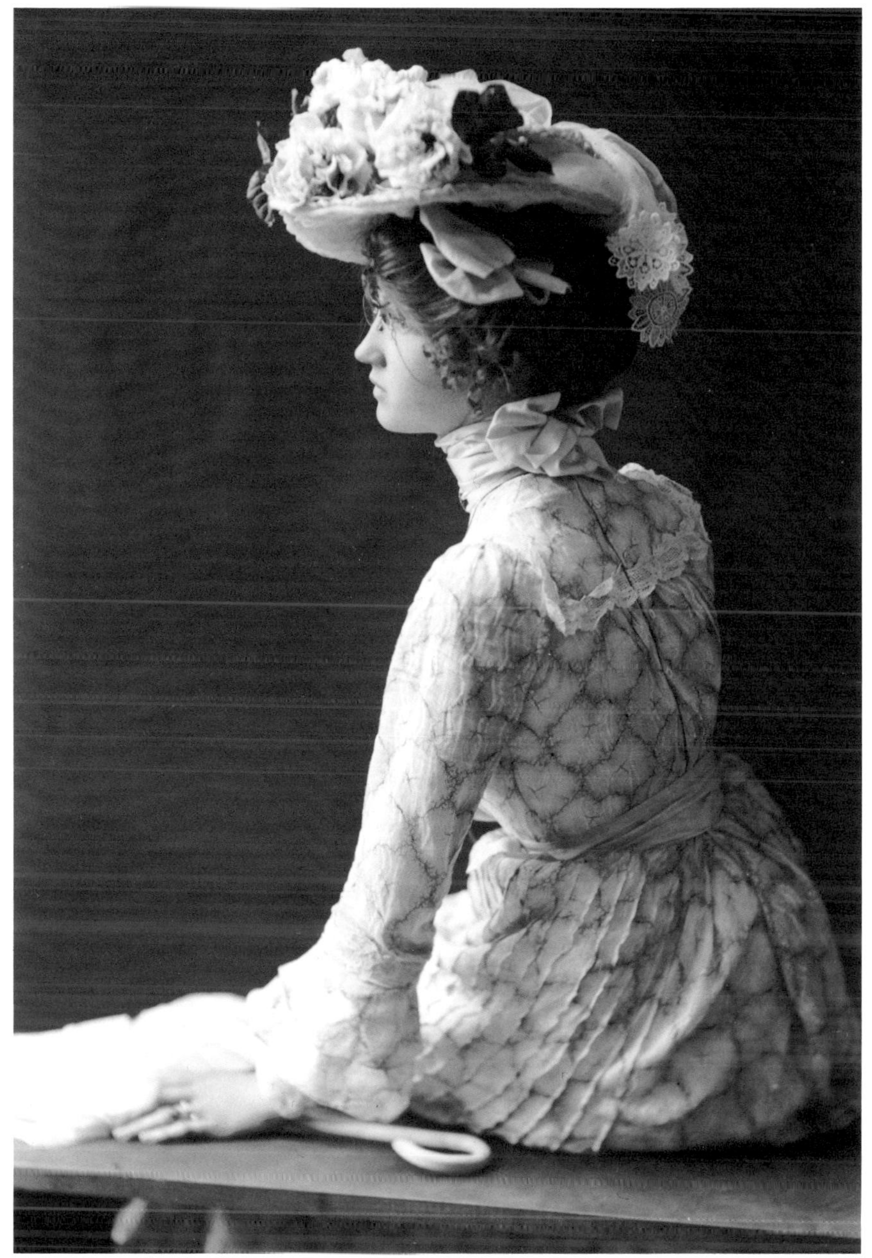

PLATE 5

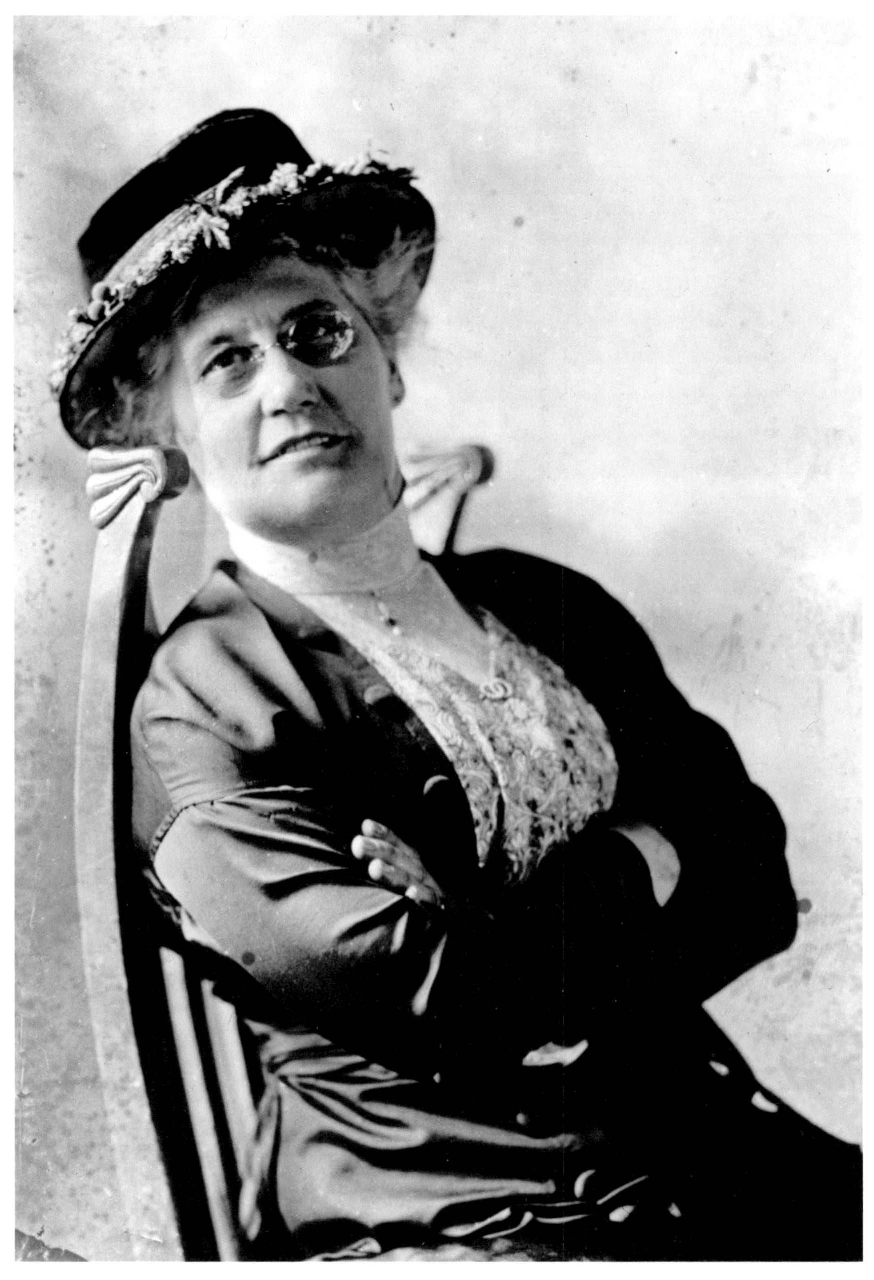

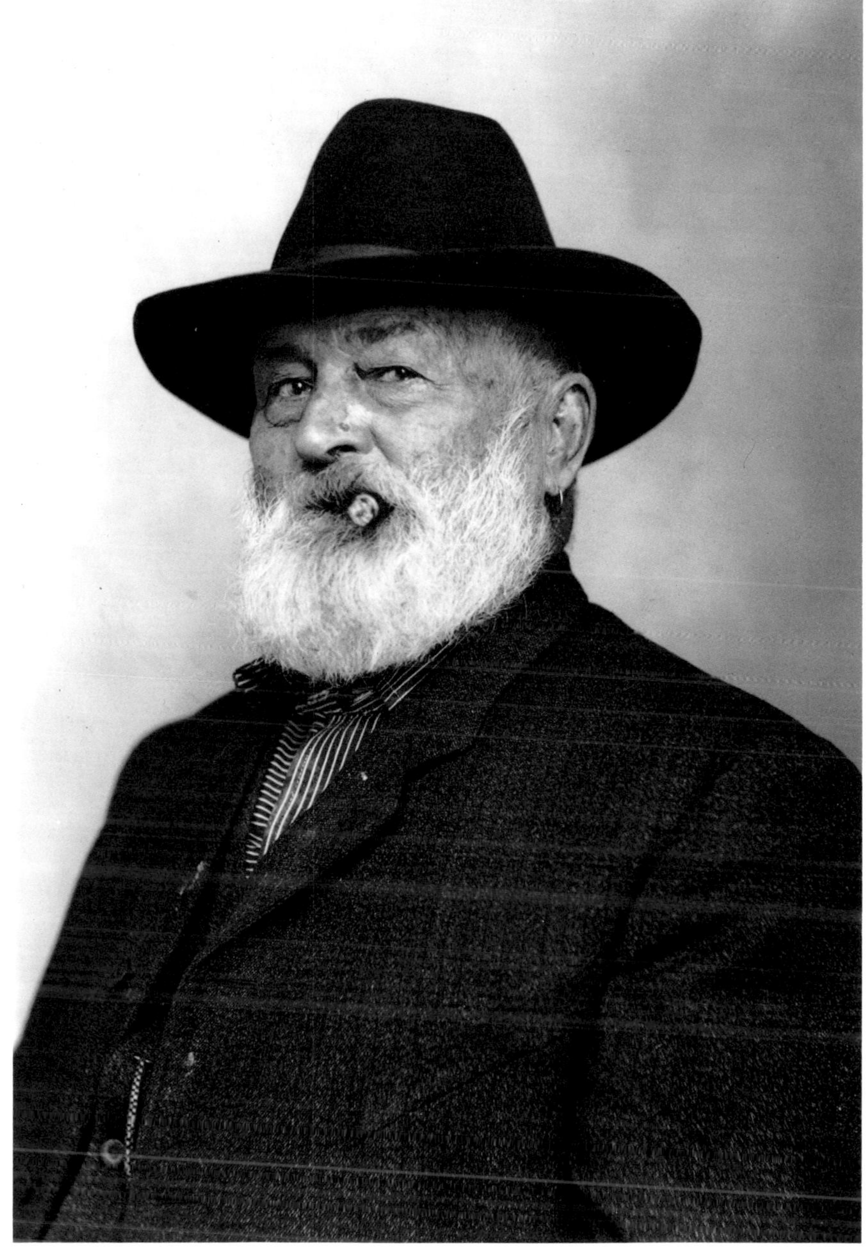

PLATE 7

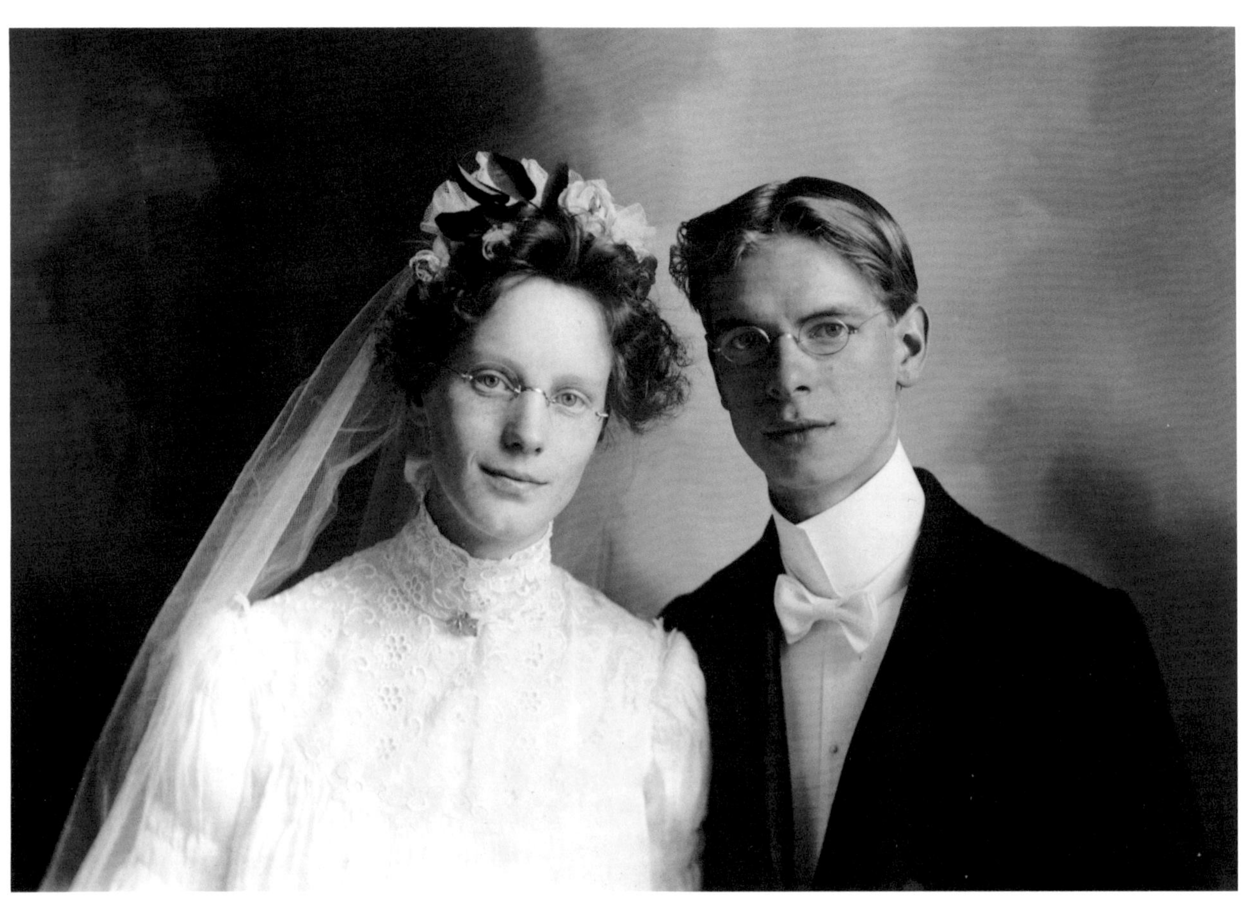

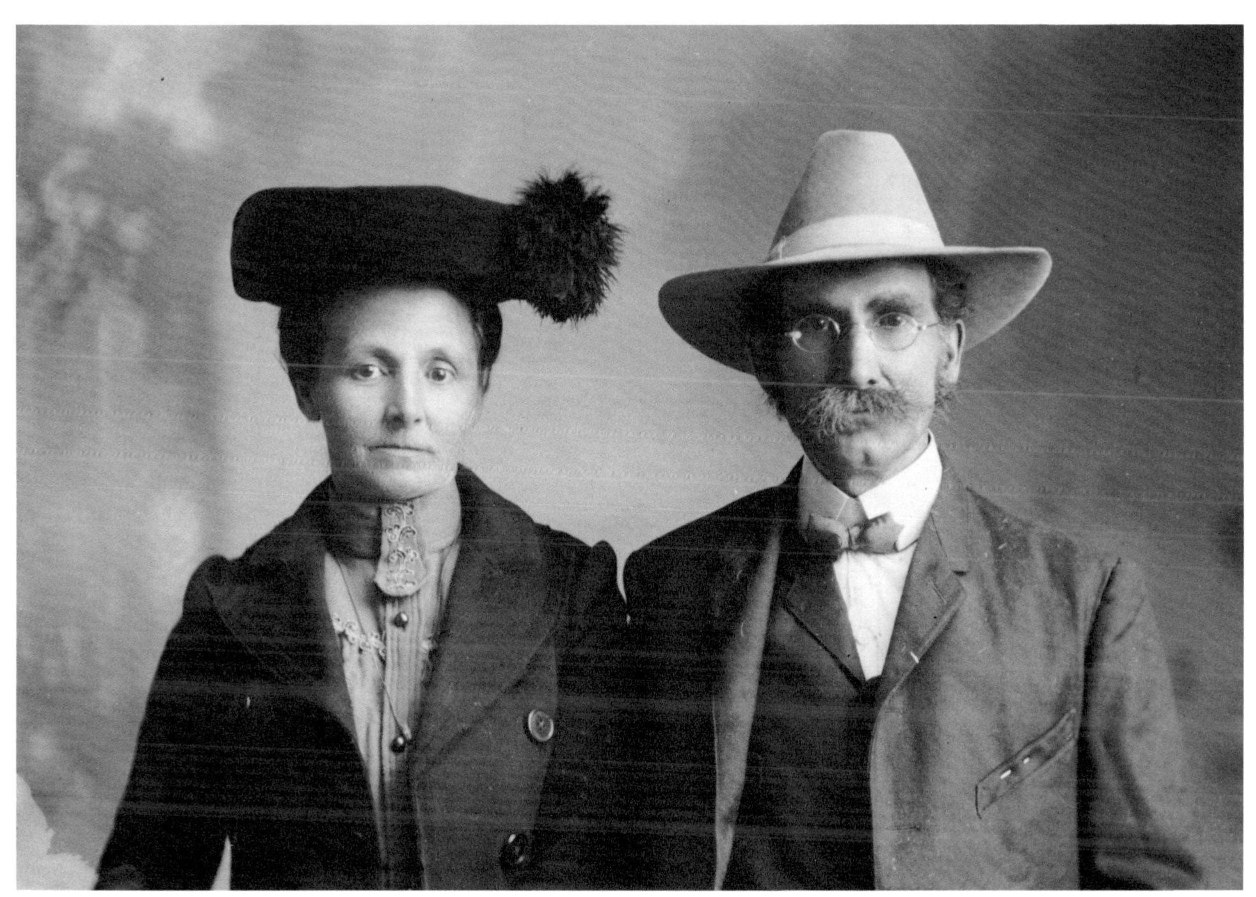

PLATE 9

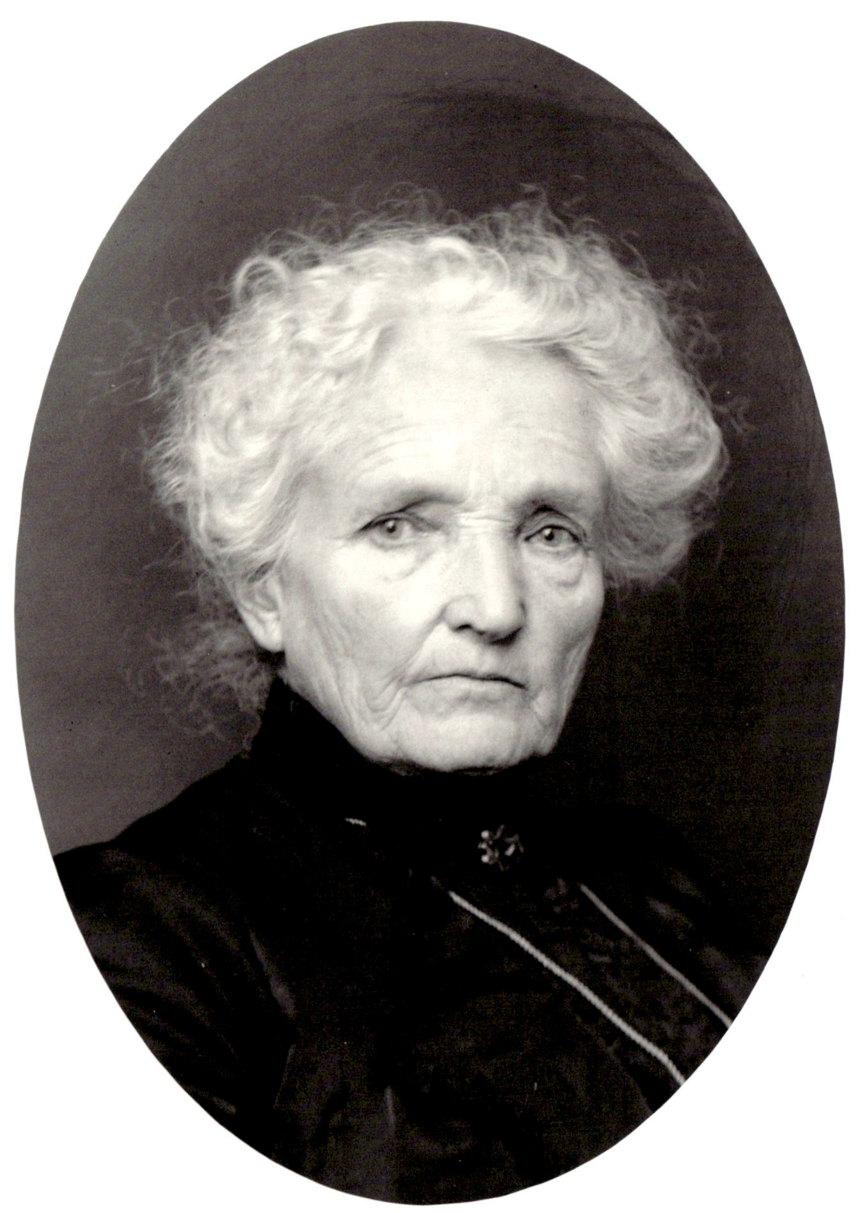

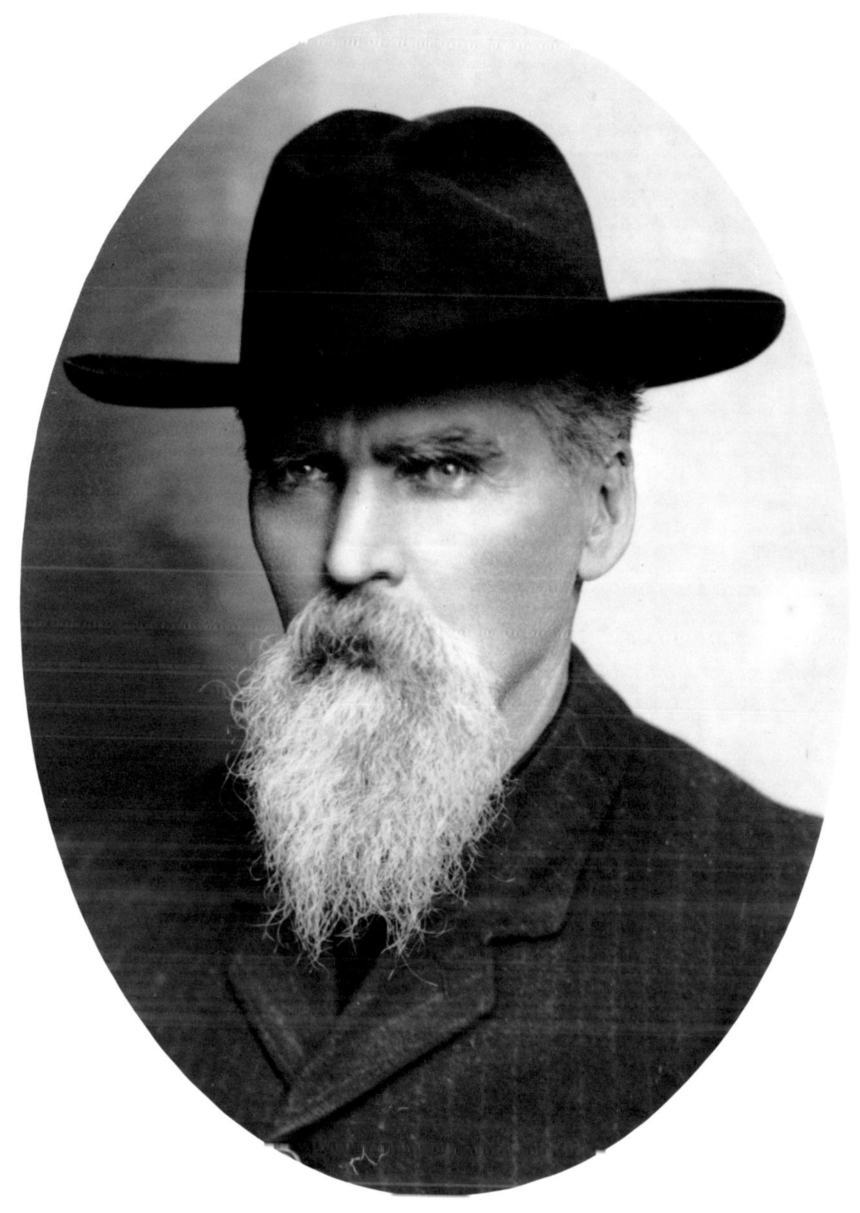

PLATE 11

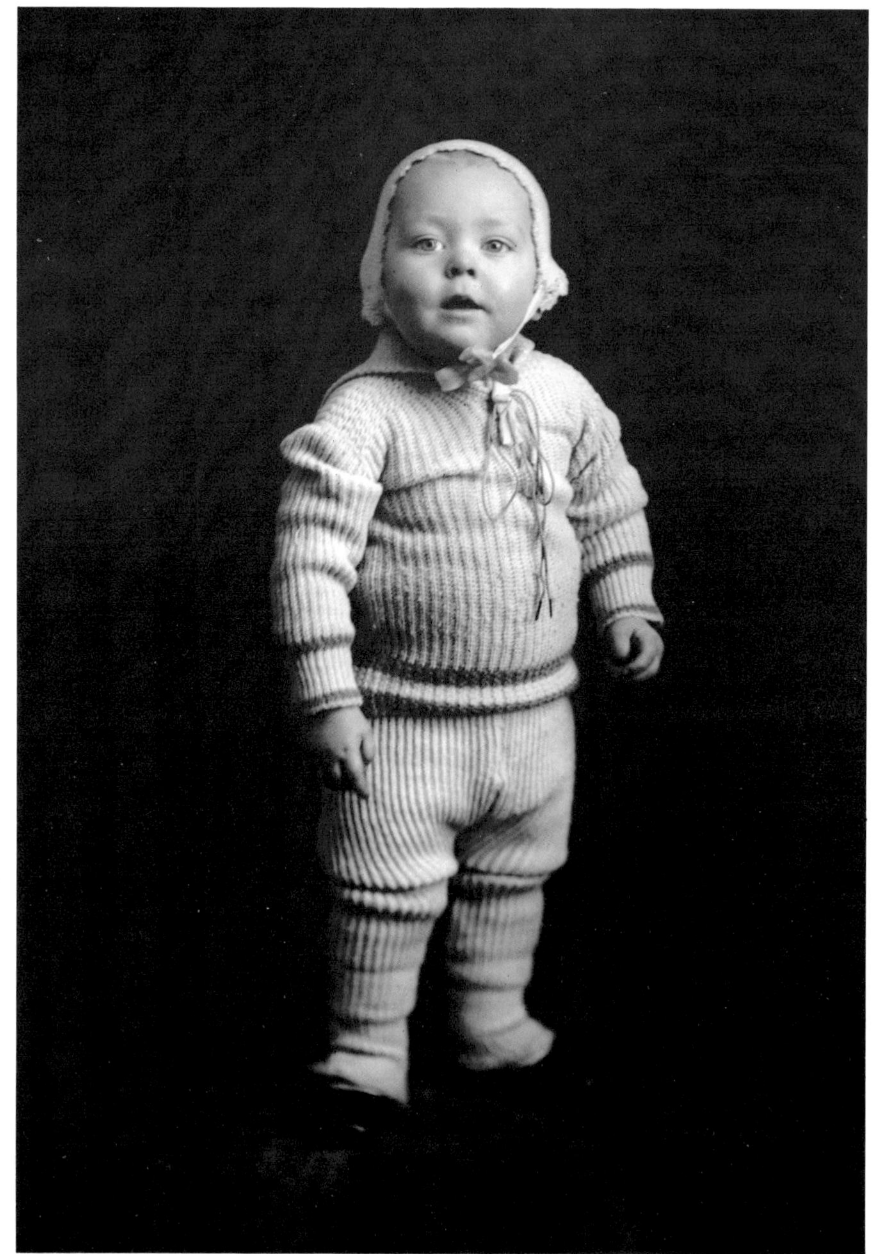

12 PLATE

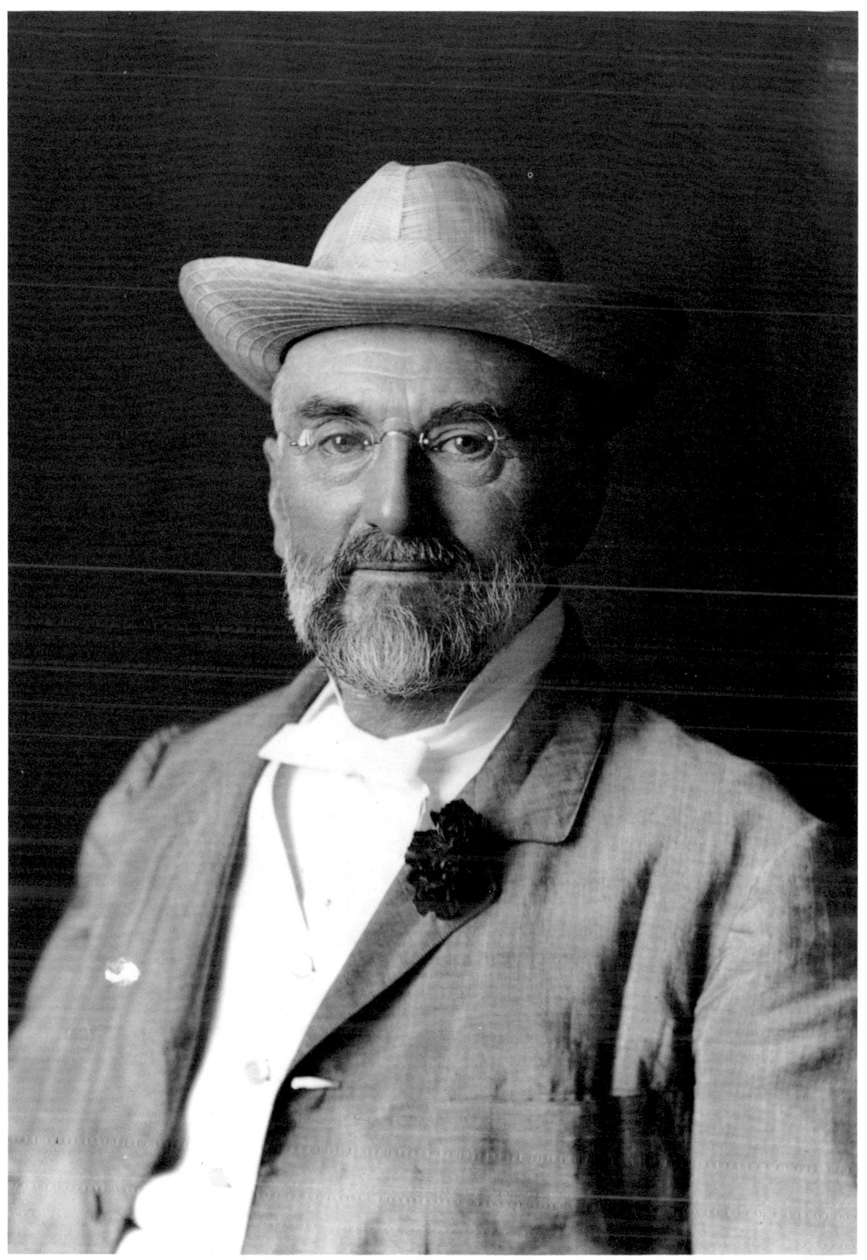

PLATE 13

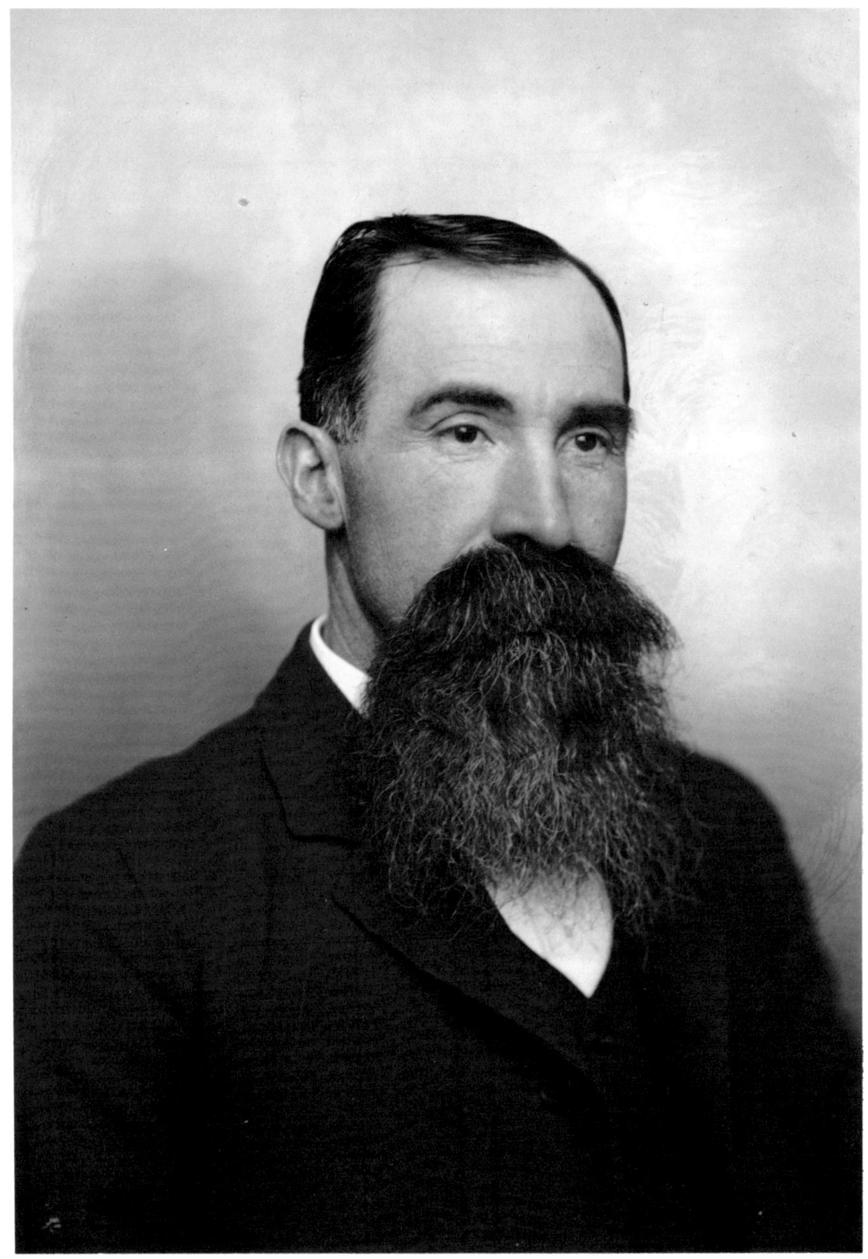

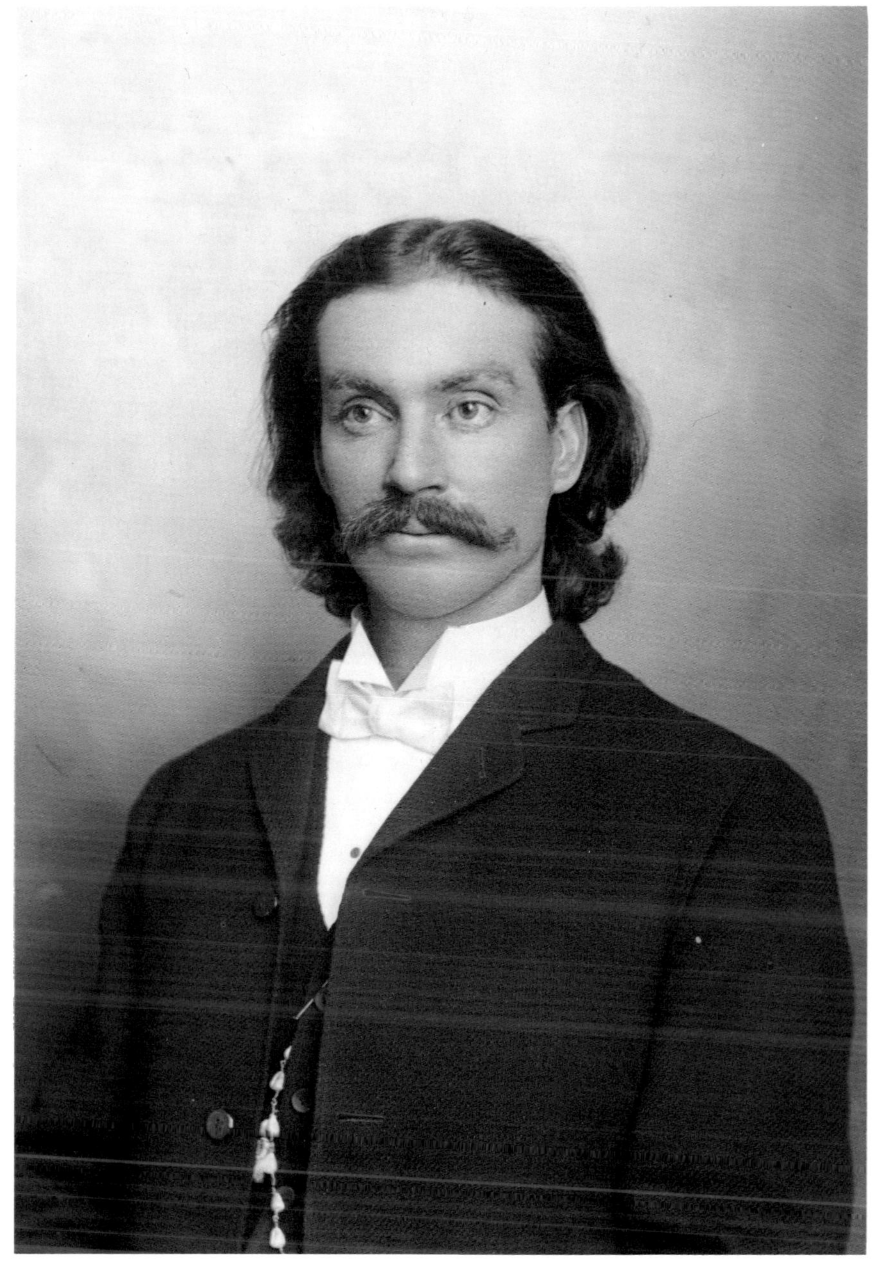

PLATE 15

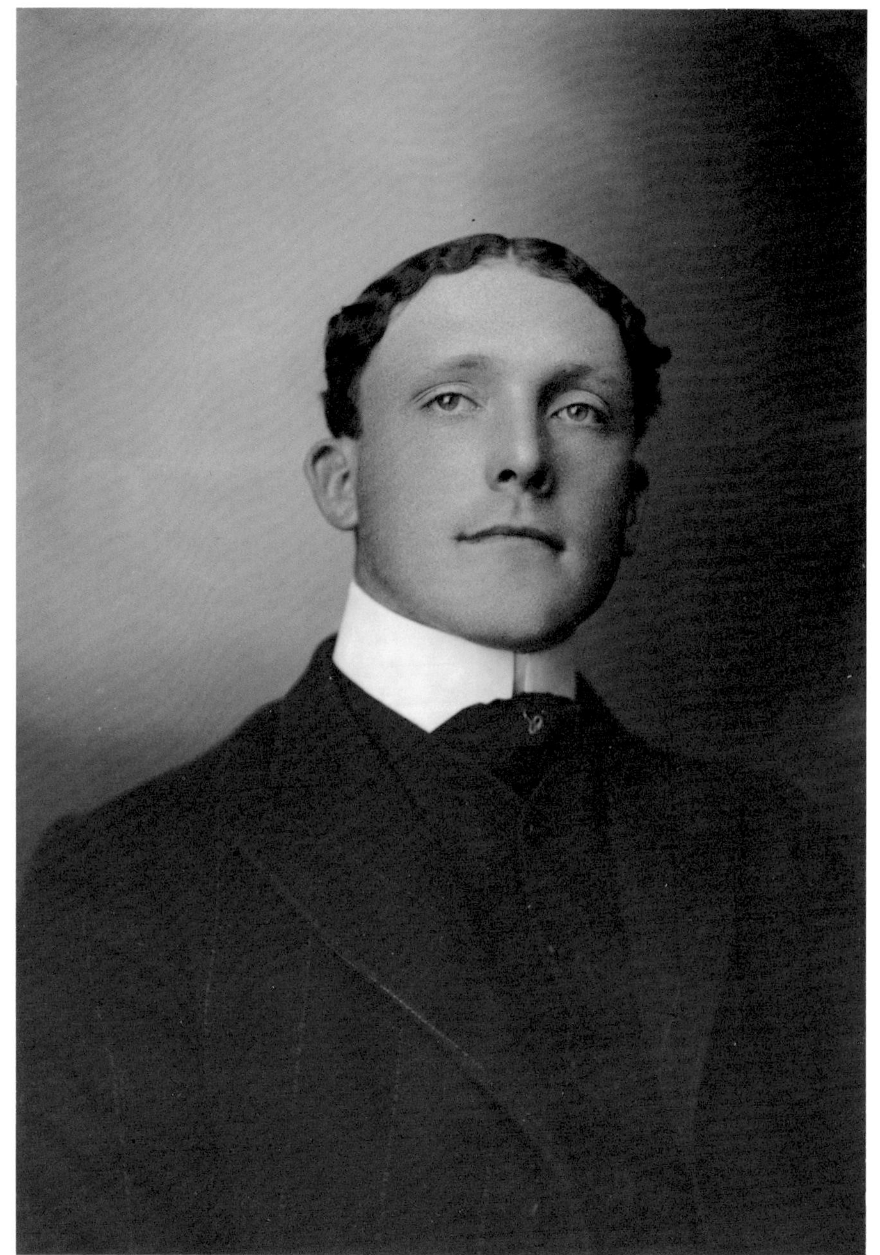

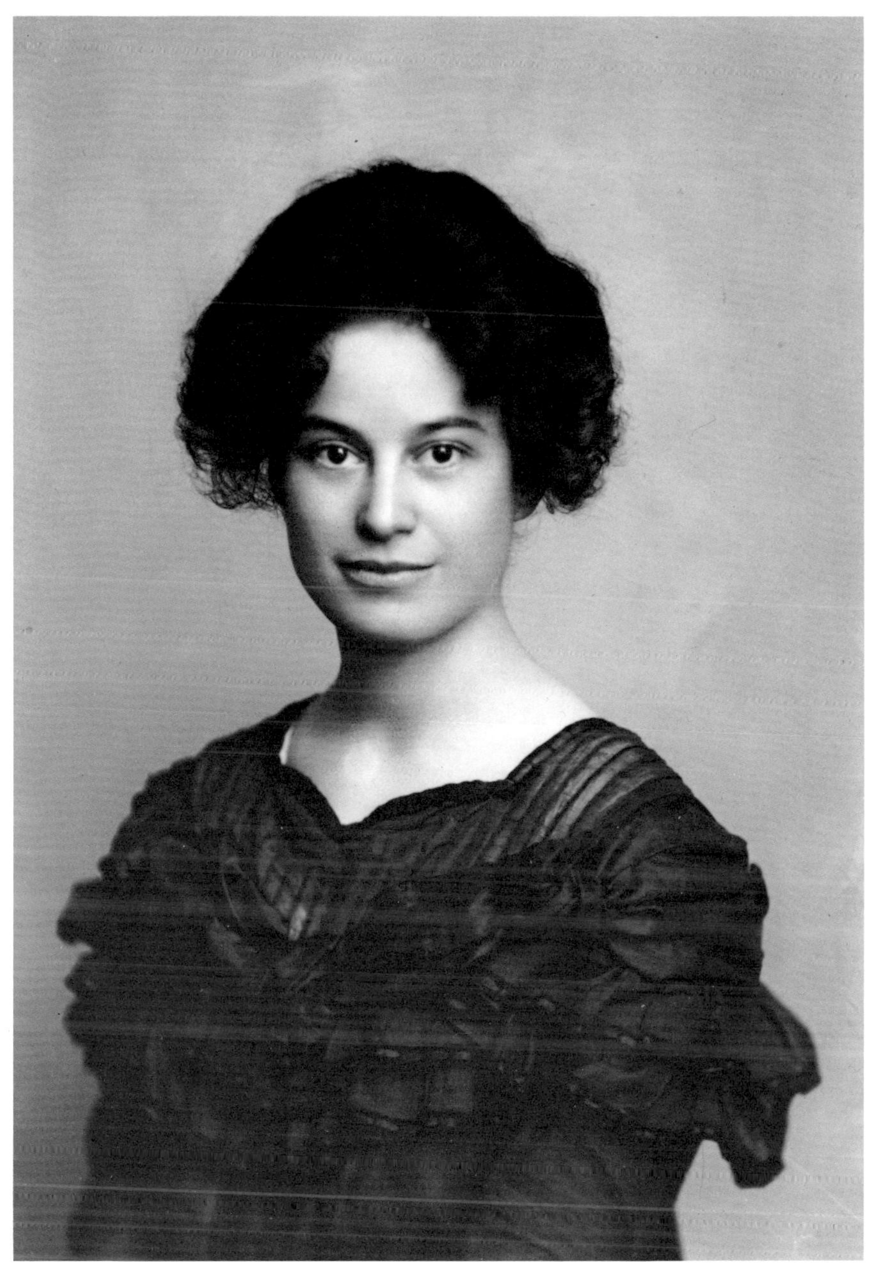

PLATE 17

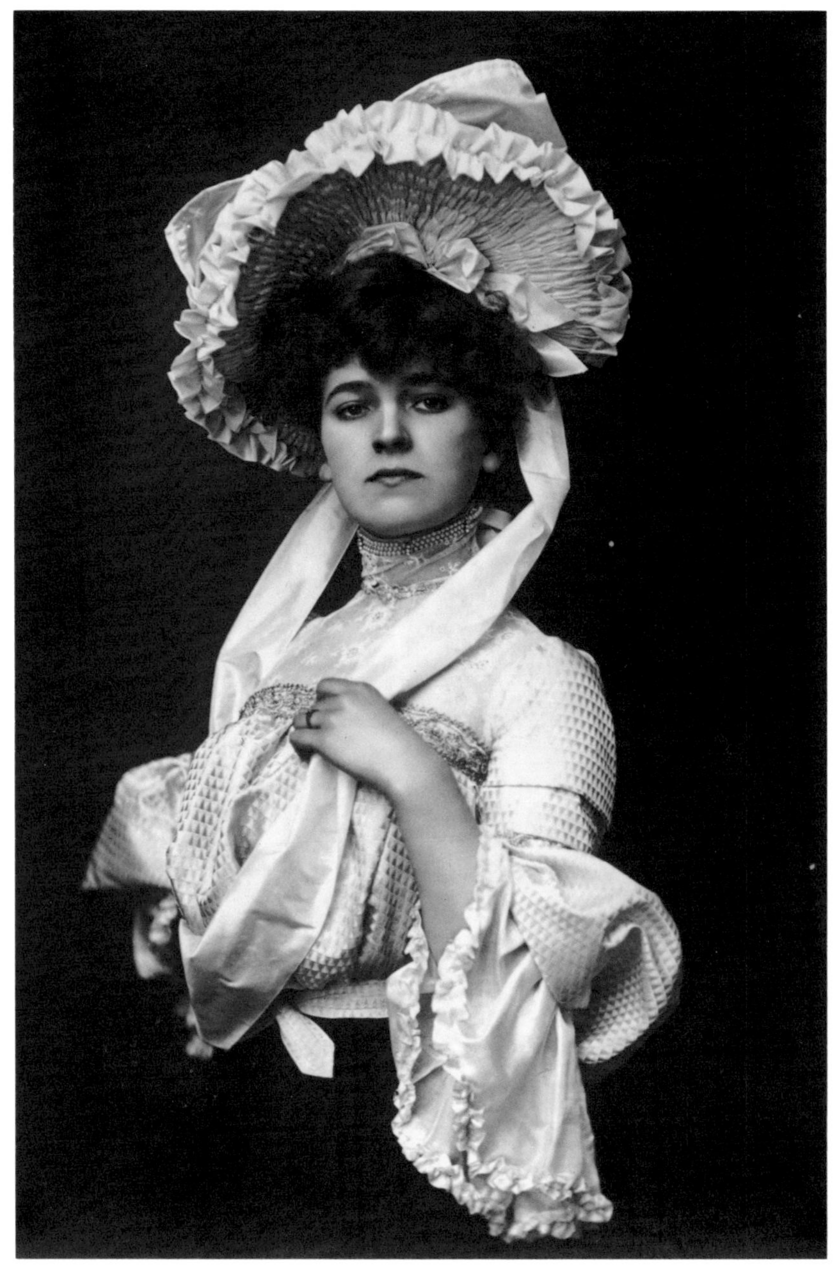

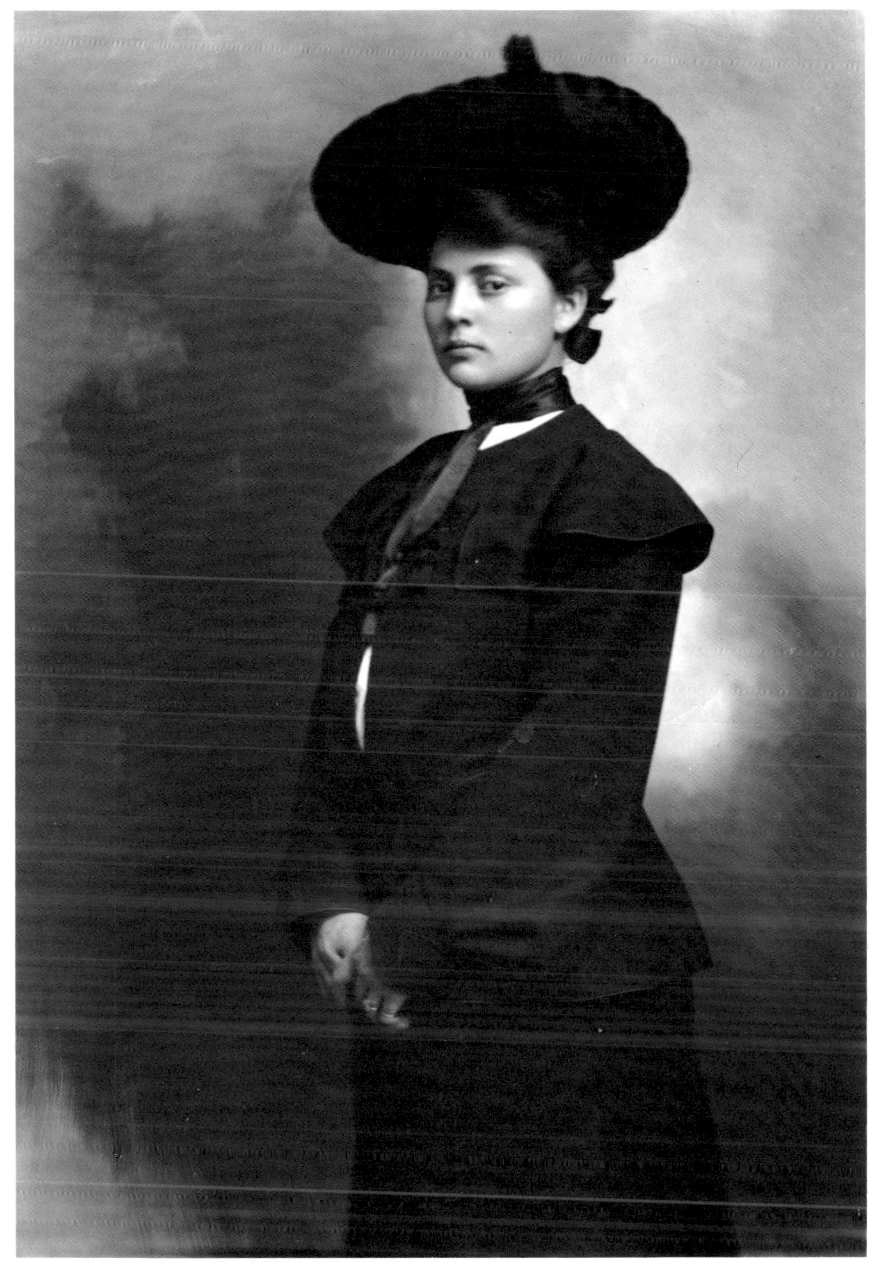

PLATE 19

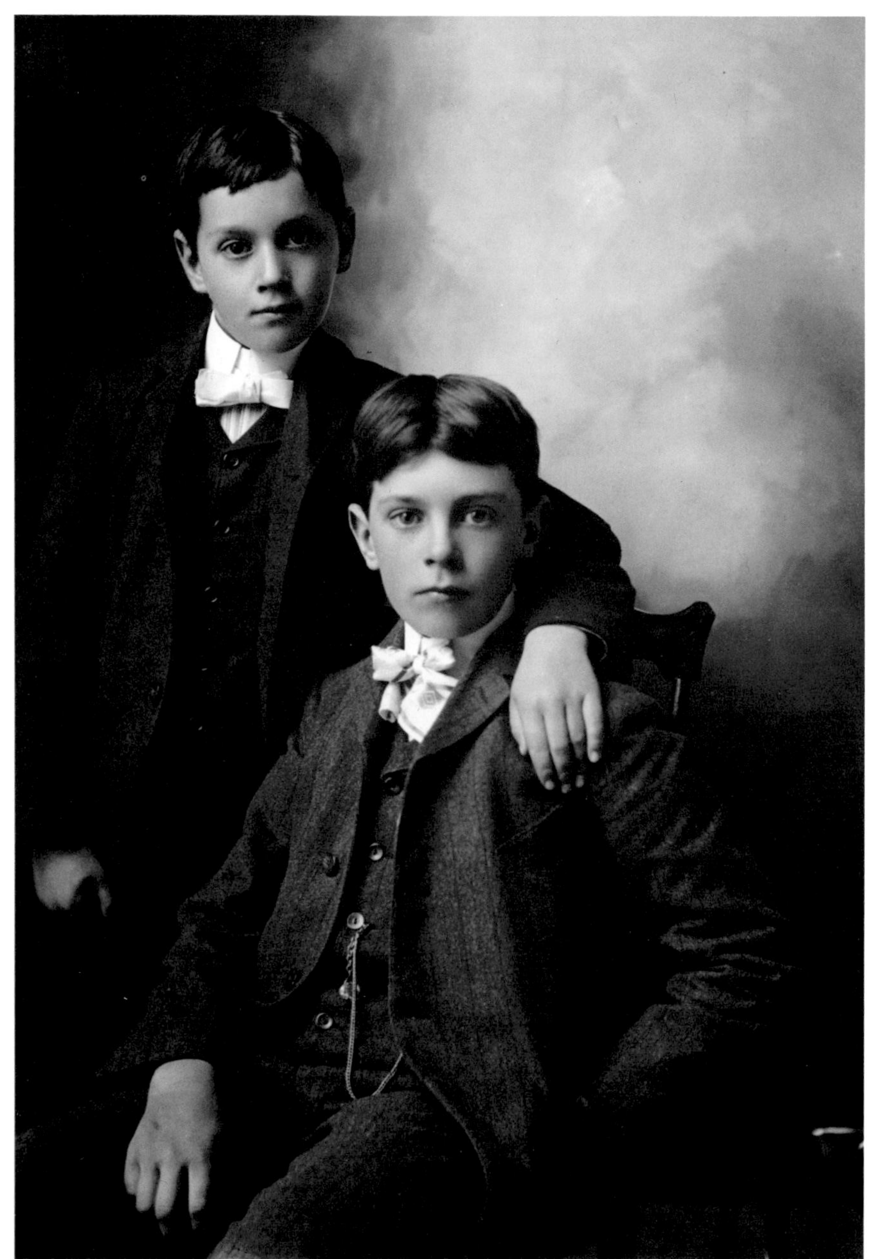

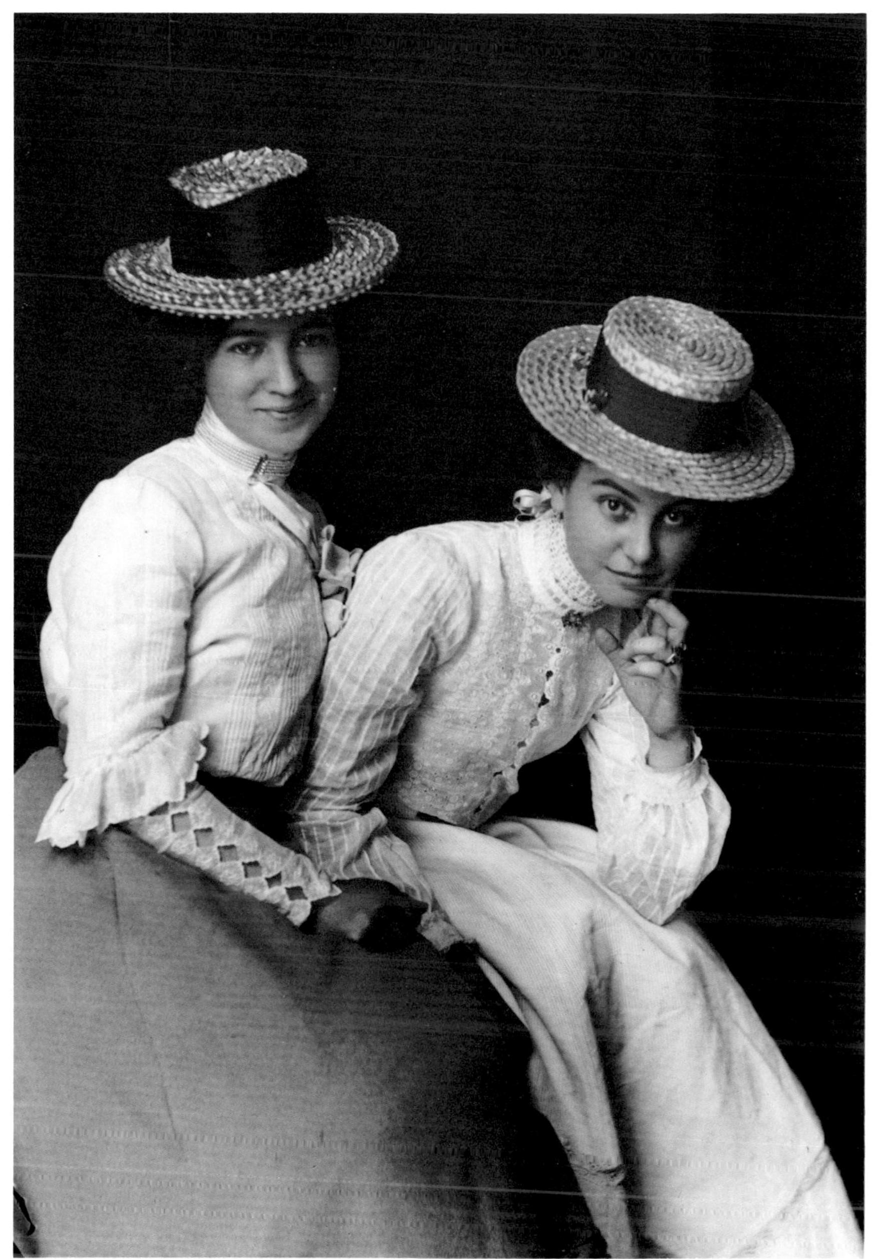

PLATE 21

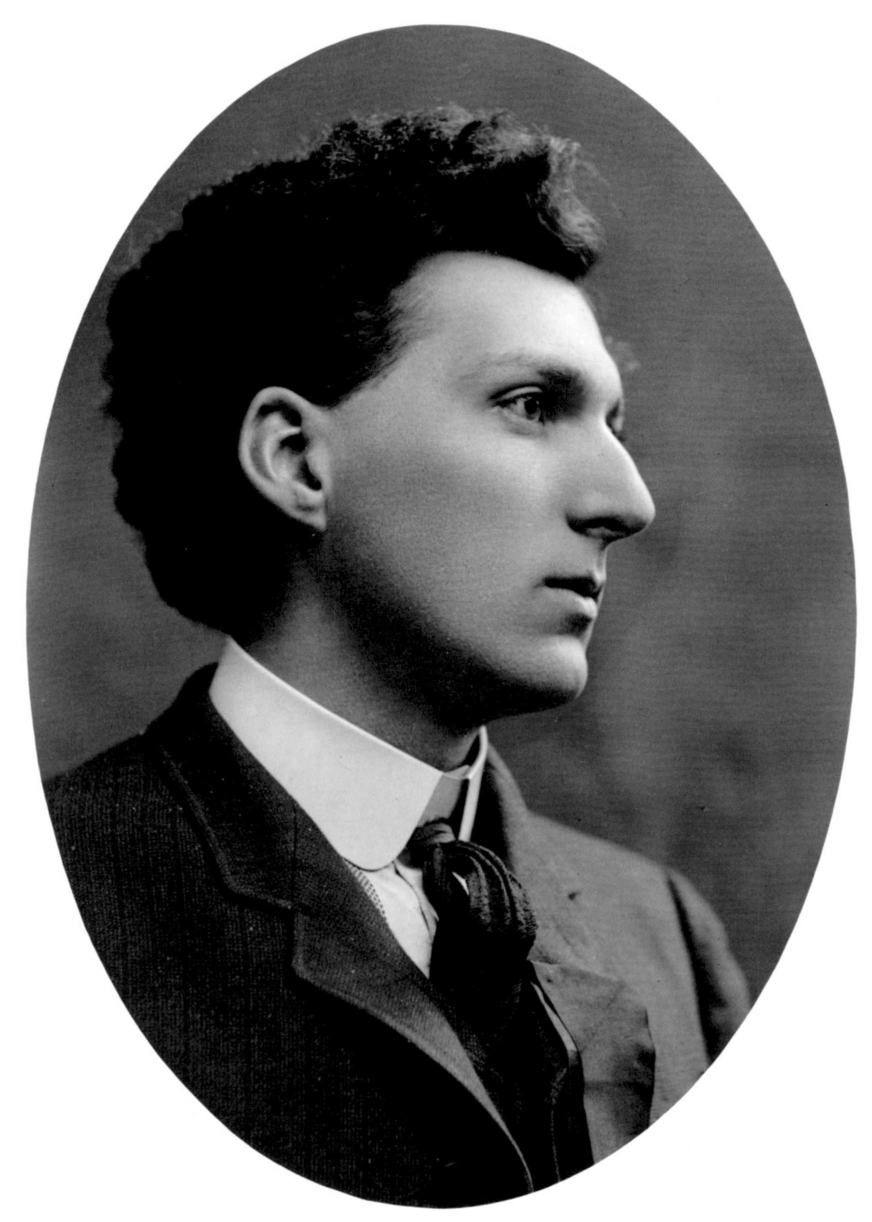

22 PLATE

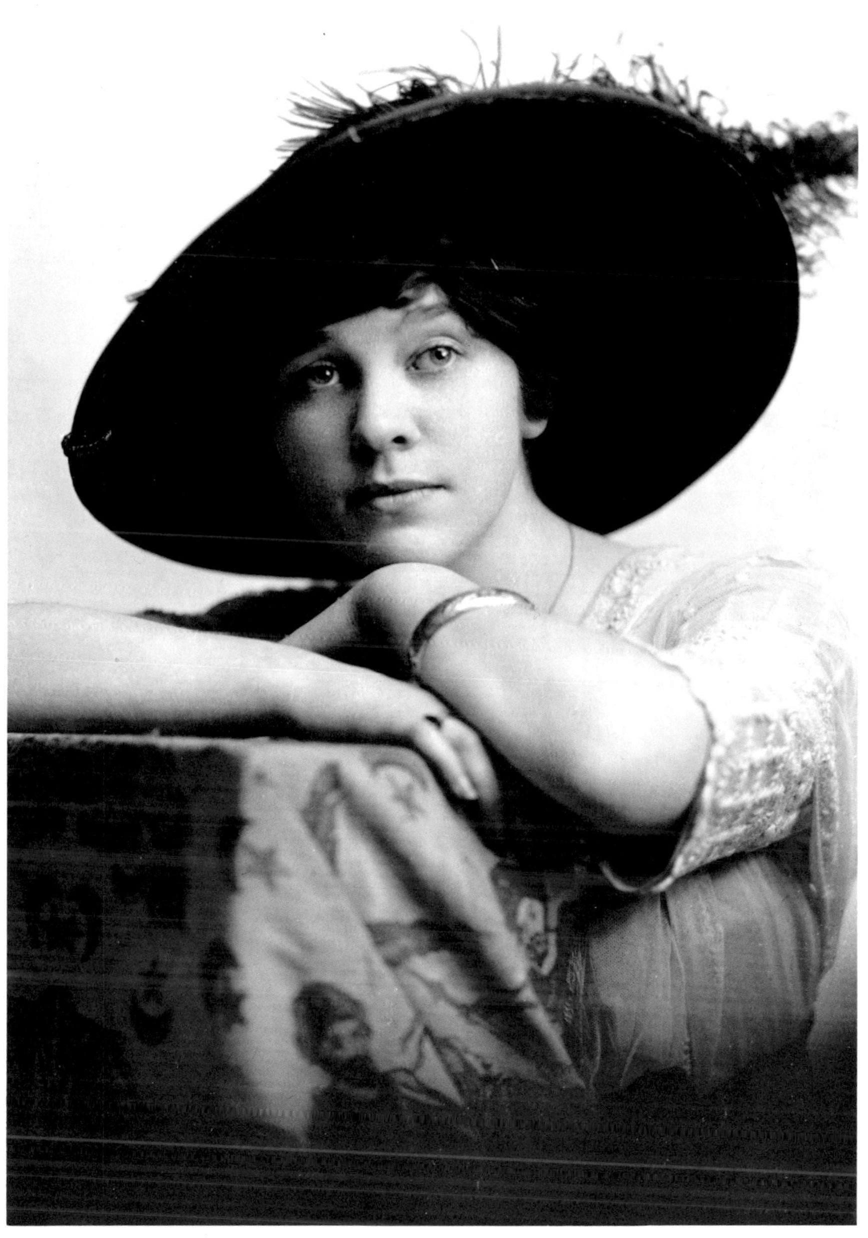

PLATE 23

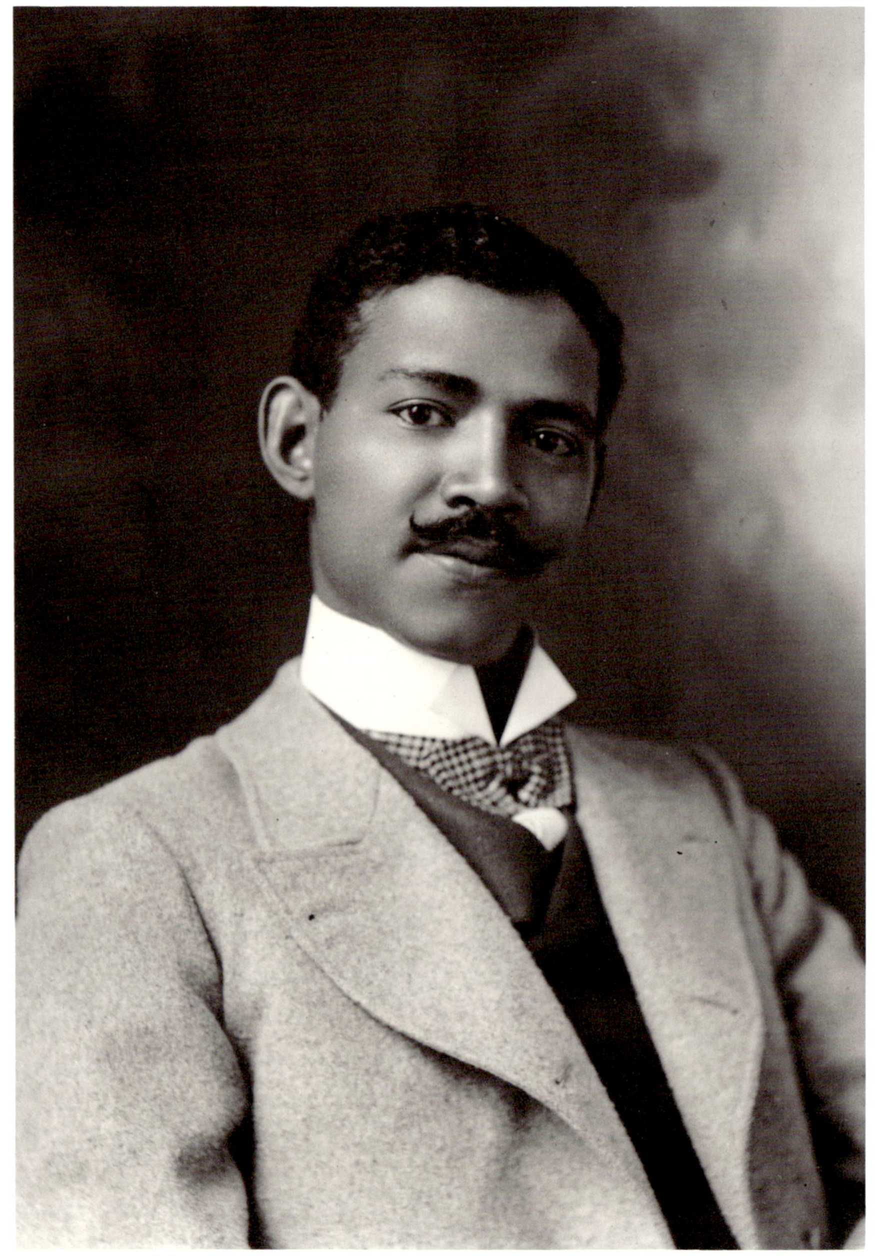

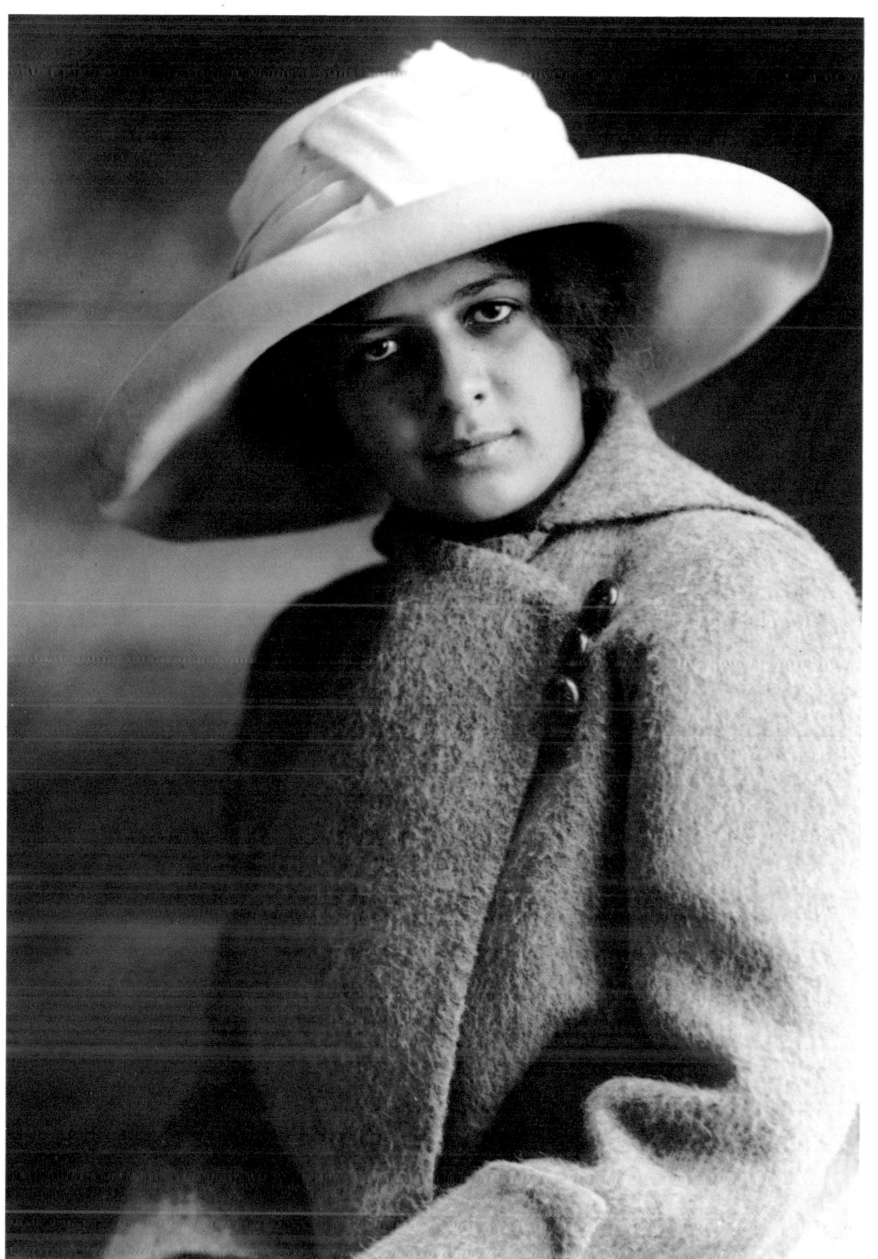

PLATE 25

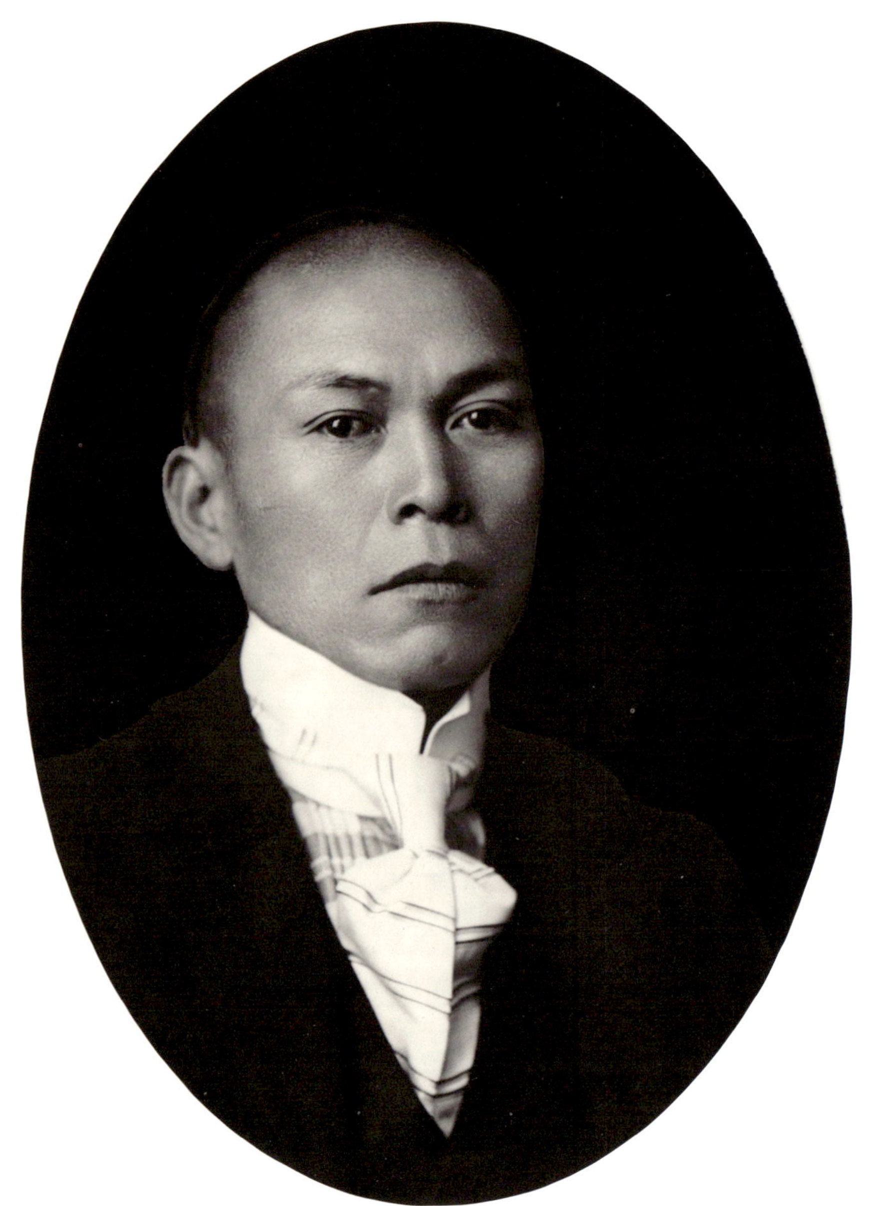

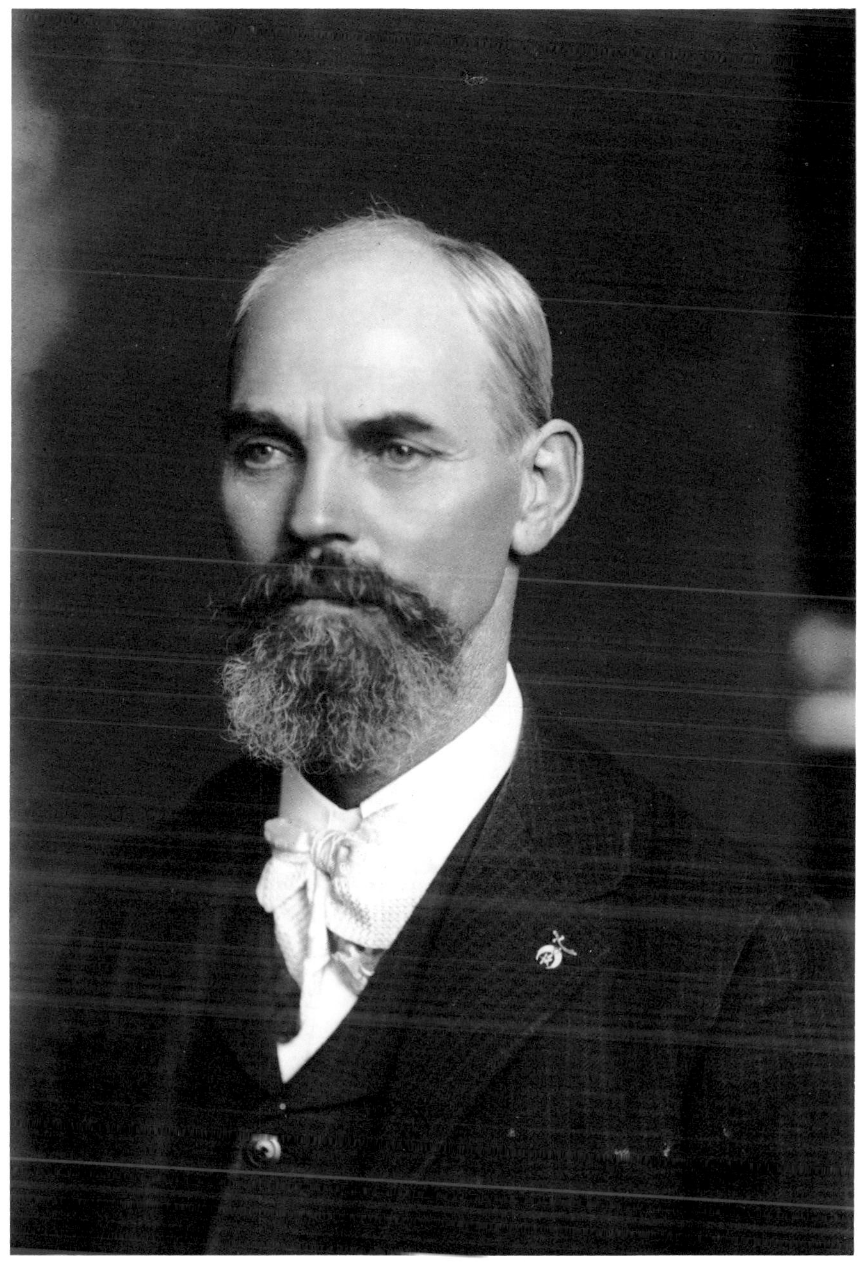

PLATE 27

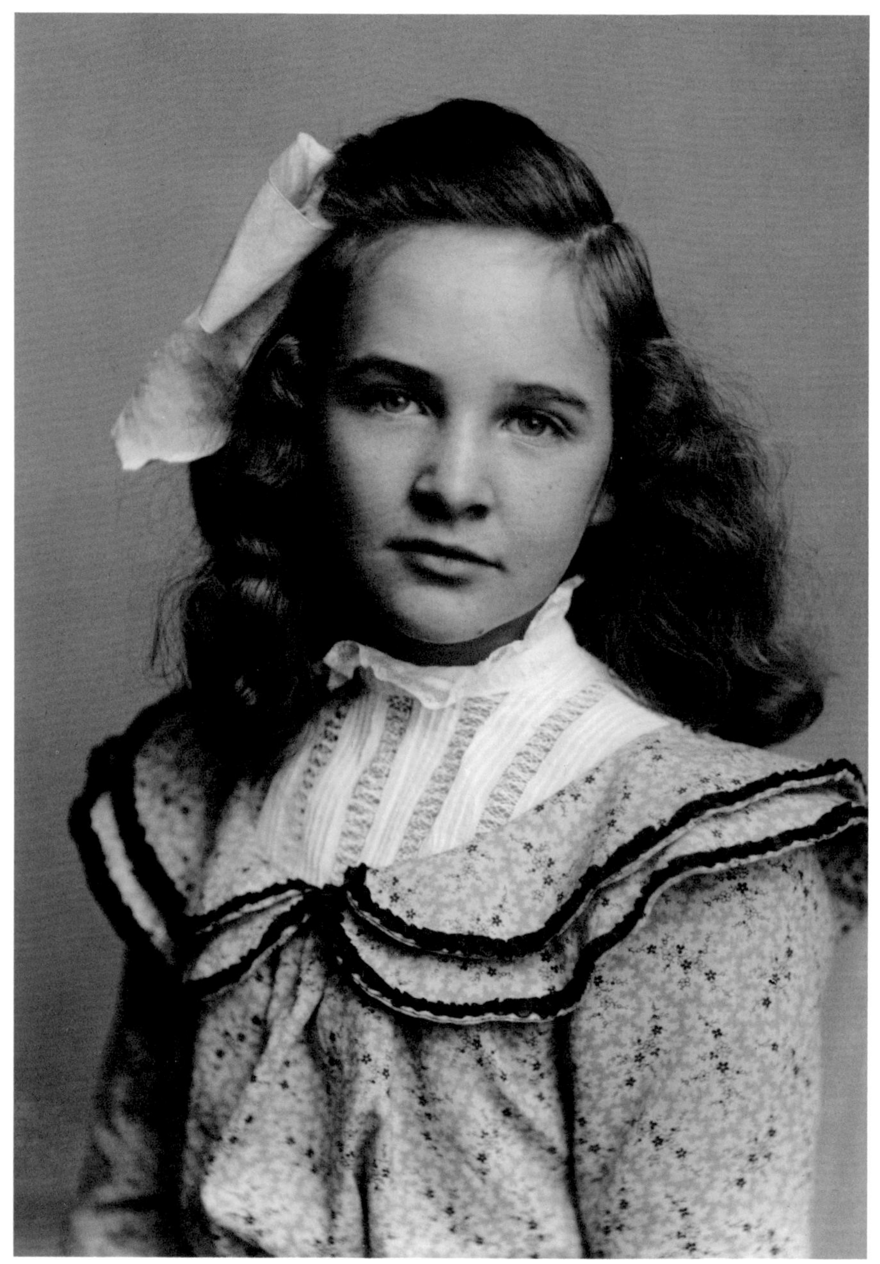

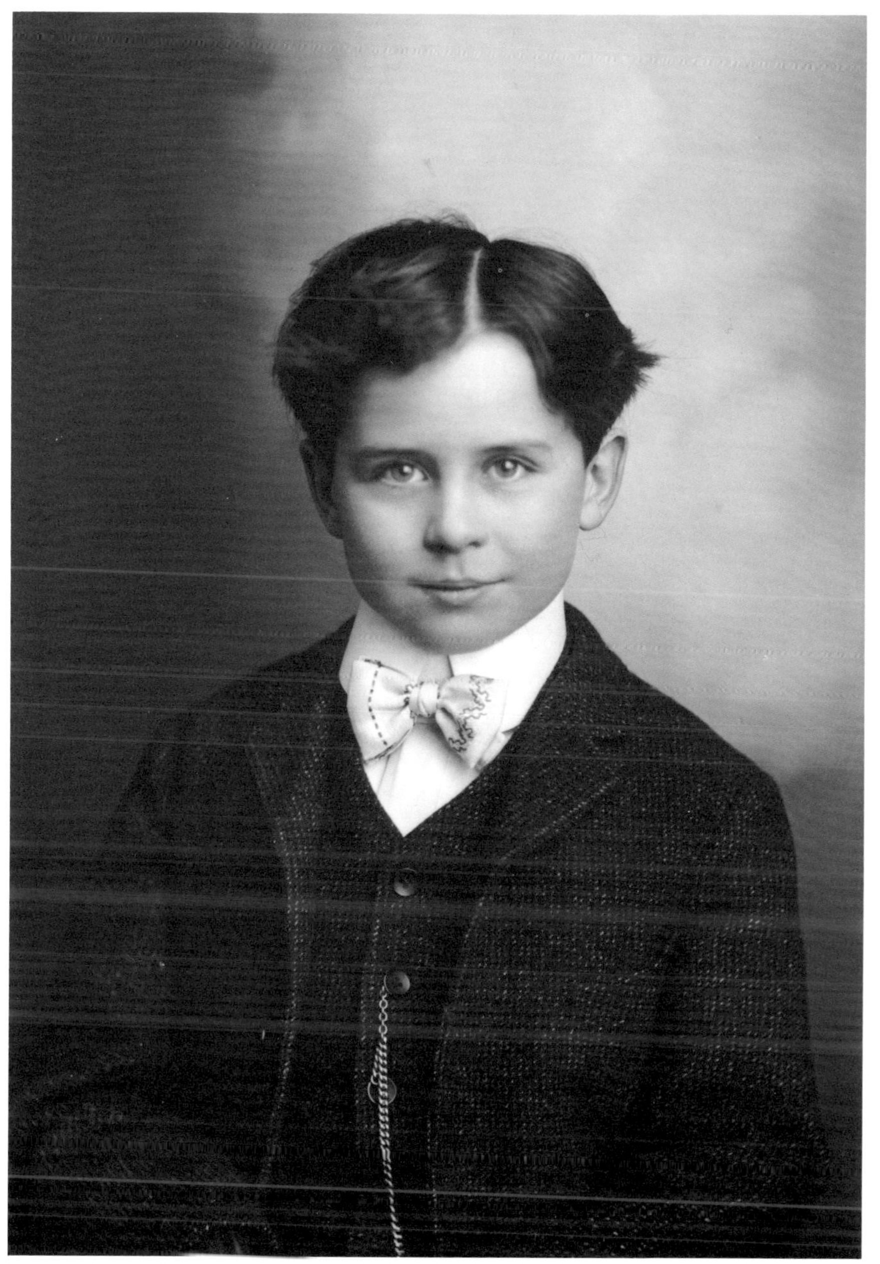

PLATE 29

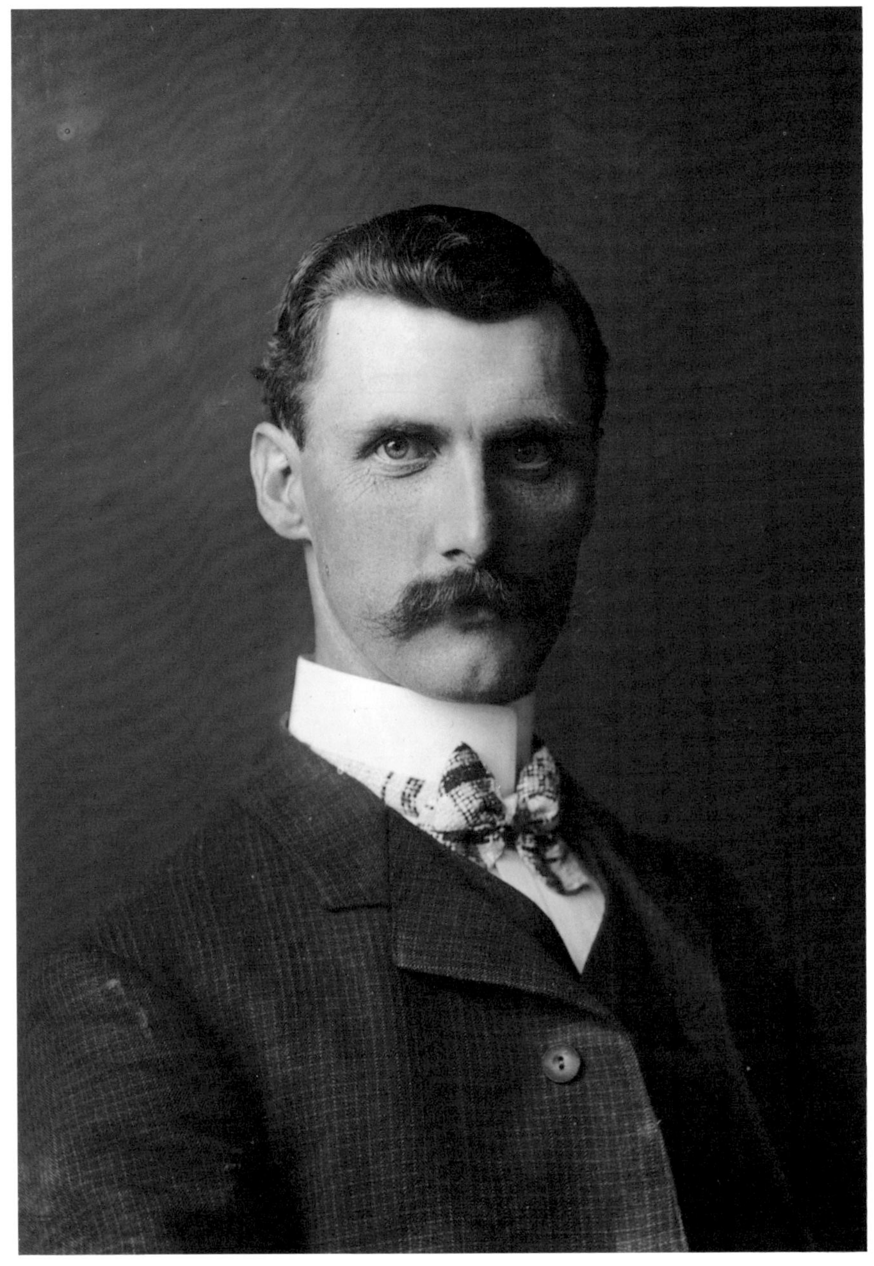

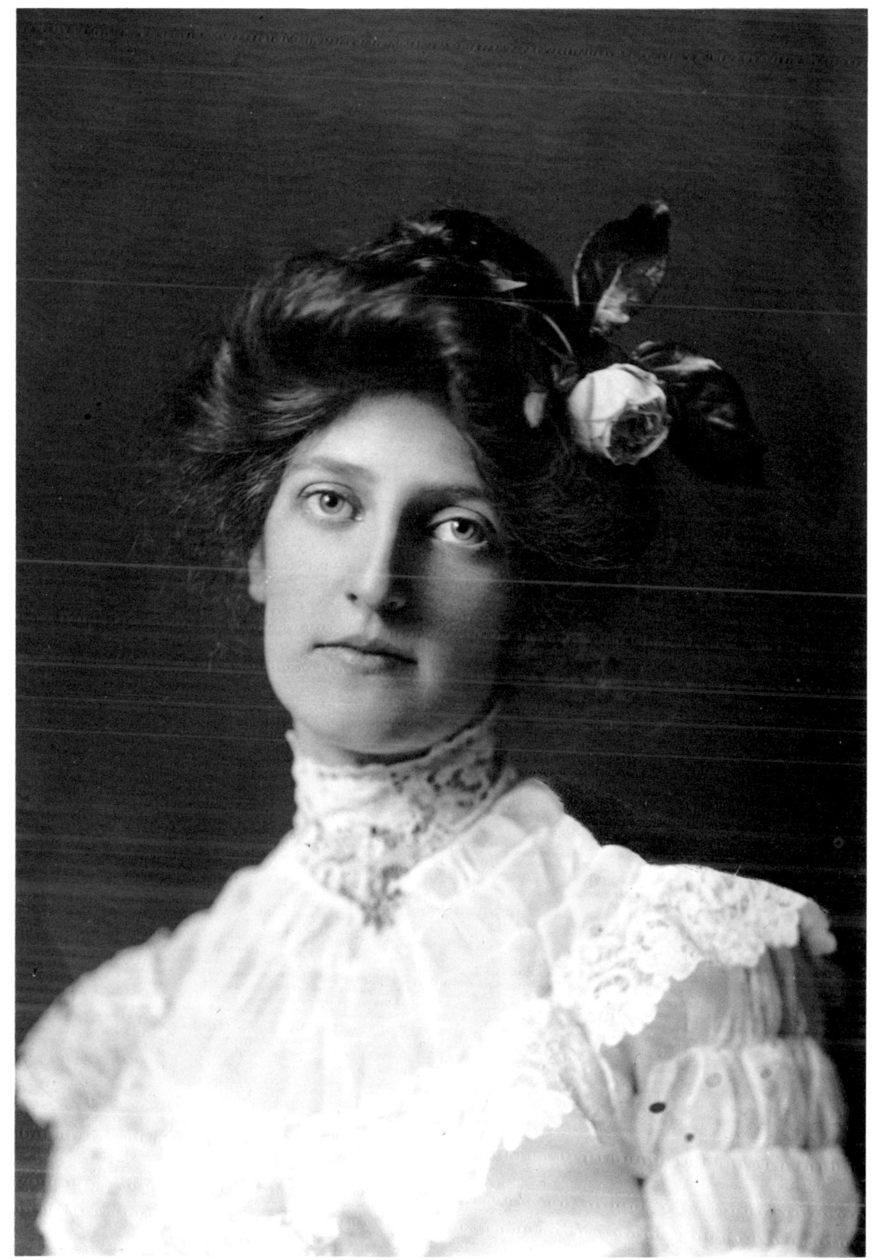

PLATE 31

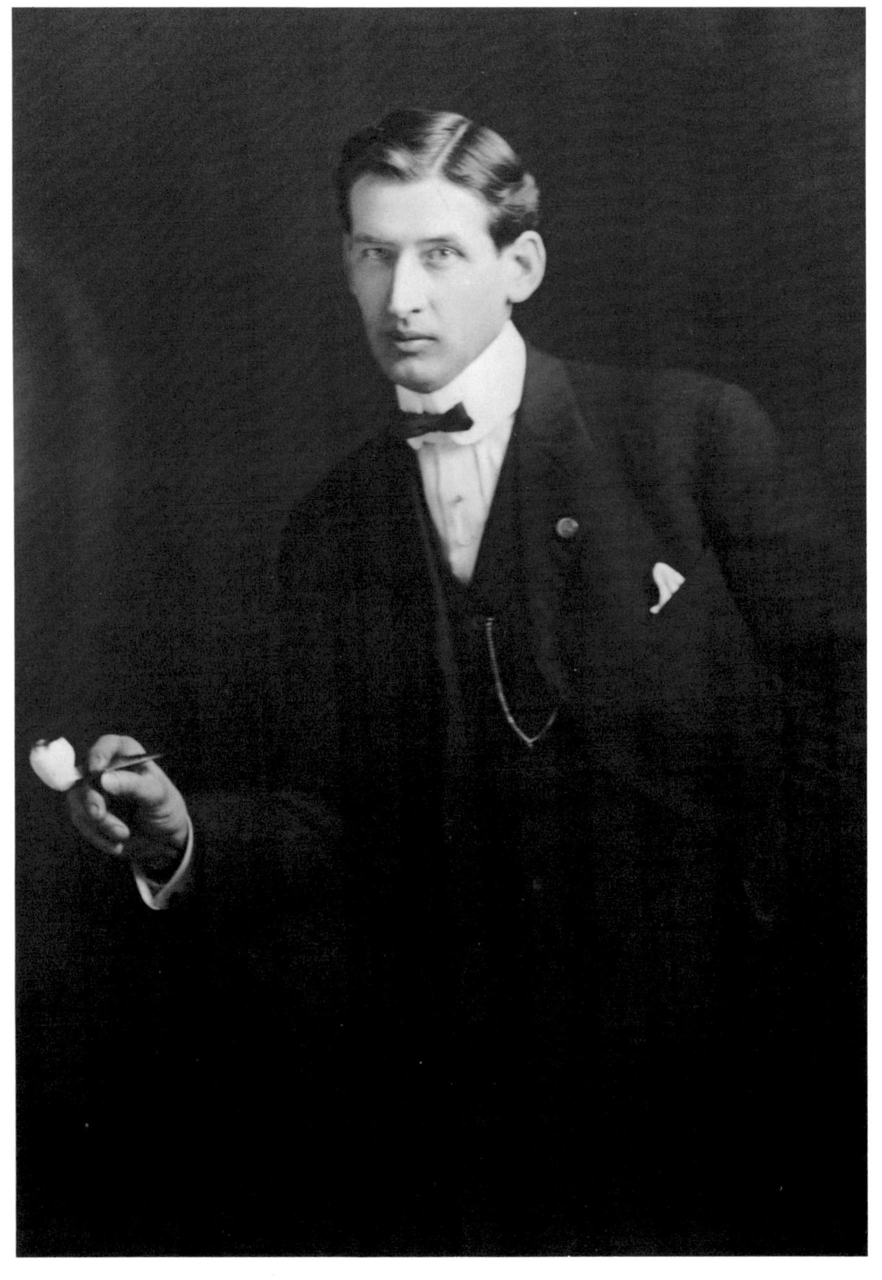

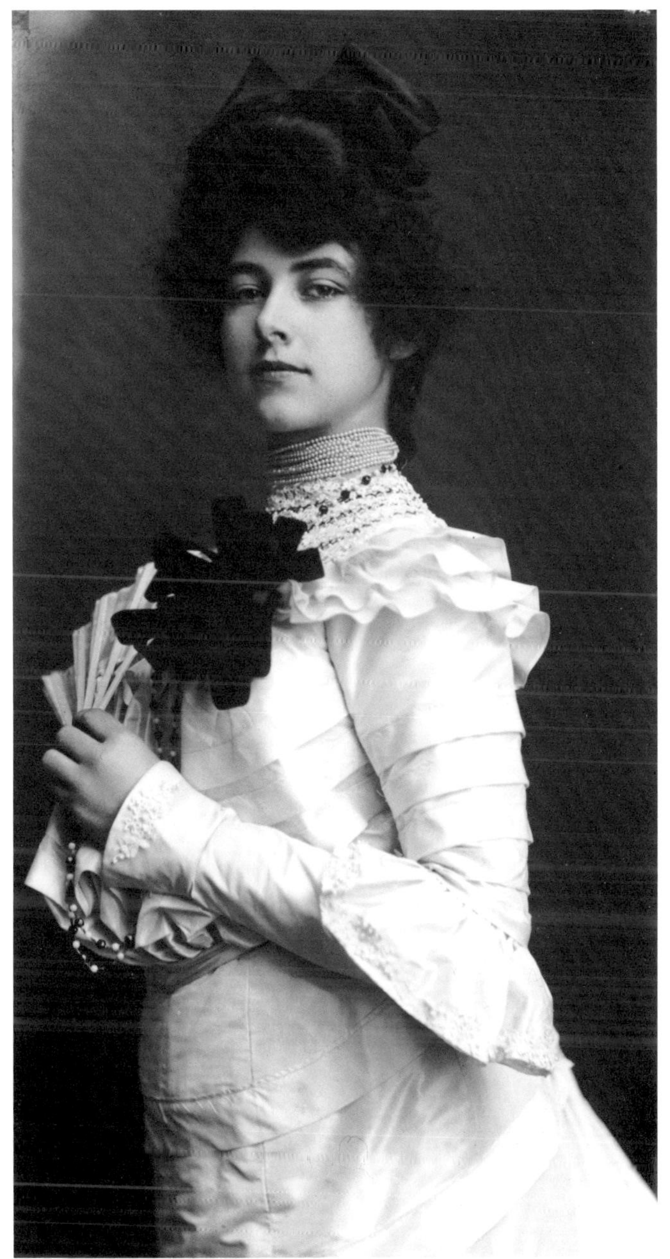

PLATE 33

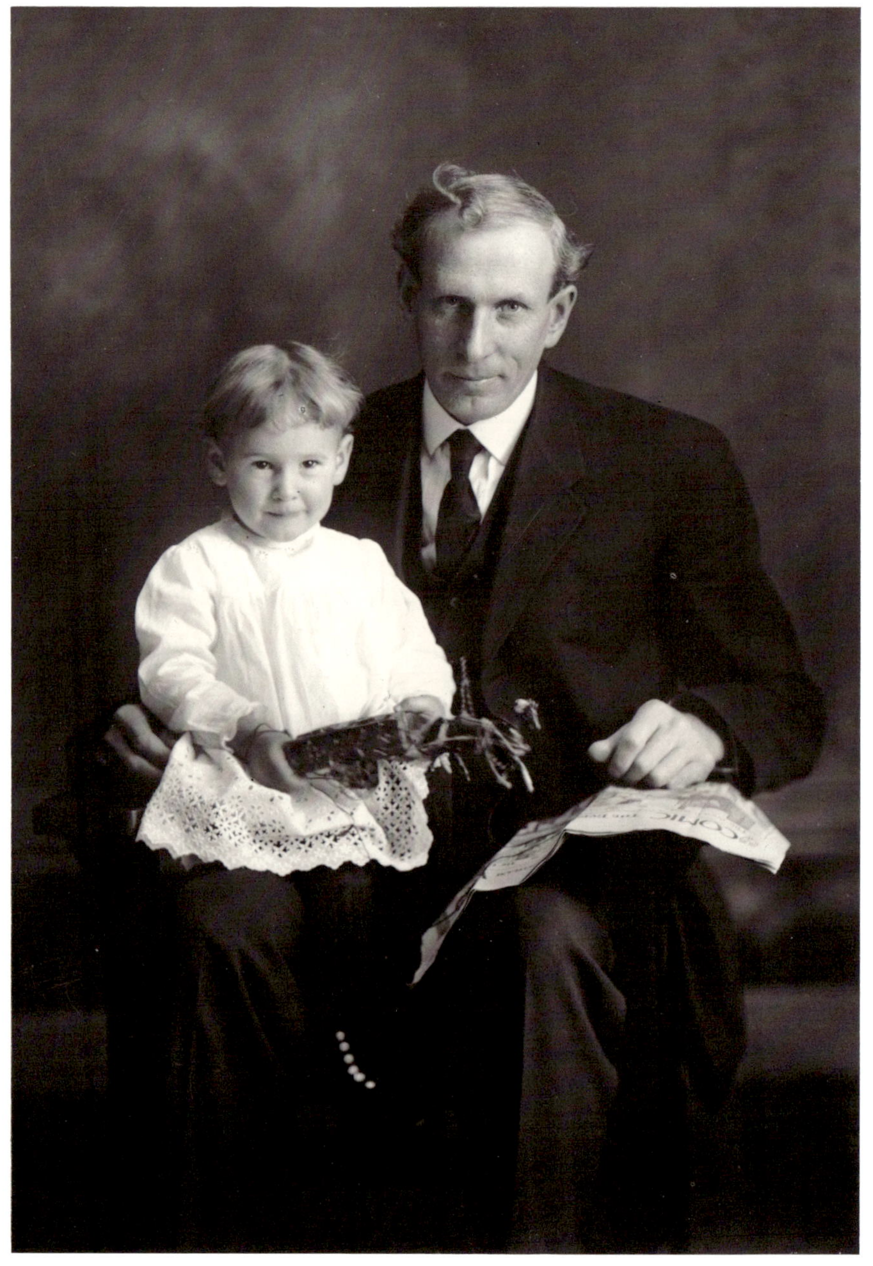

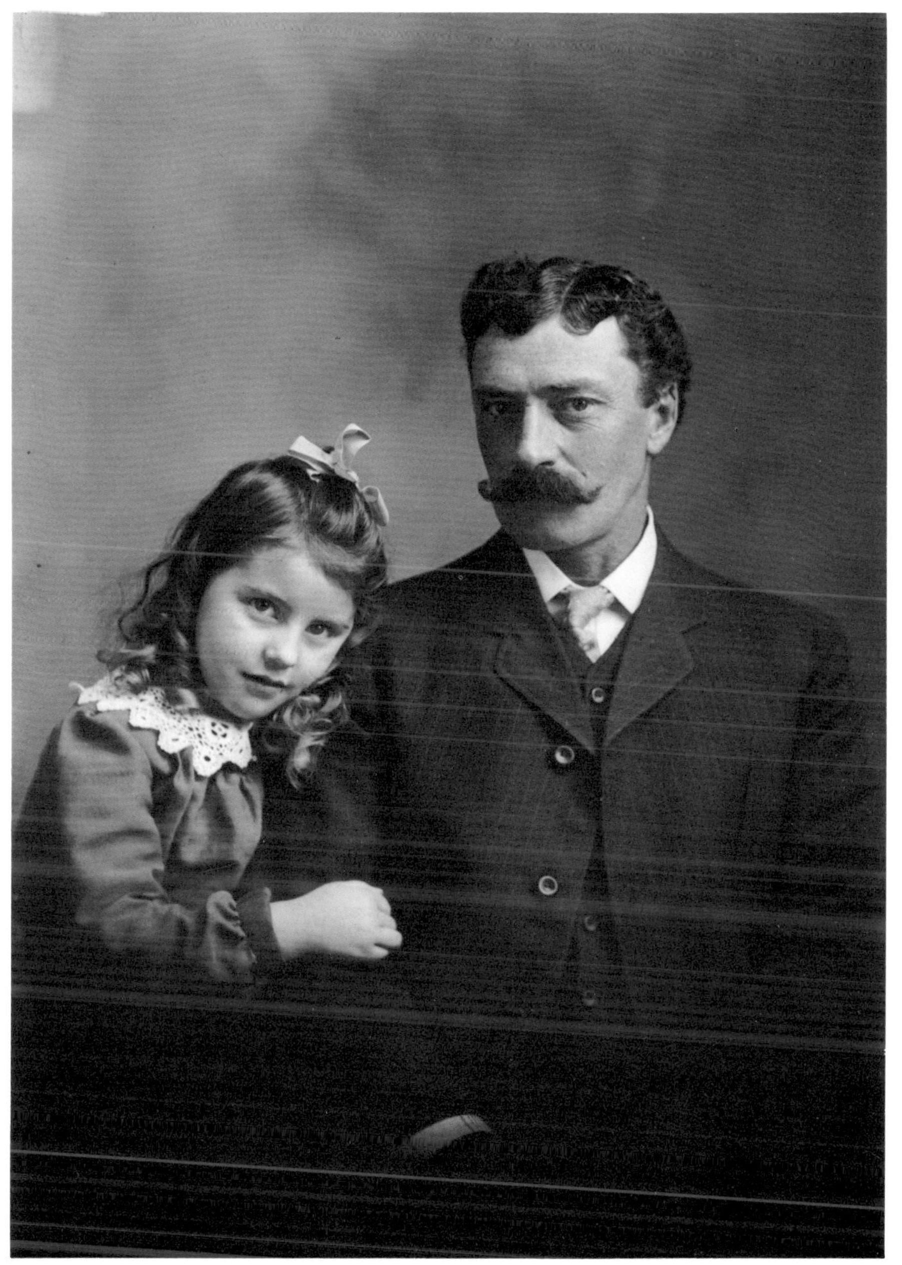

PLATE 35

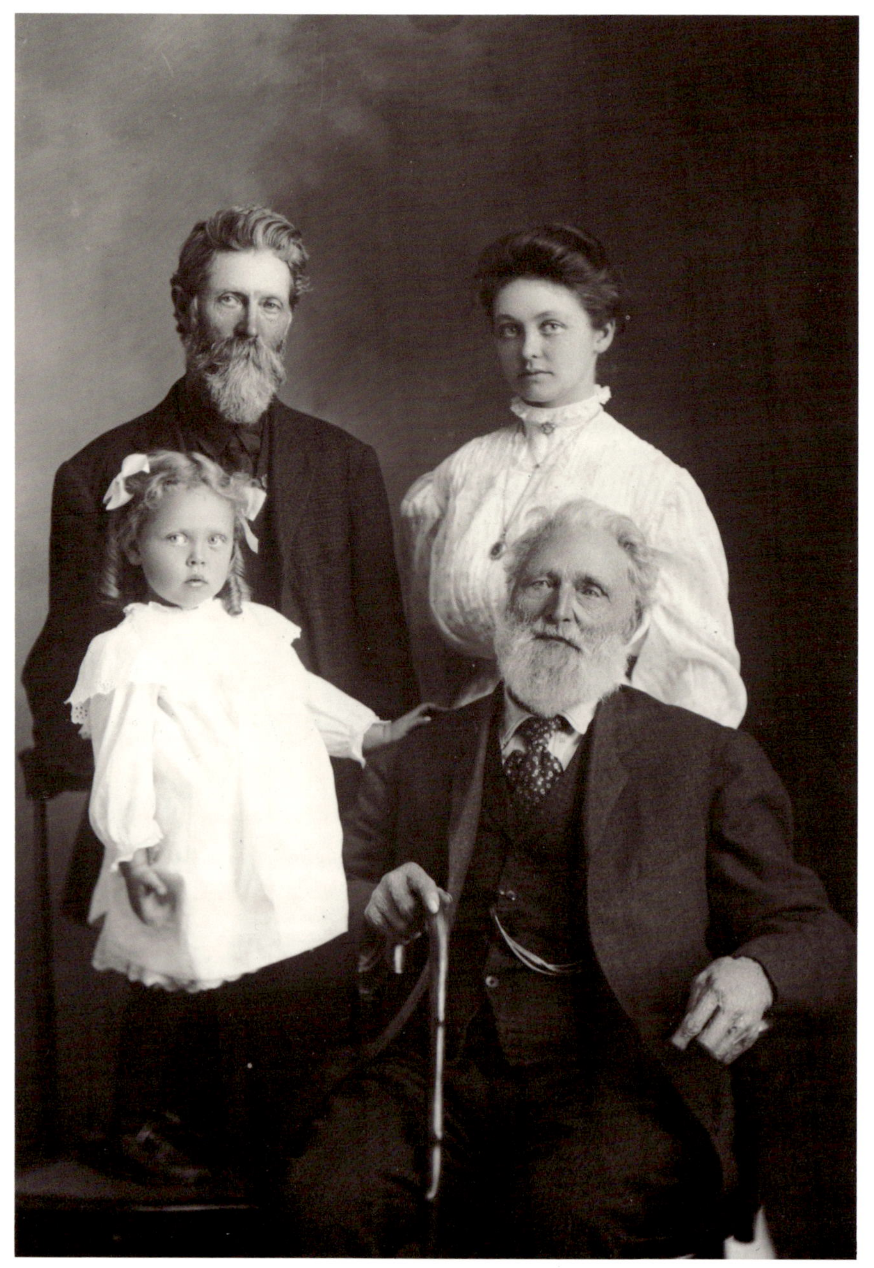

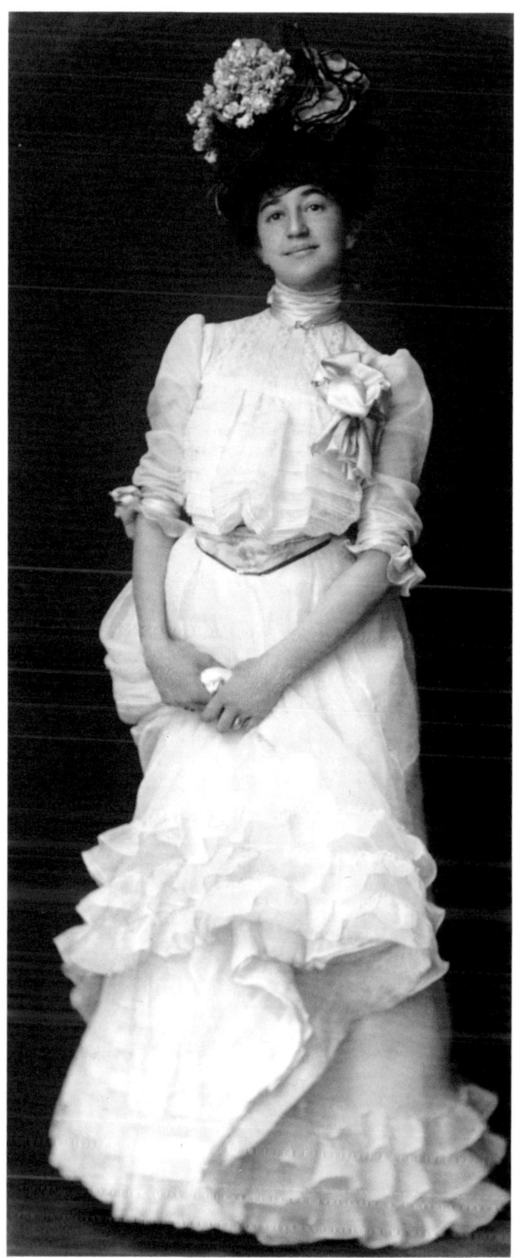

PLATE 37

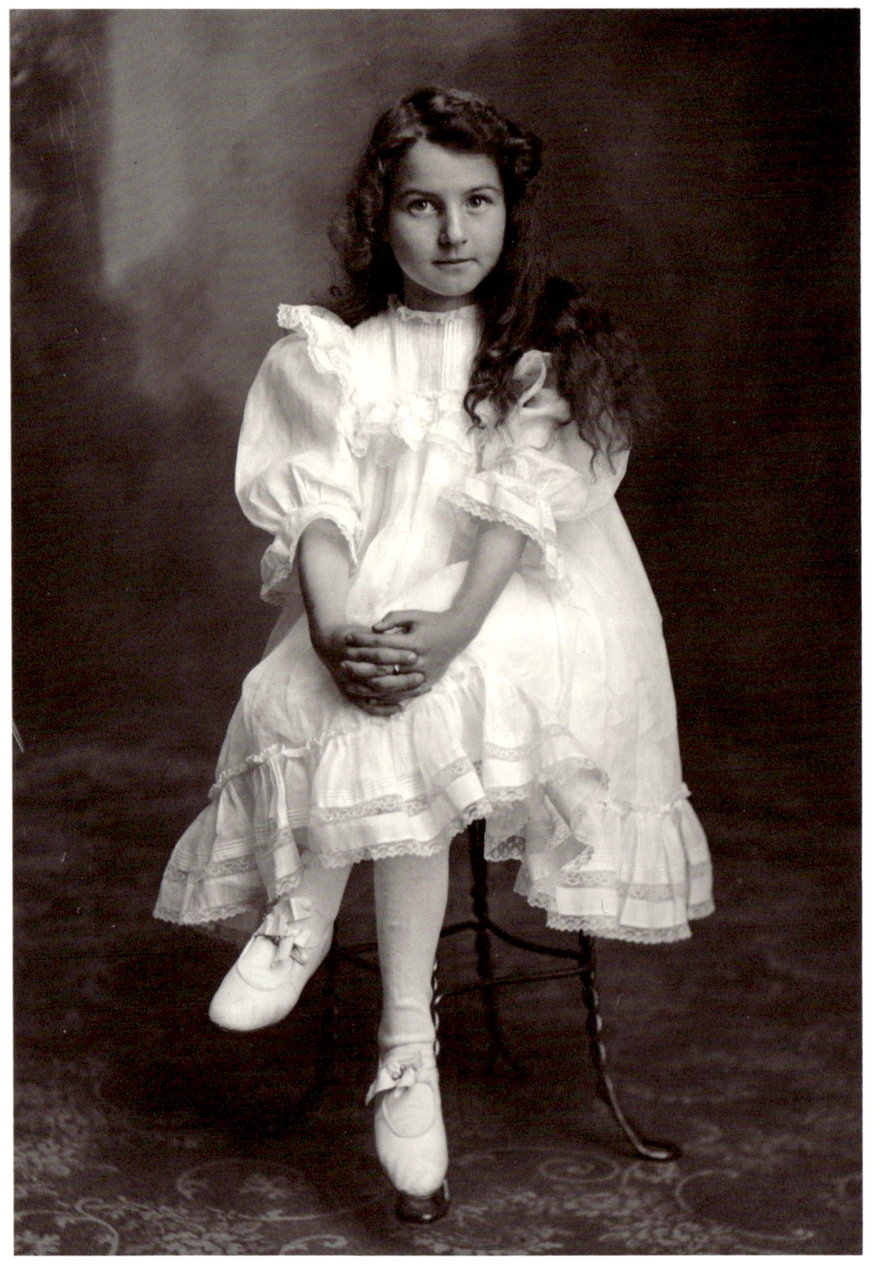

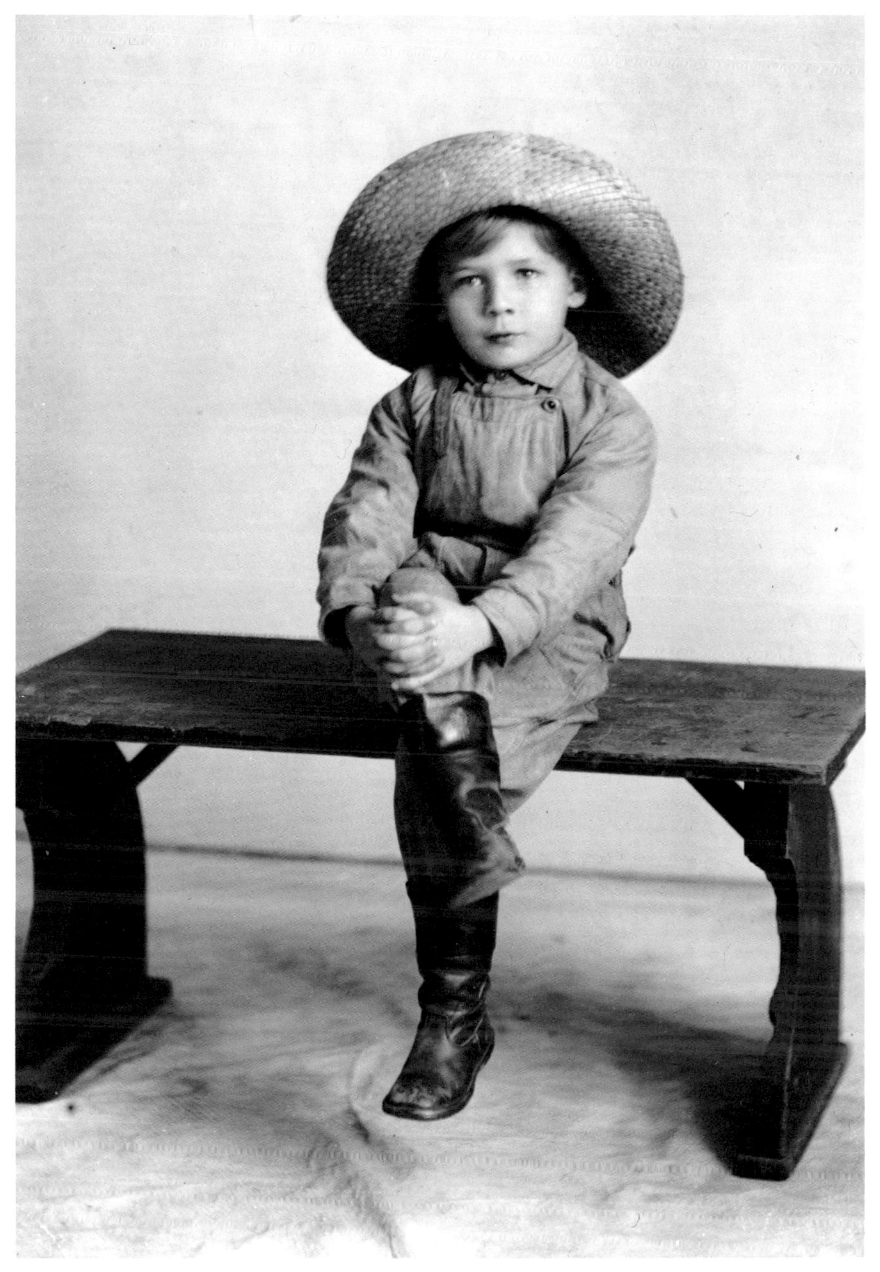

PLATE 39

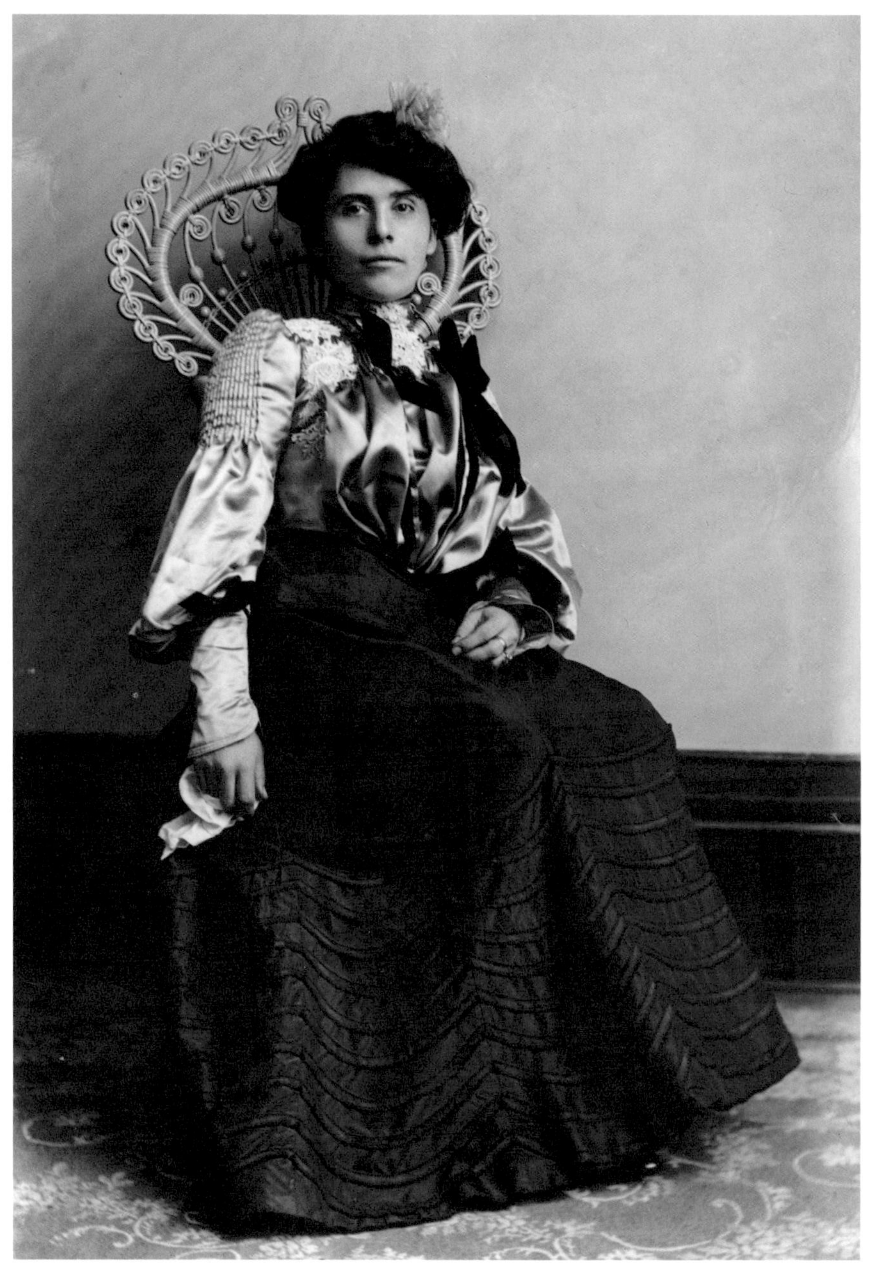

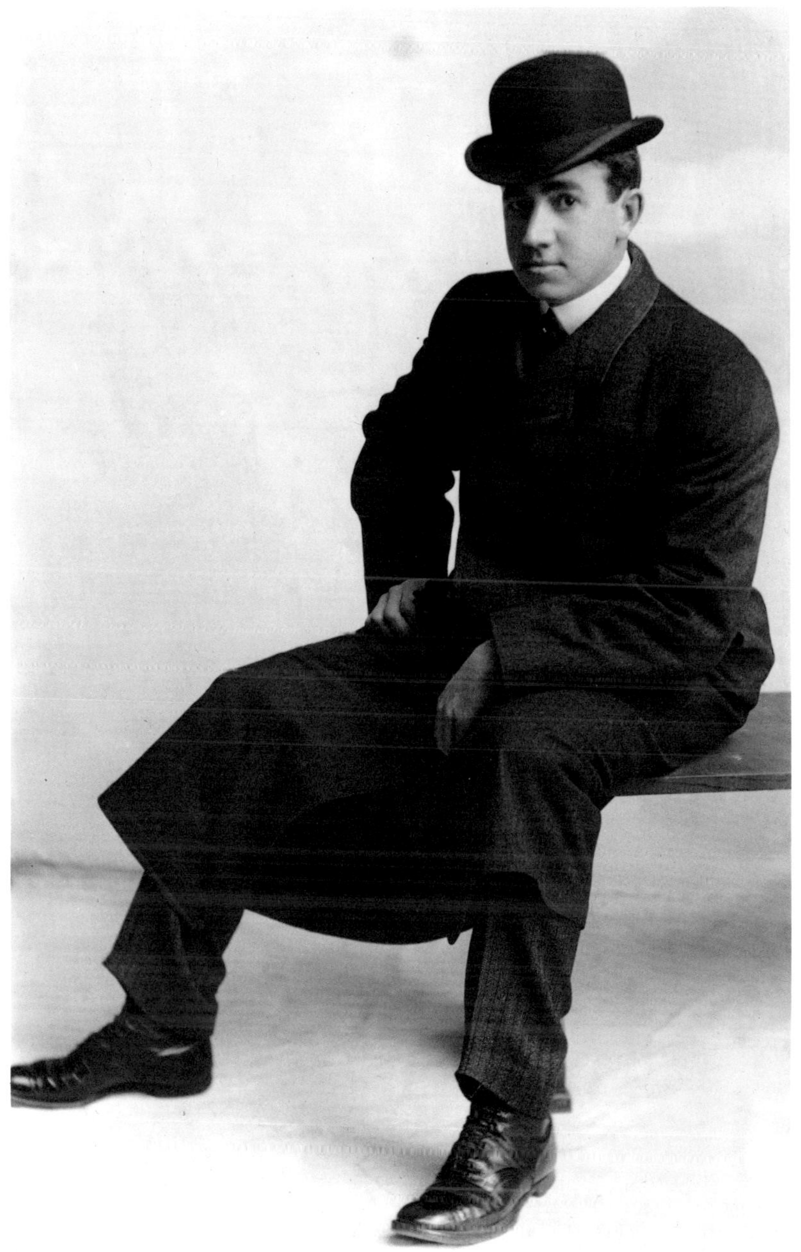

PLATE 41

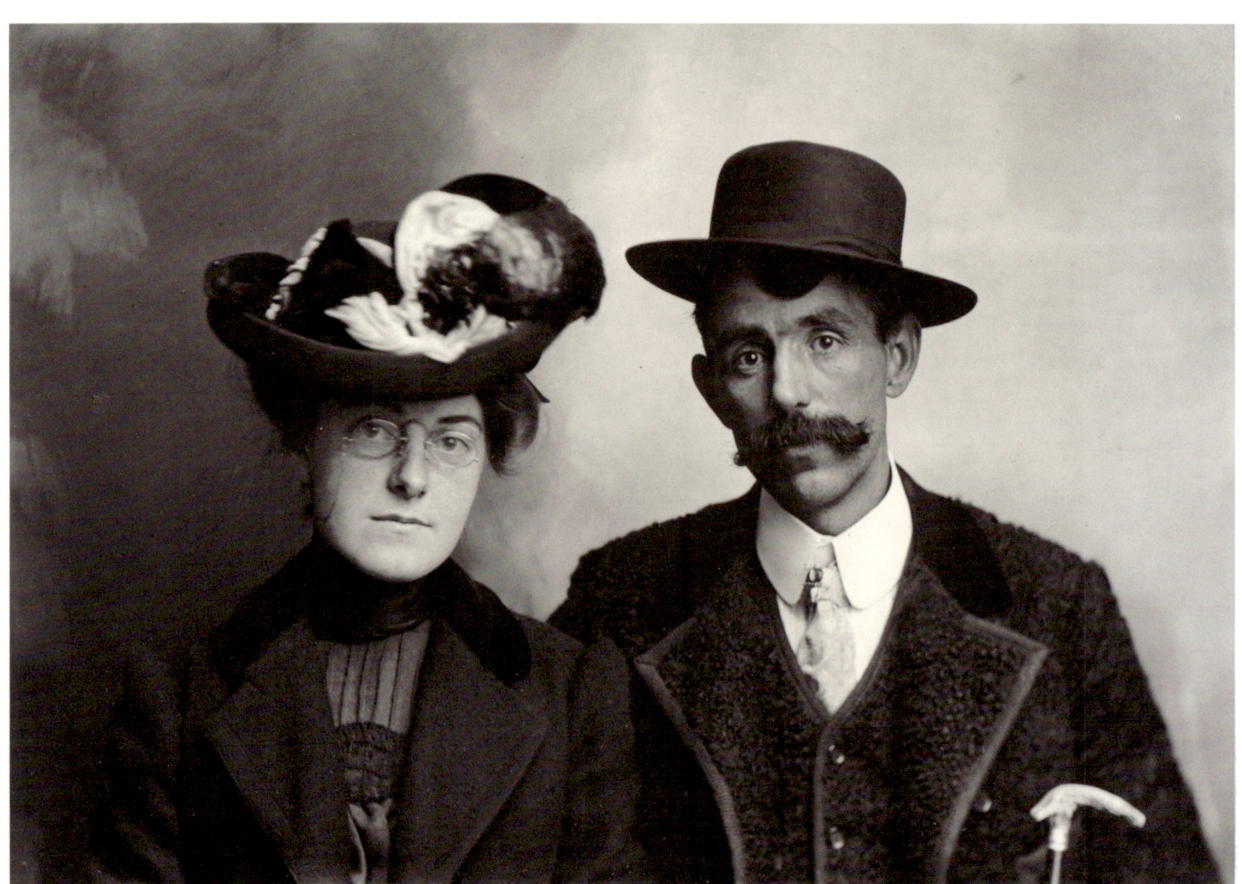

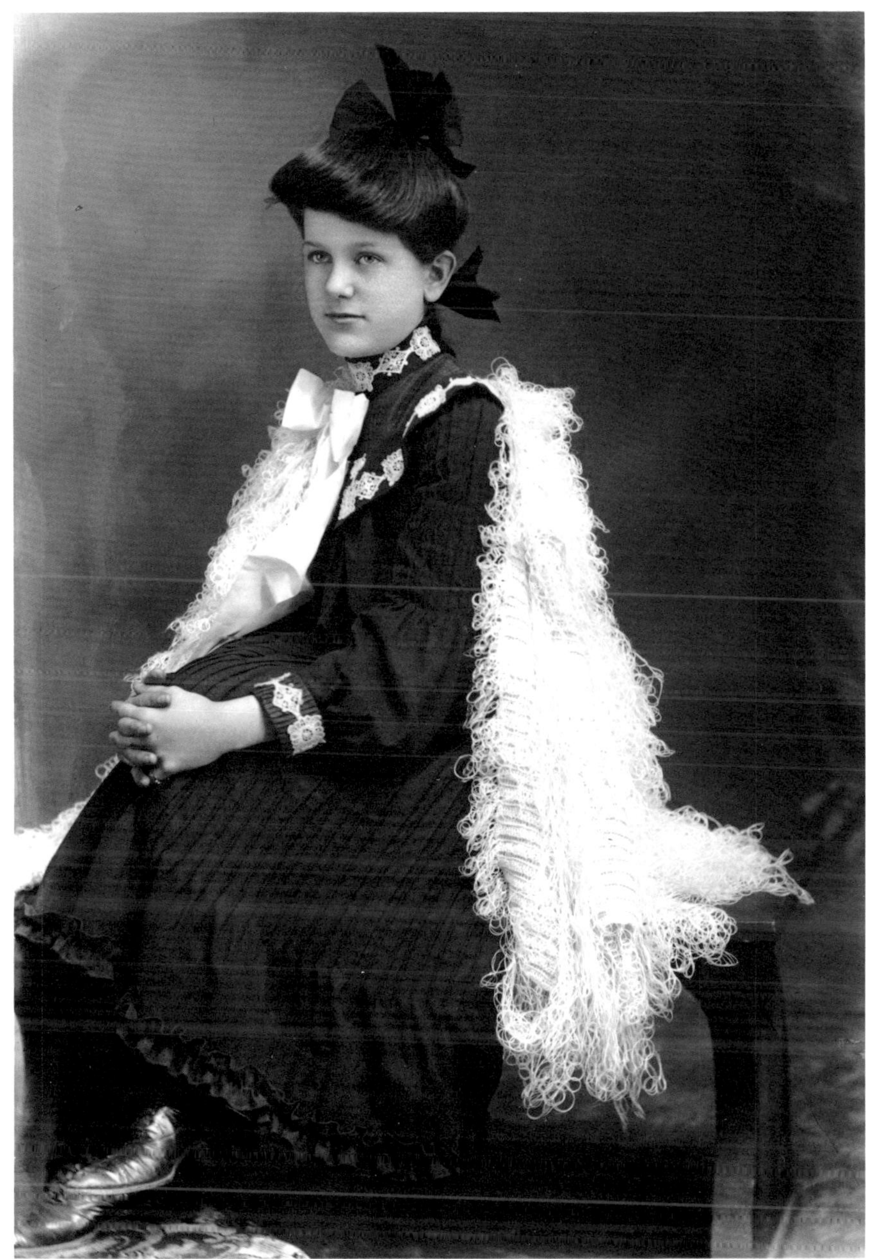

PLATE 43

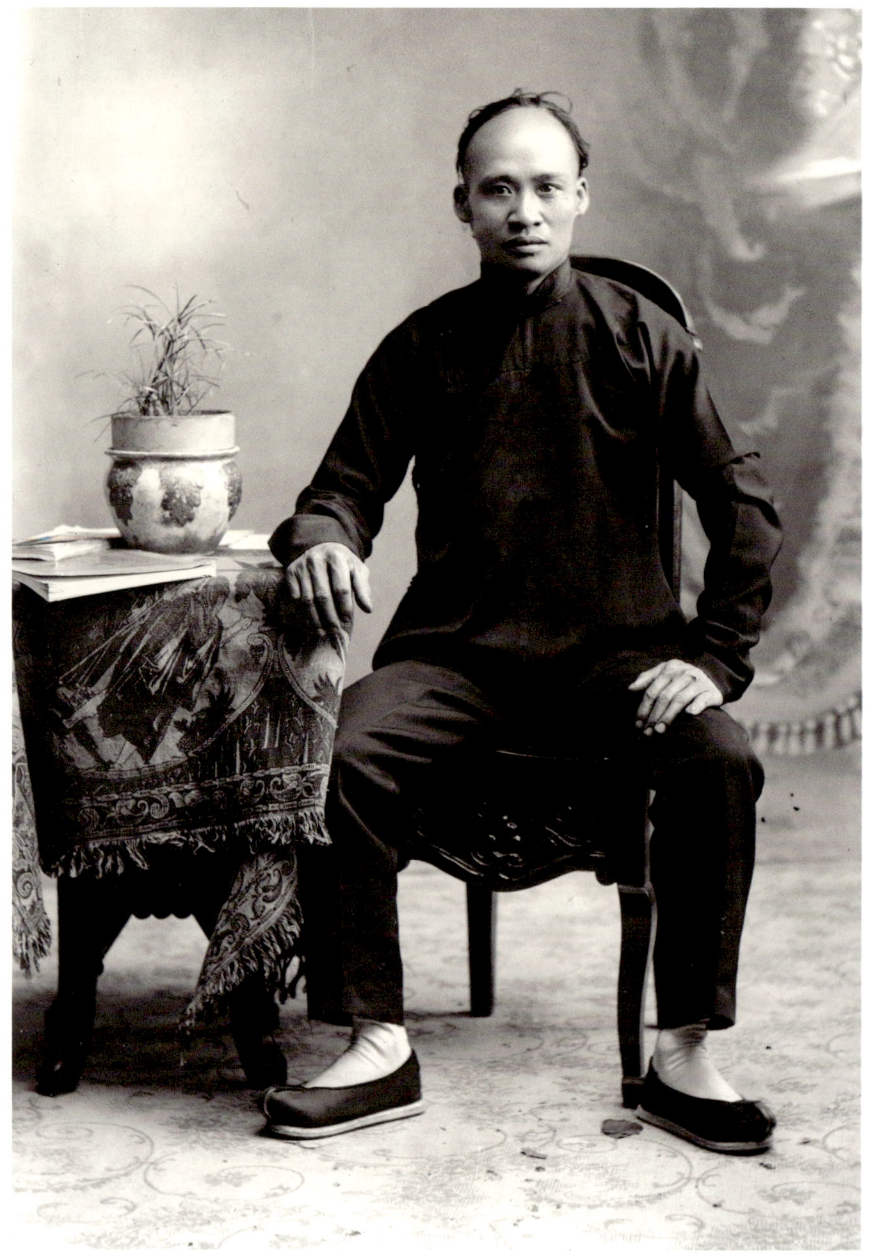

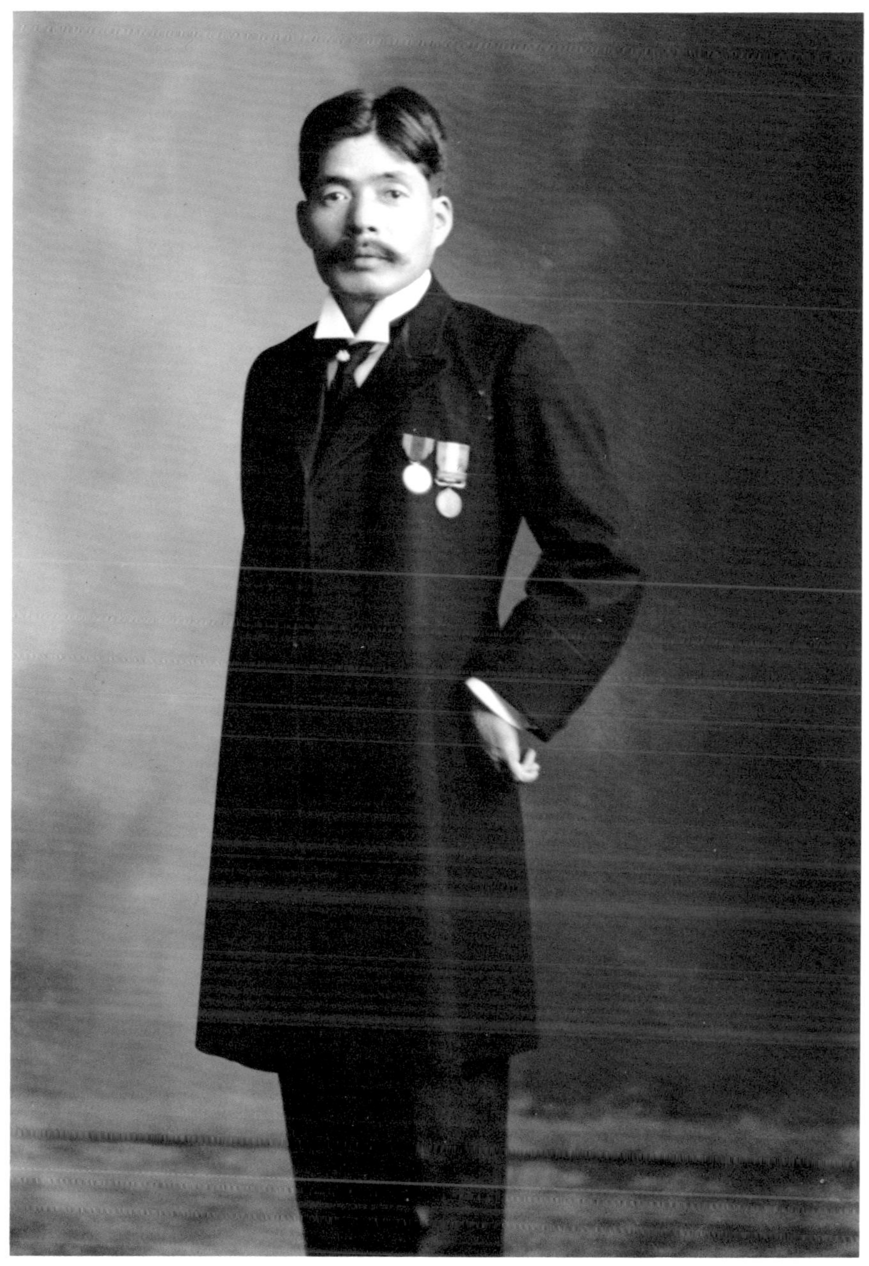

PLATE 45

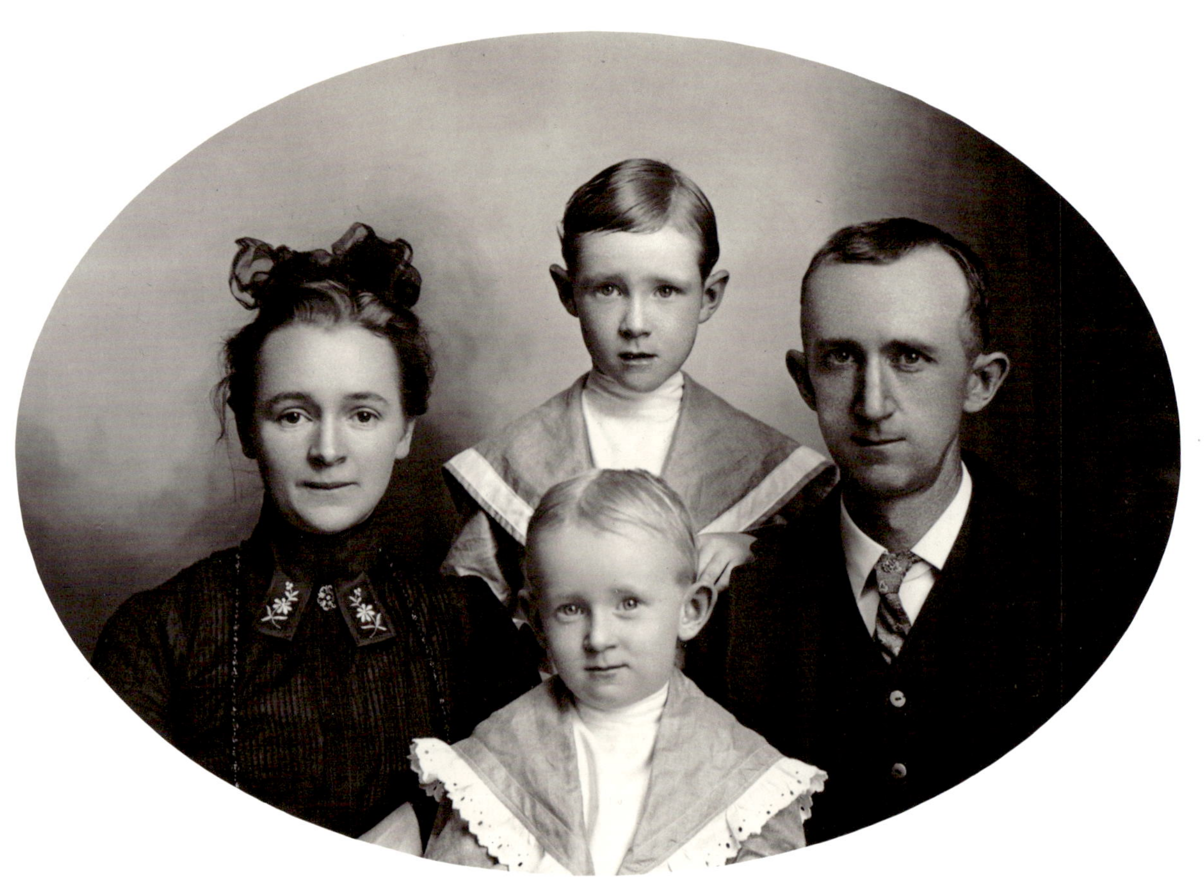

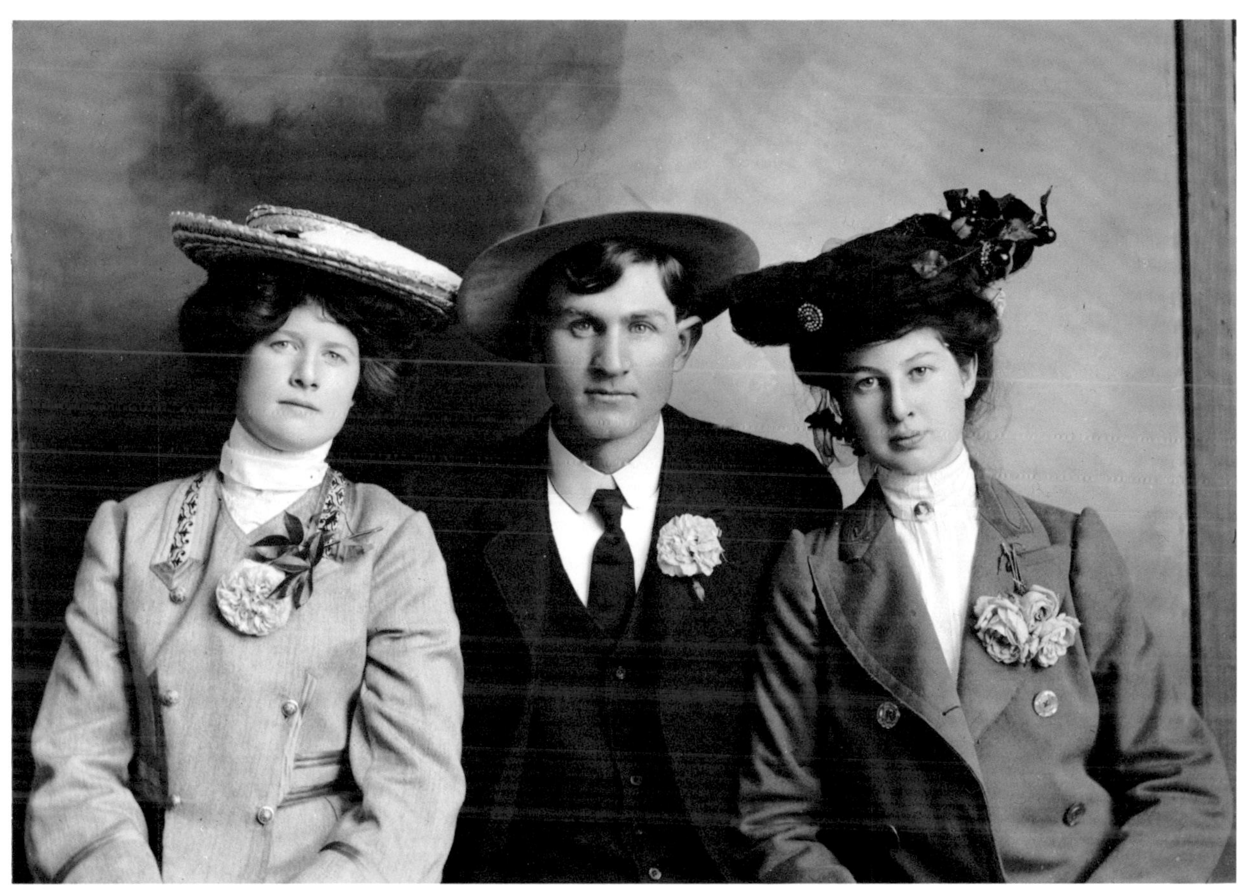

PLATE 47

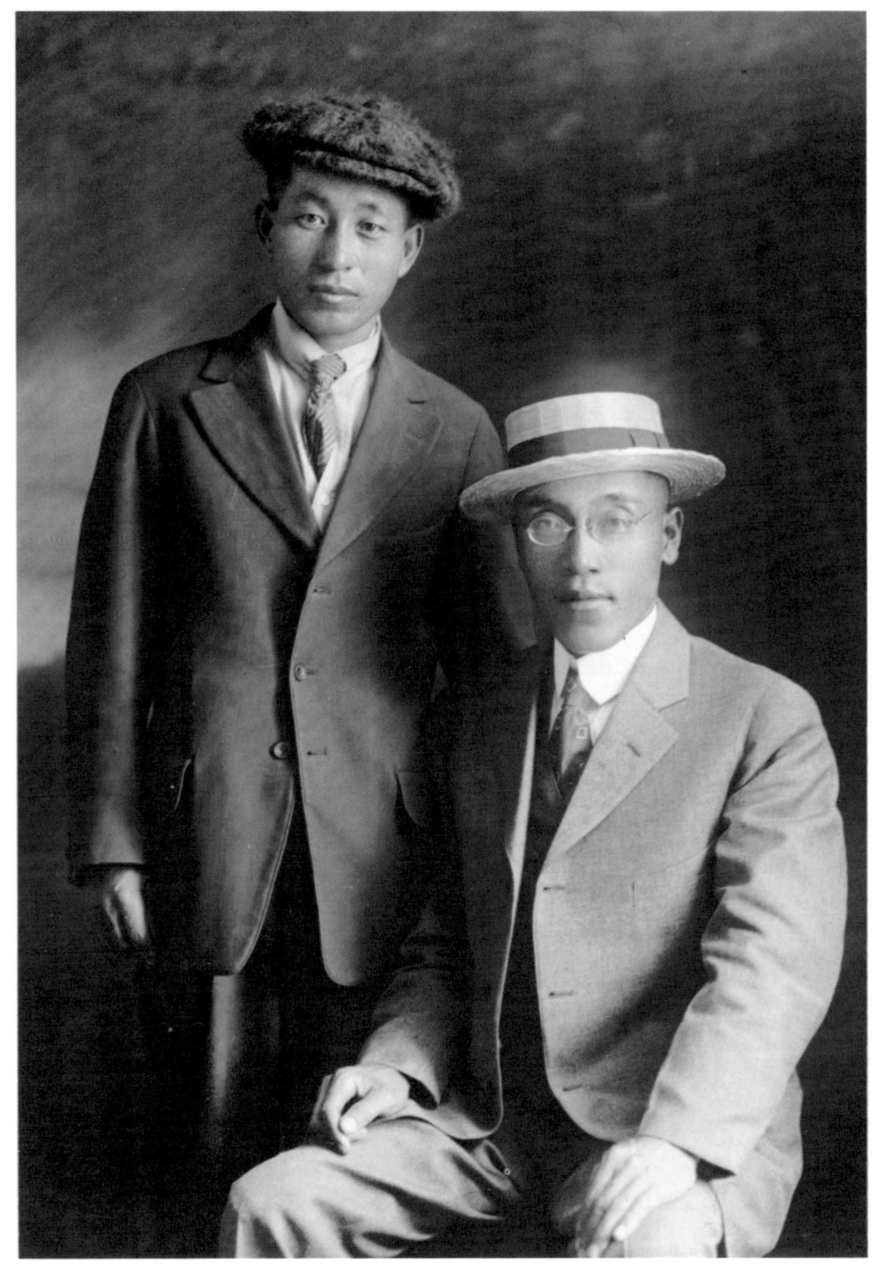

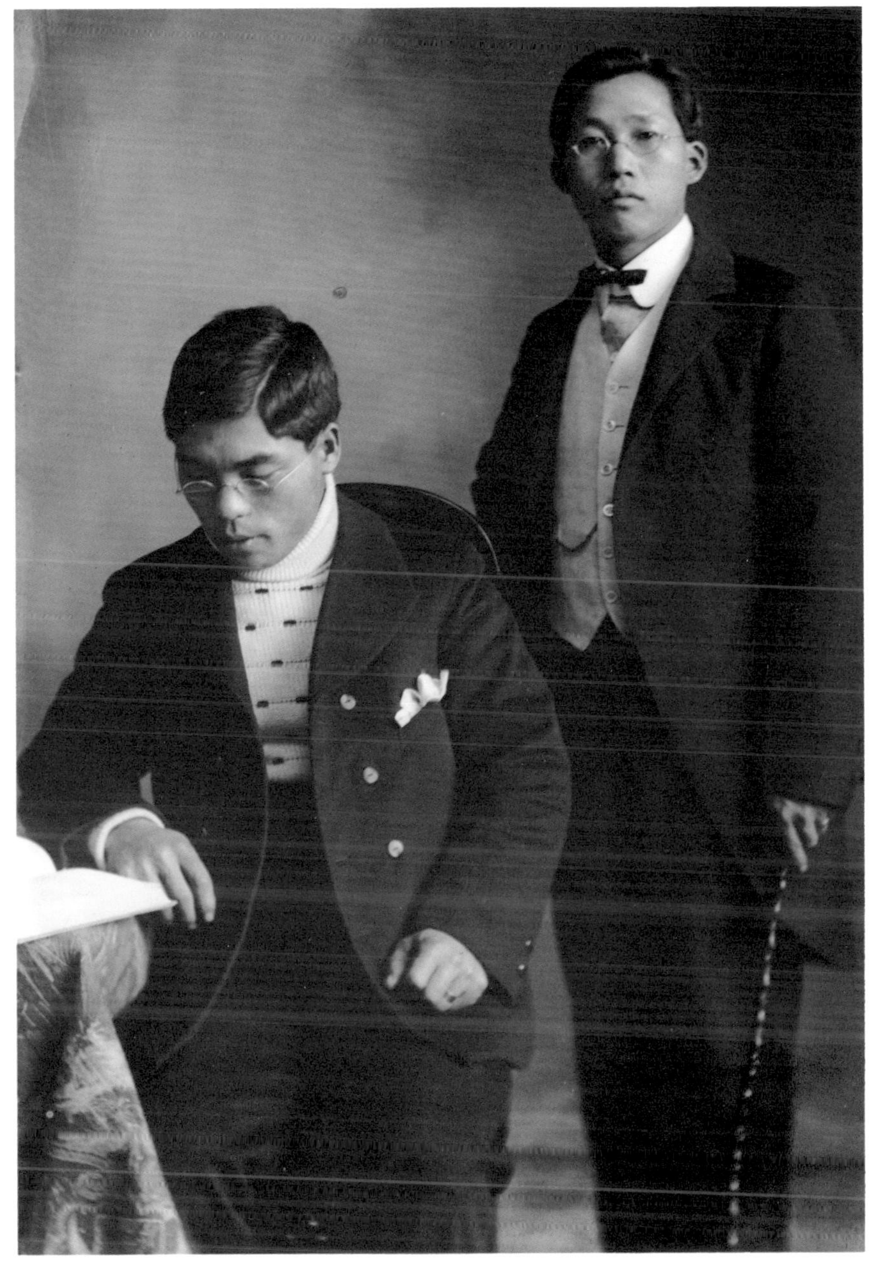

PLATE 49

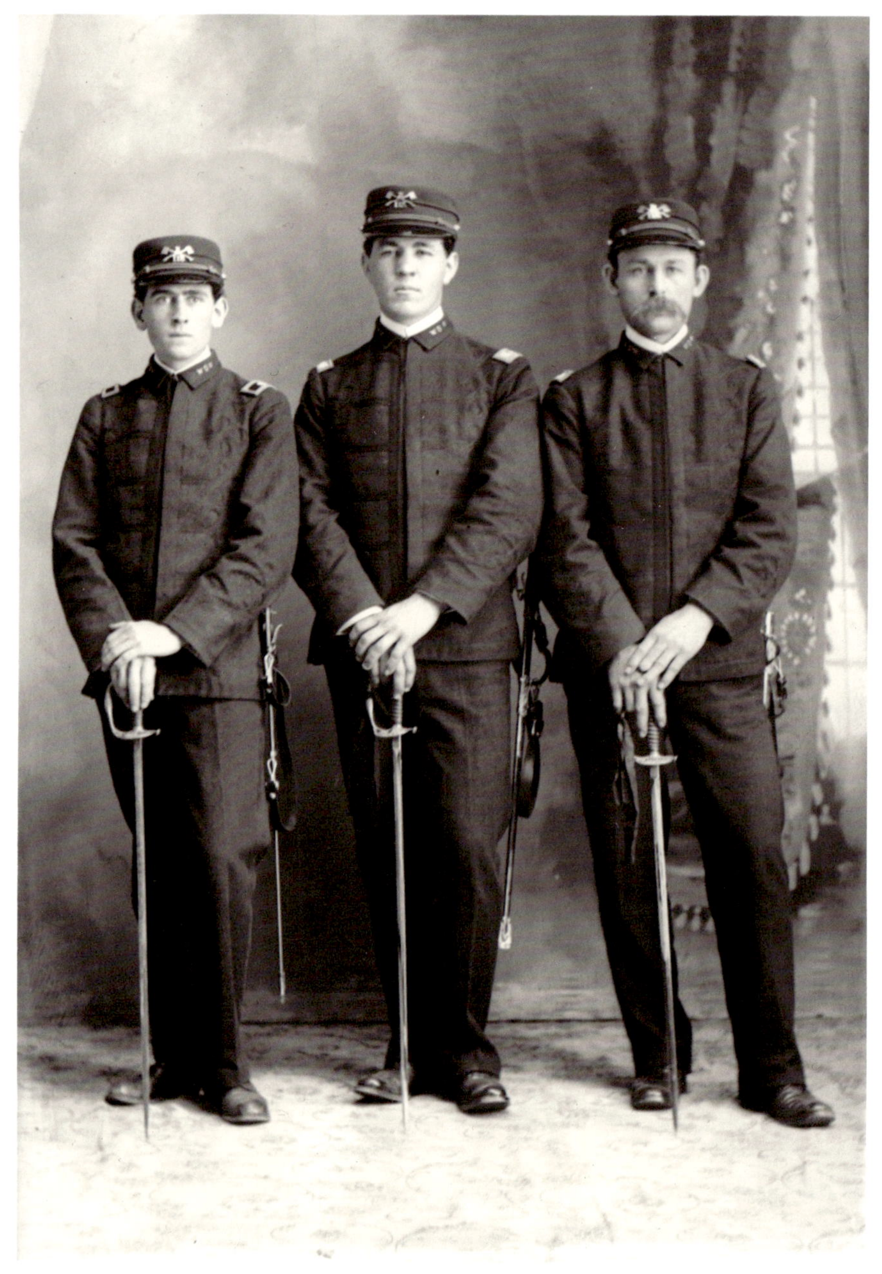

50 PLATE

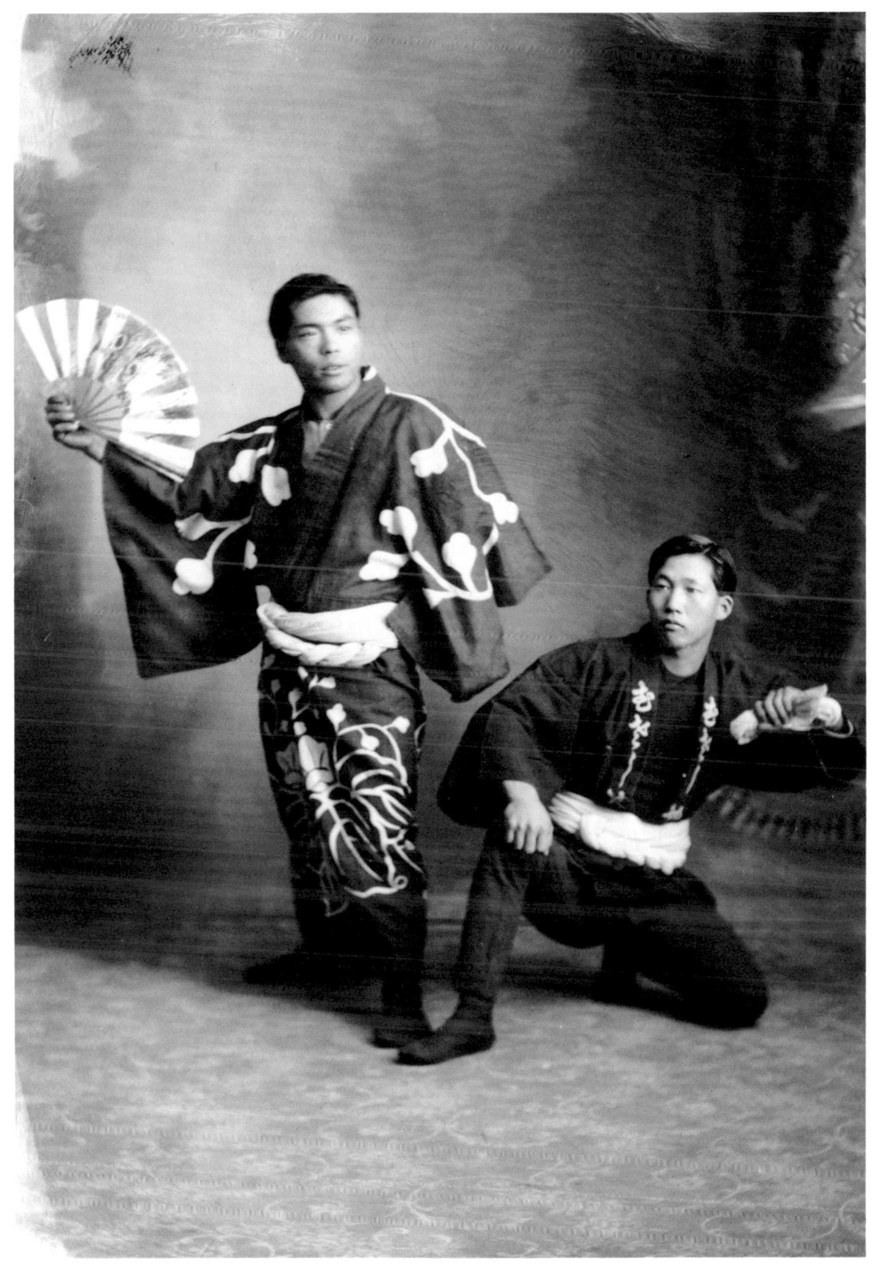

PLATE 51

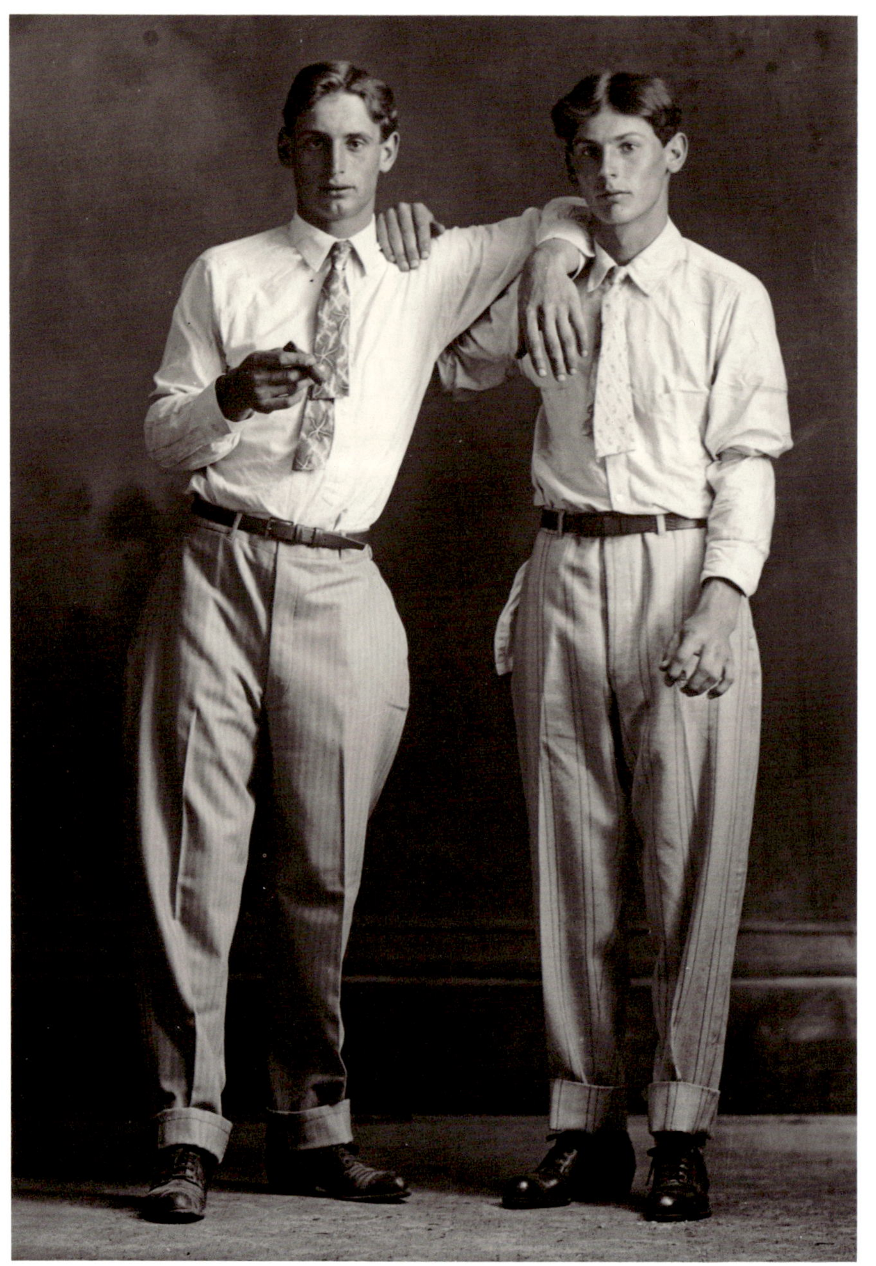

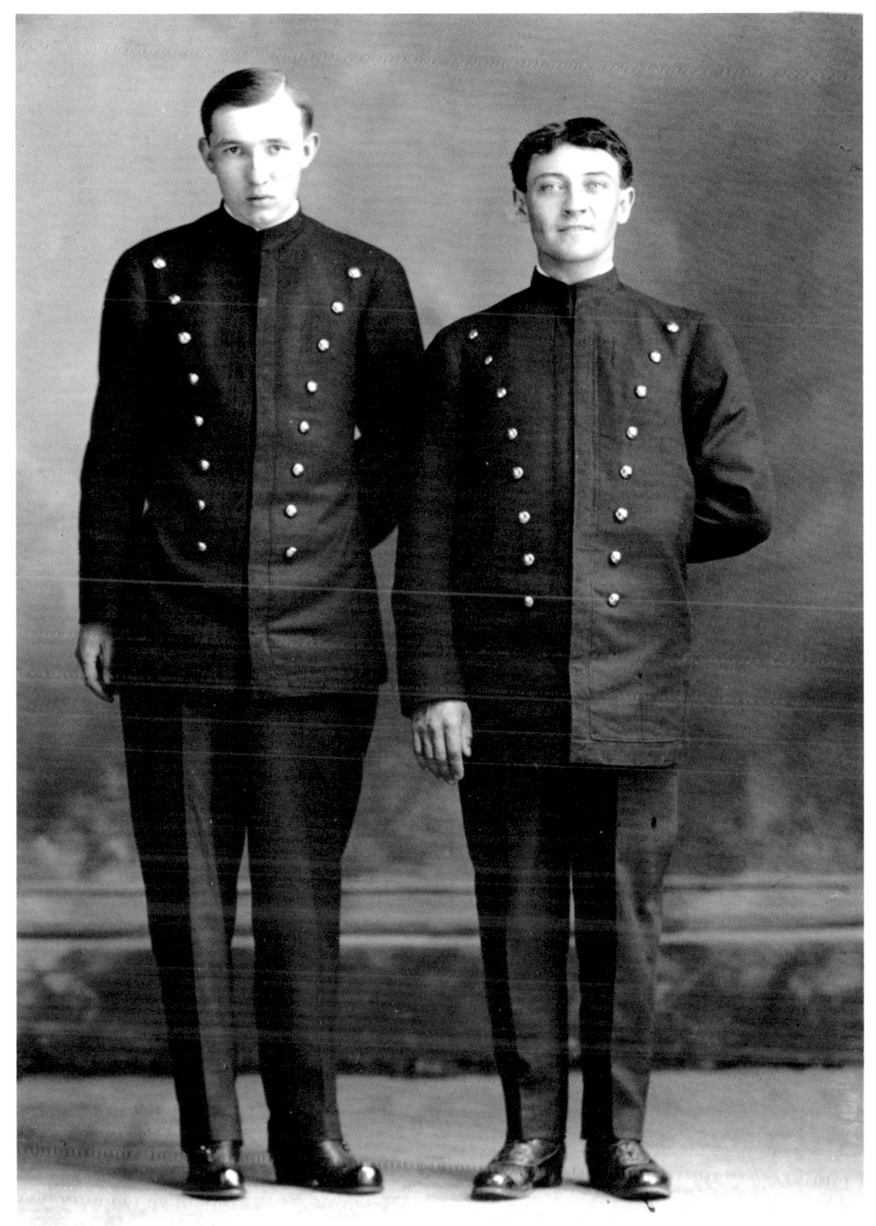

PLATE 53

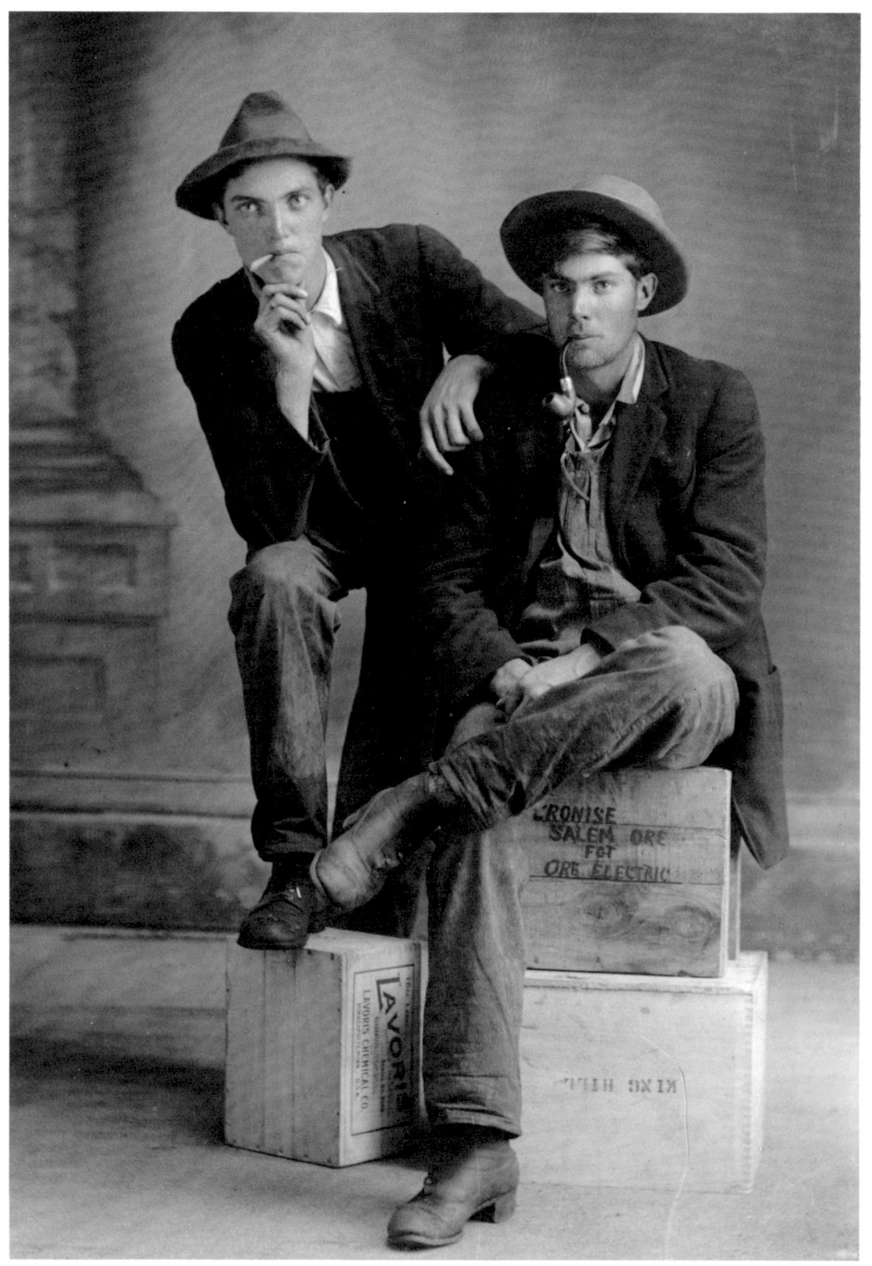
CRONISE
SALEM ORE
Fgt
ORE ELECTRIC
LAVORIS
LAVORIS CHEMICAL CO.

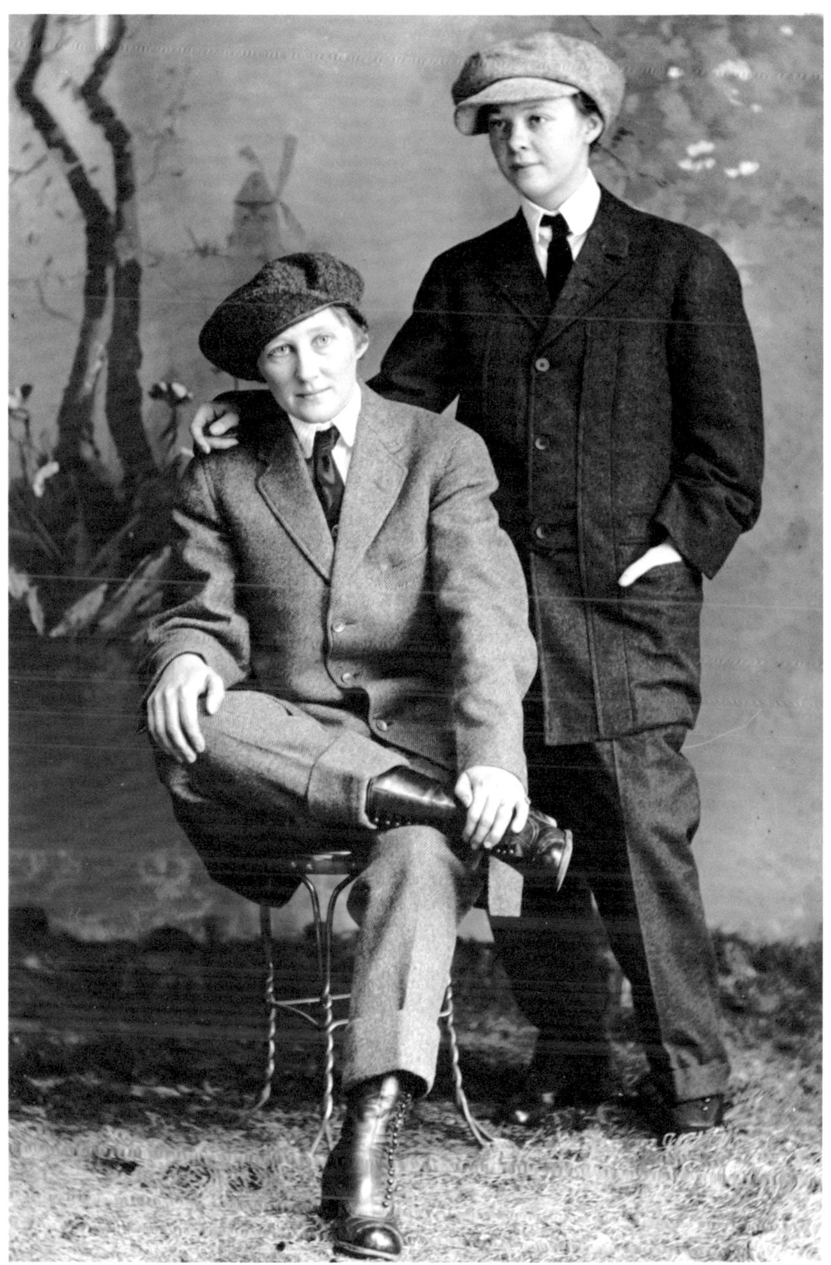

PLATE 55

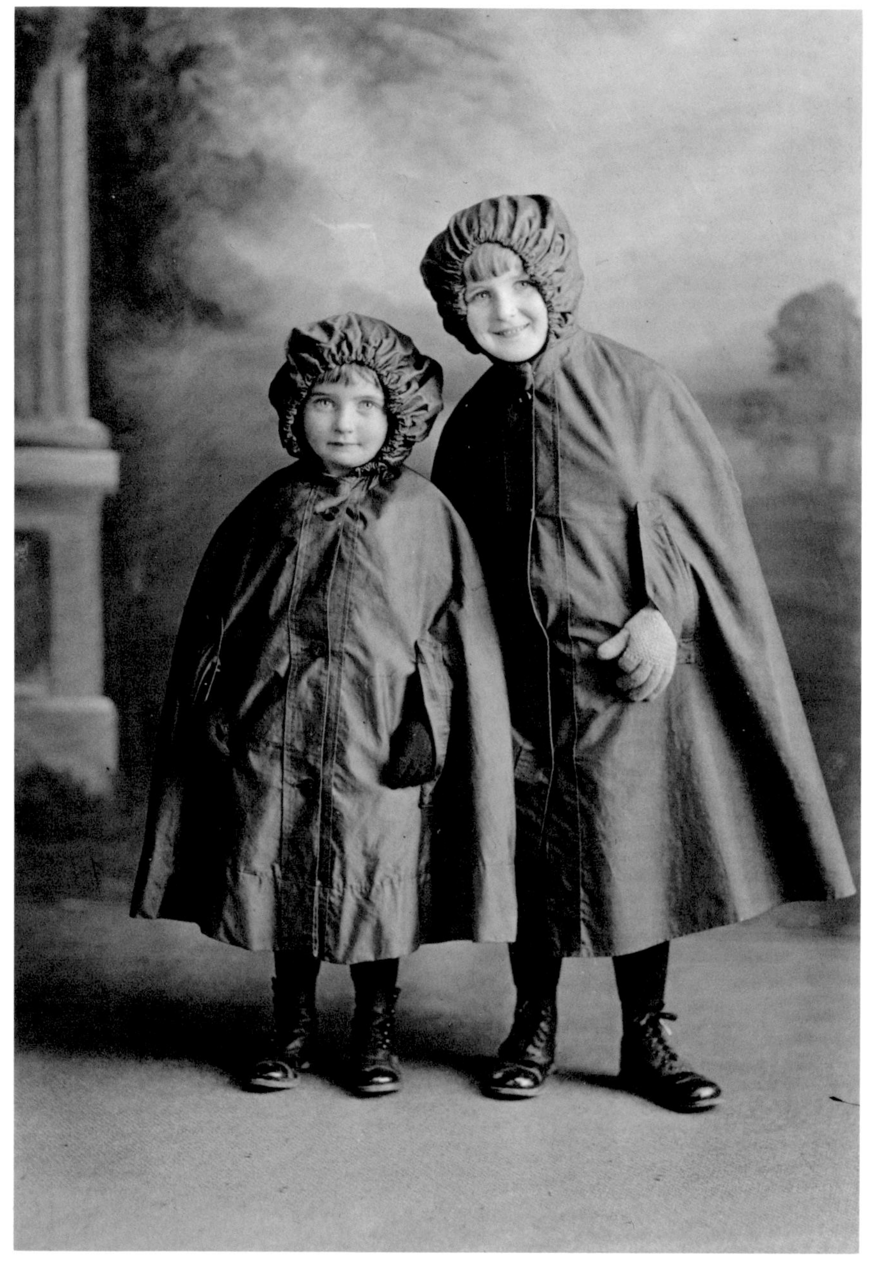

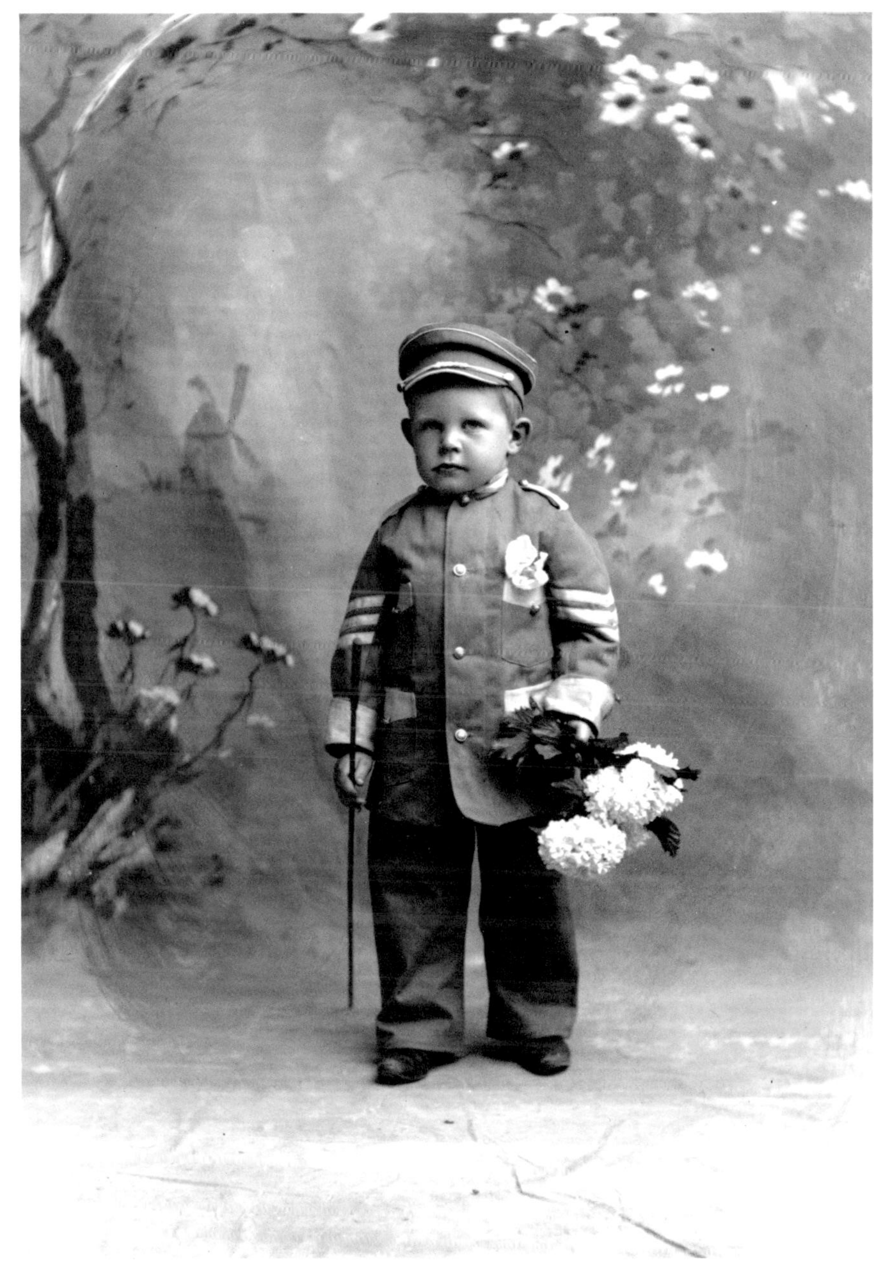

PLATE 57

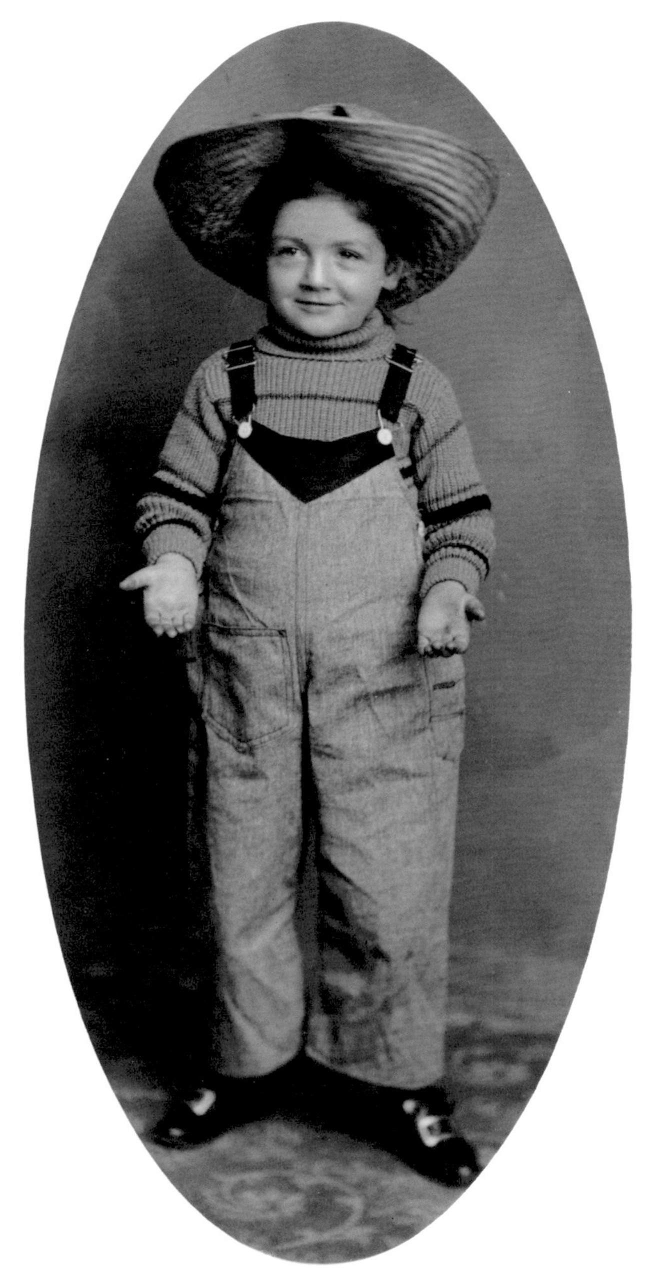

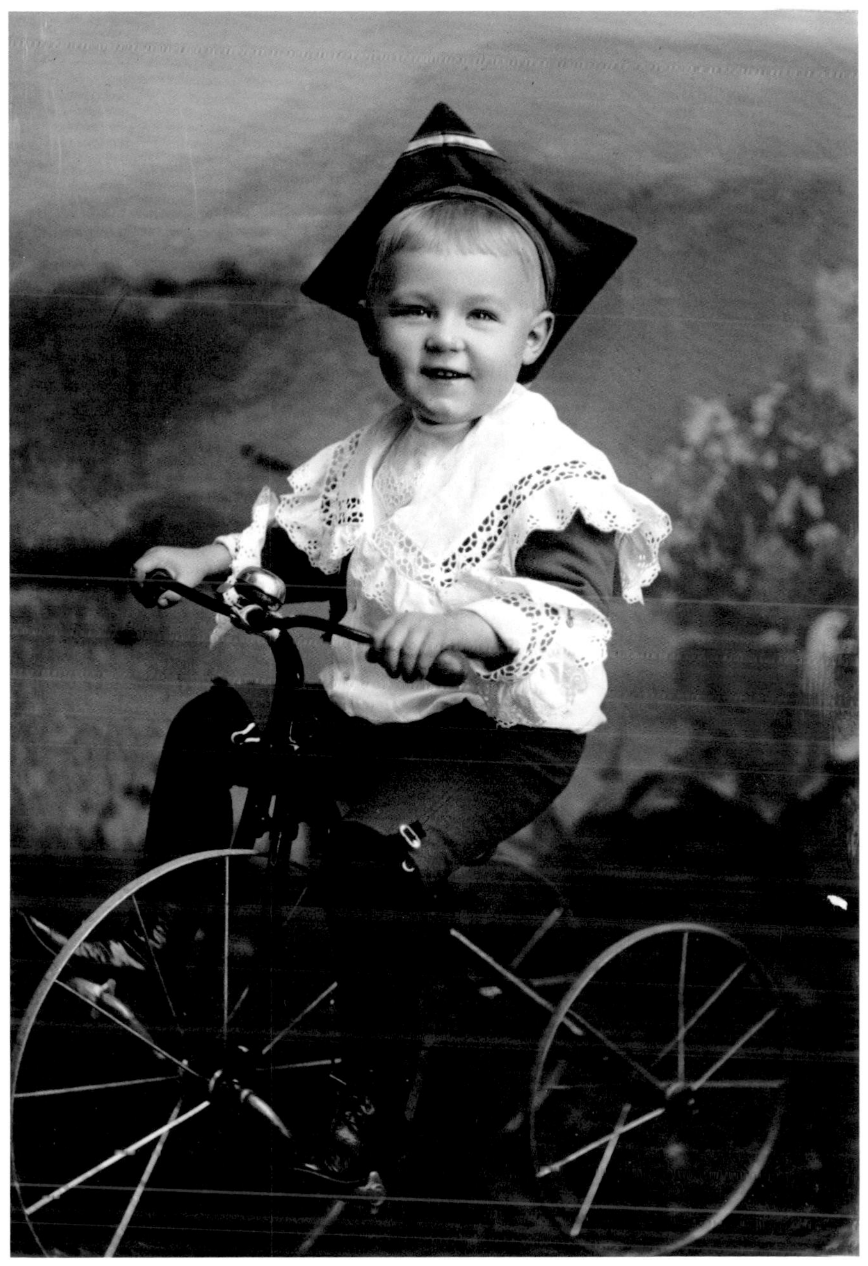

PLATE 59

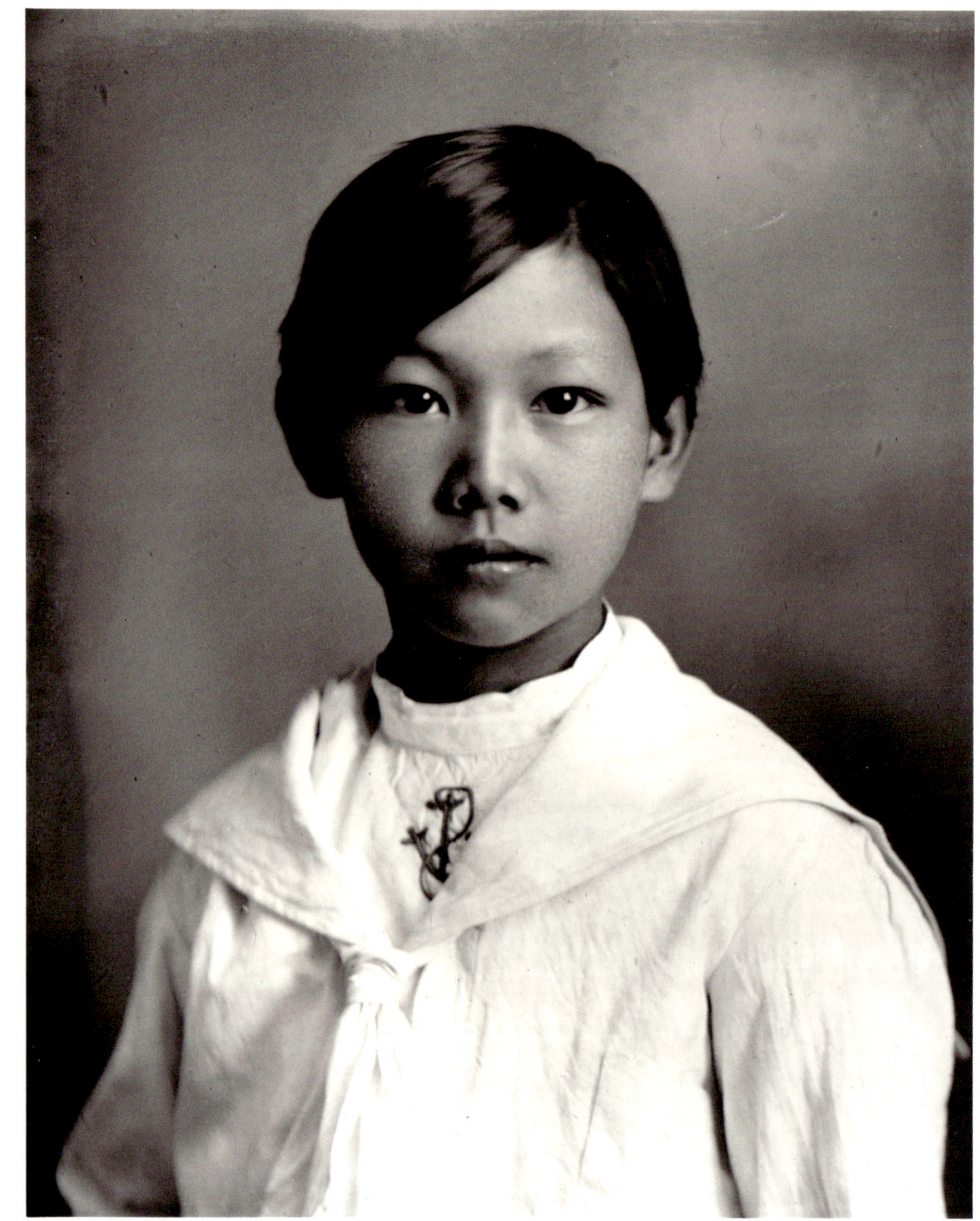

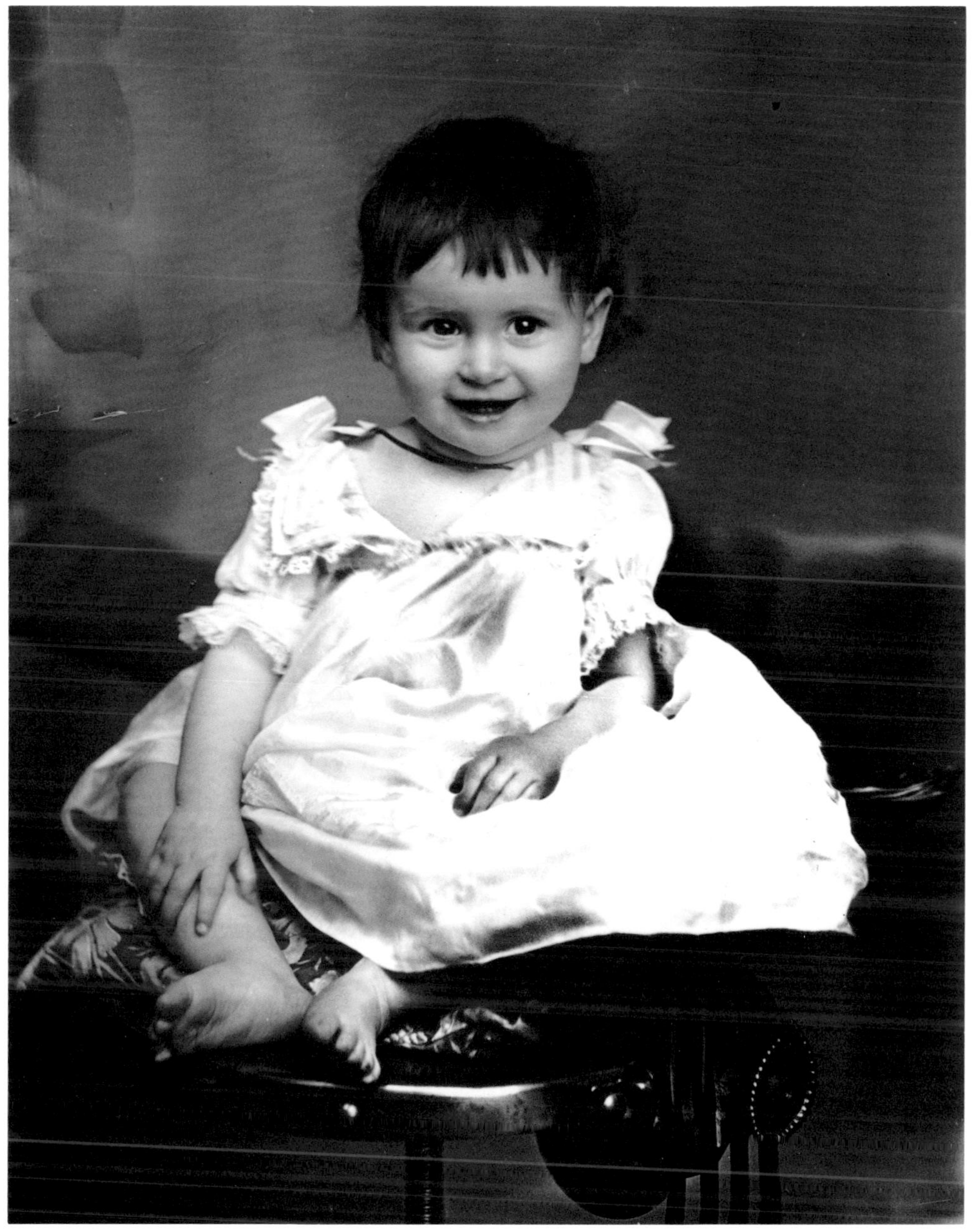

PLATE 61

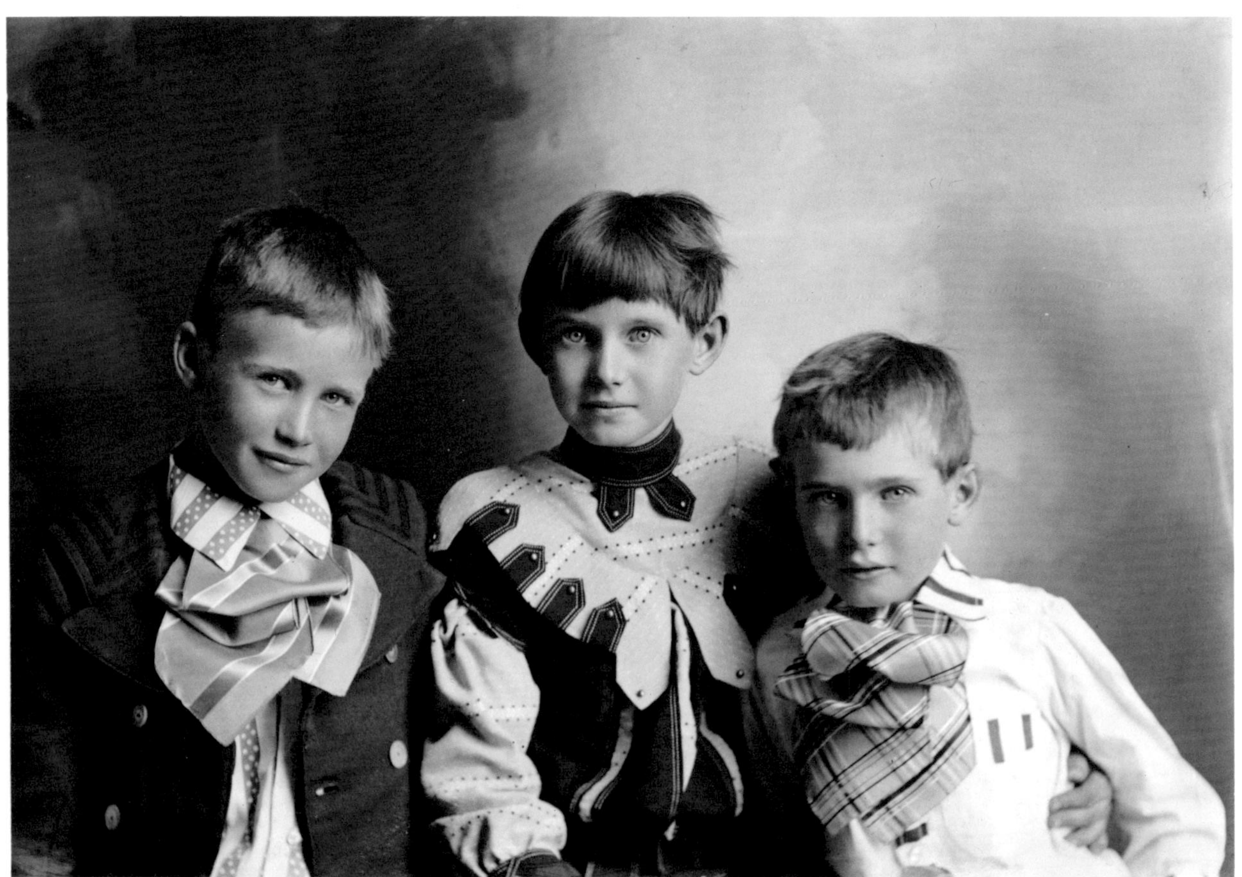

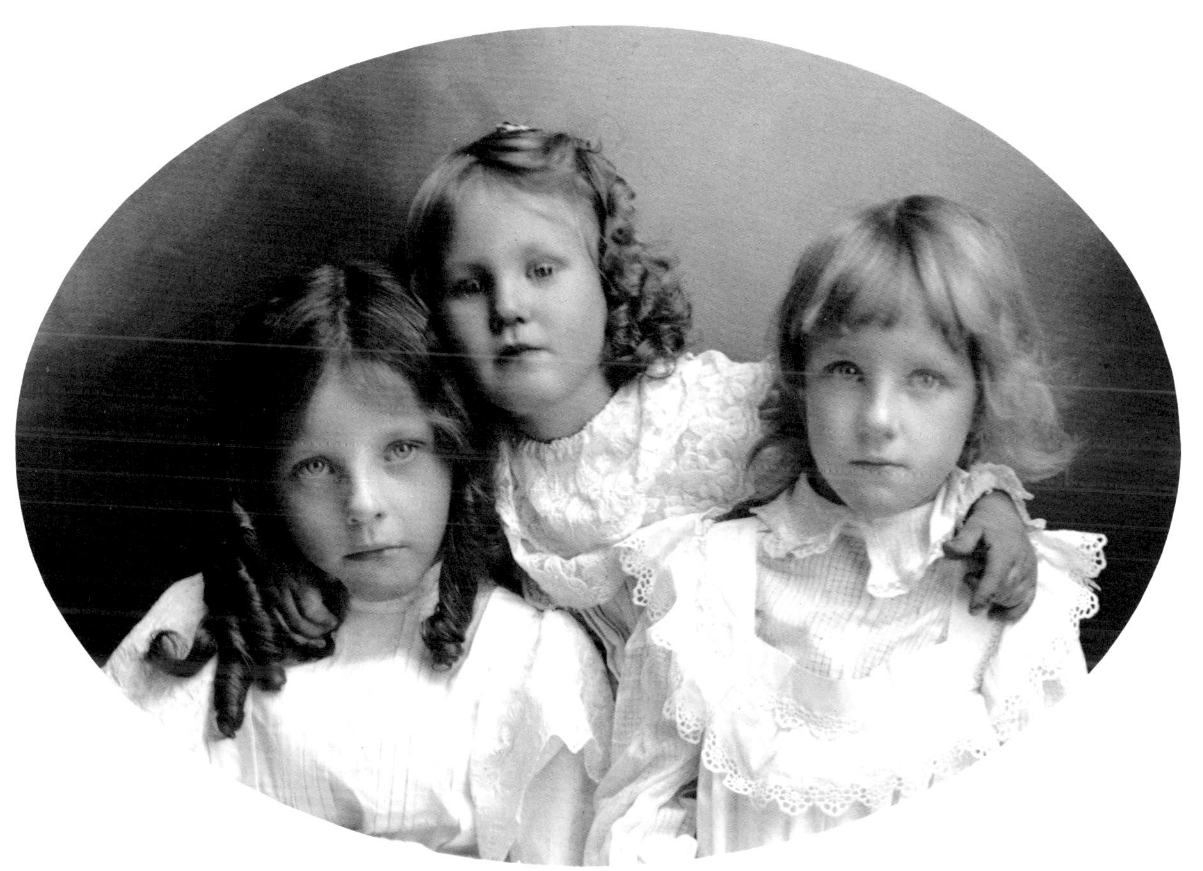

PLATE 63

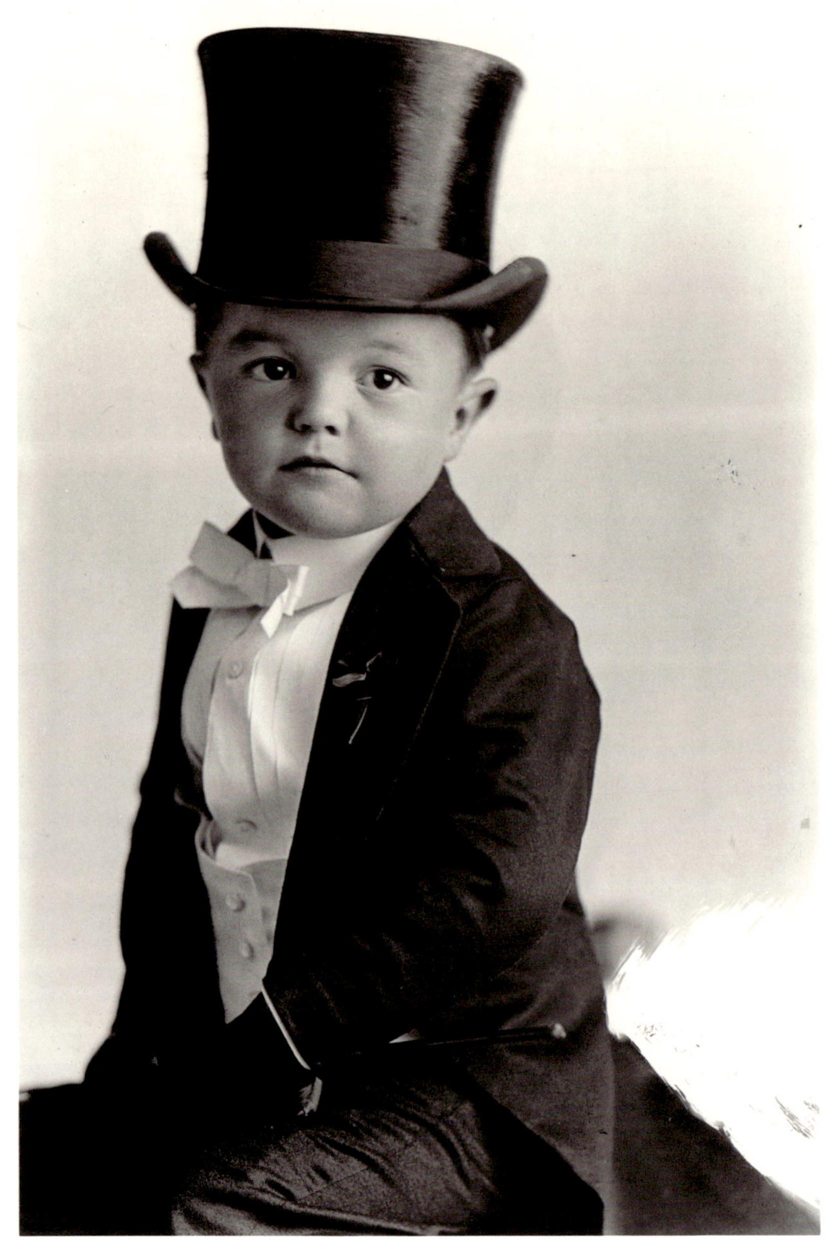

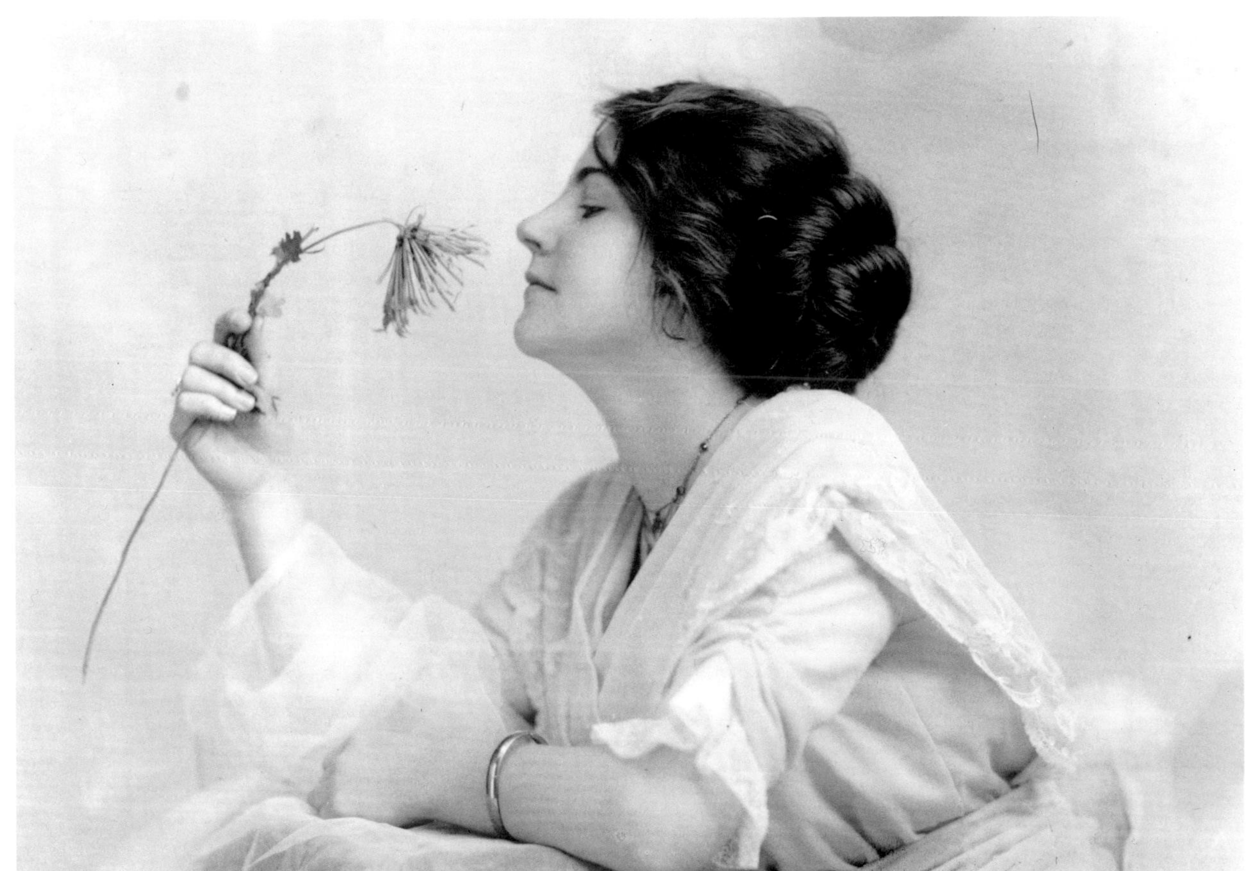

PLATE 65

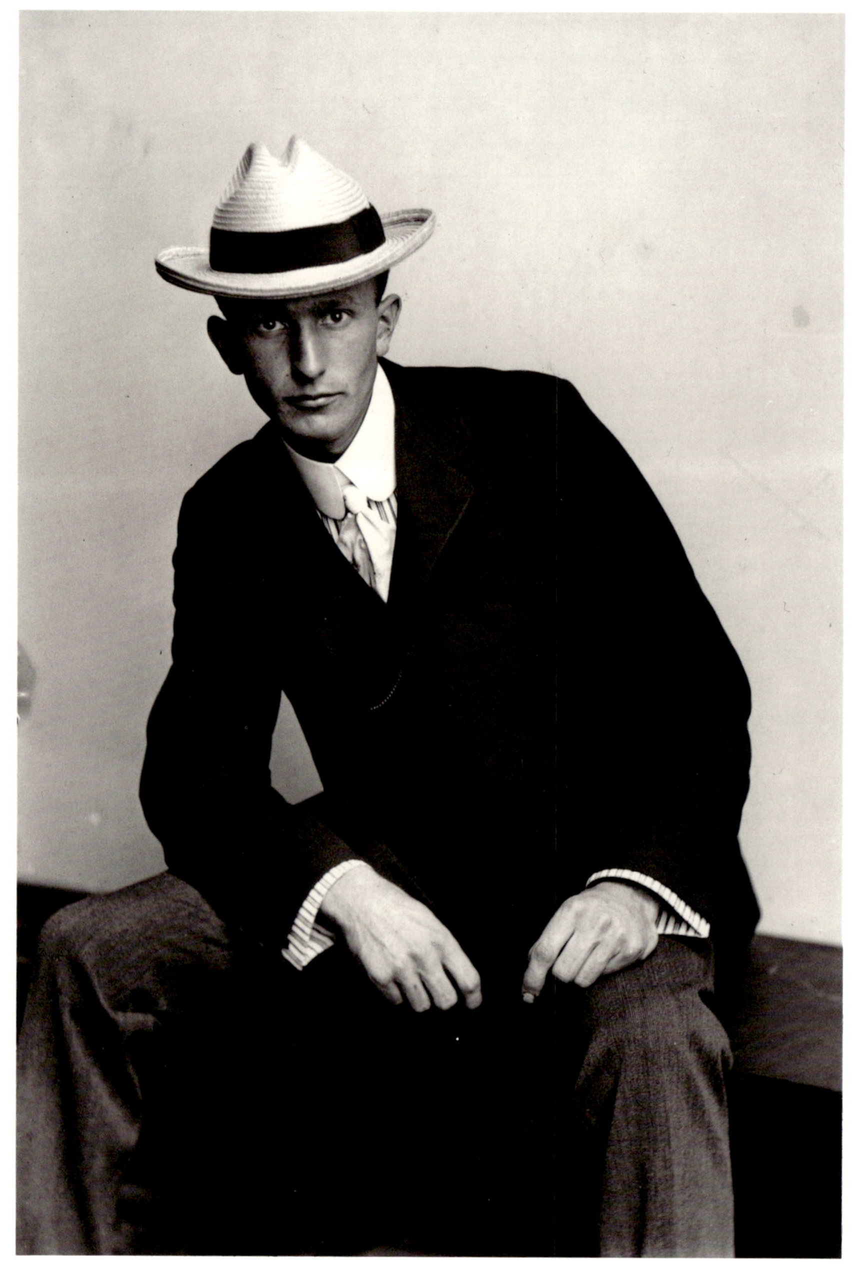

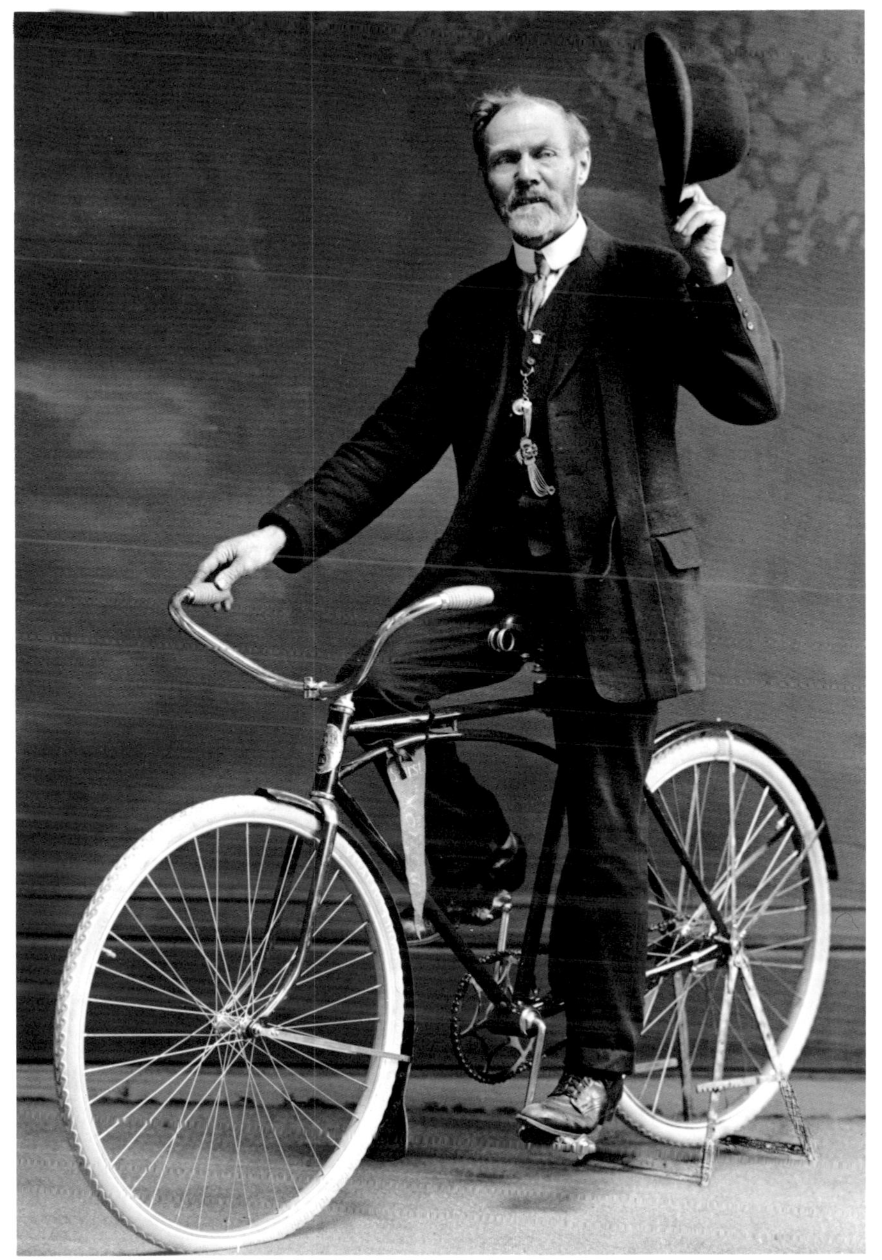

PLATE 67

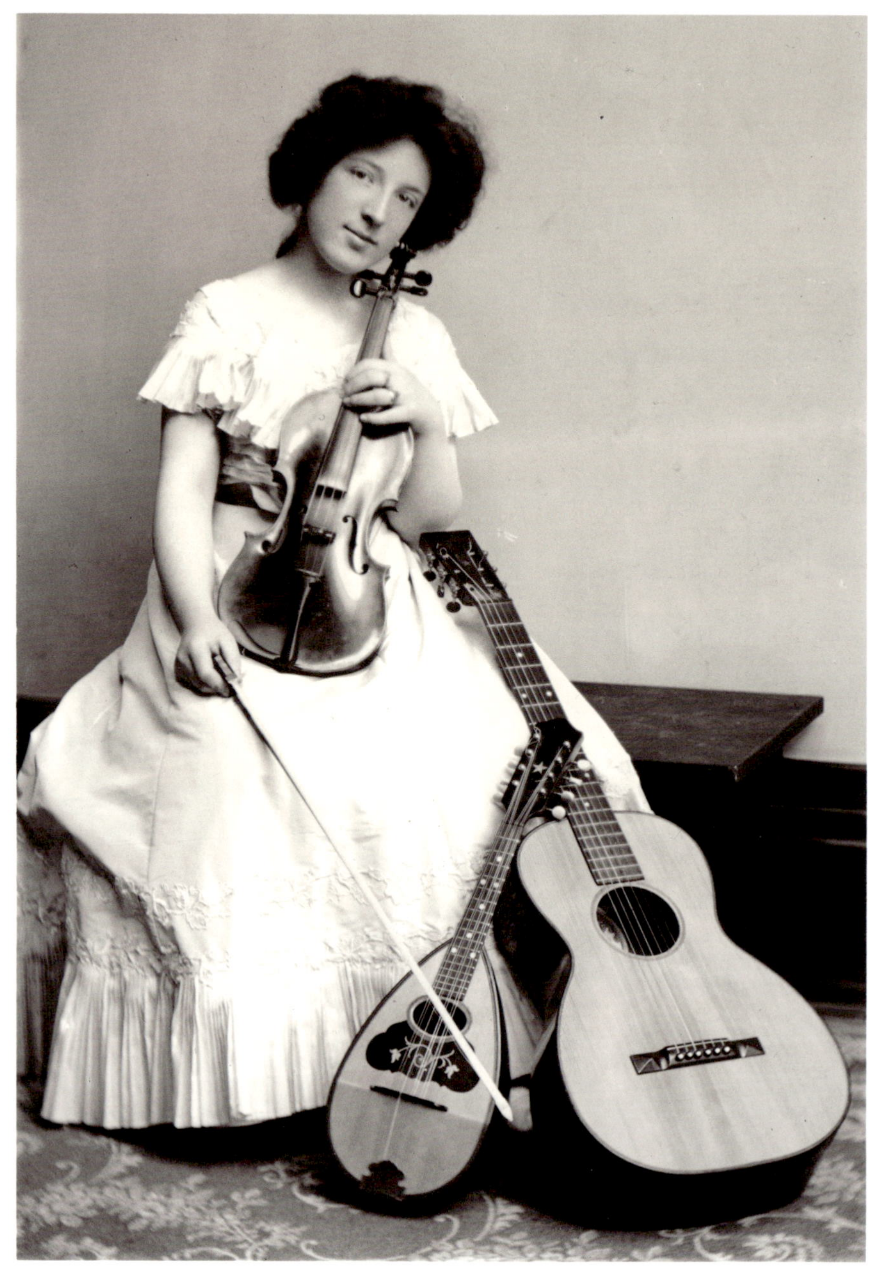

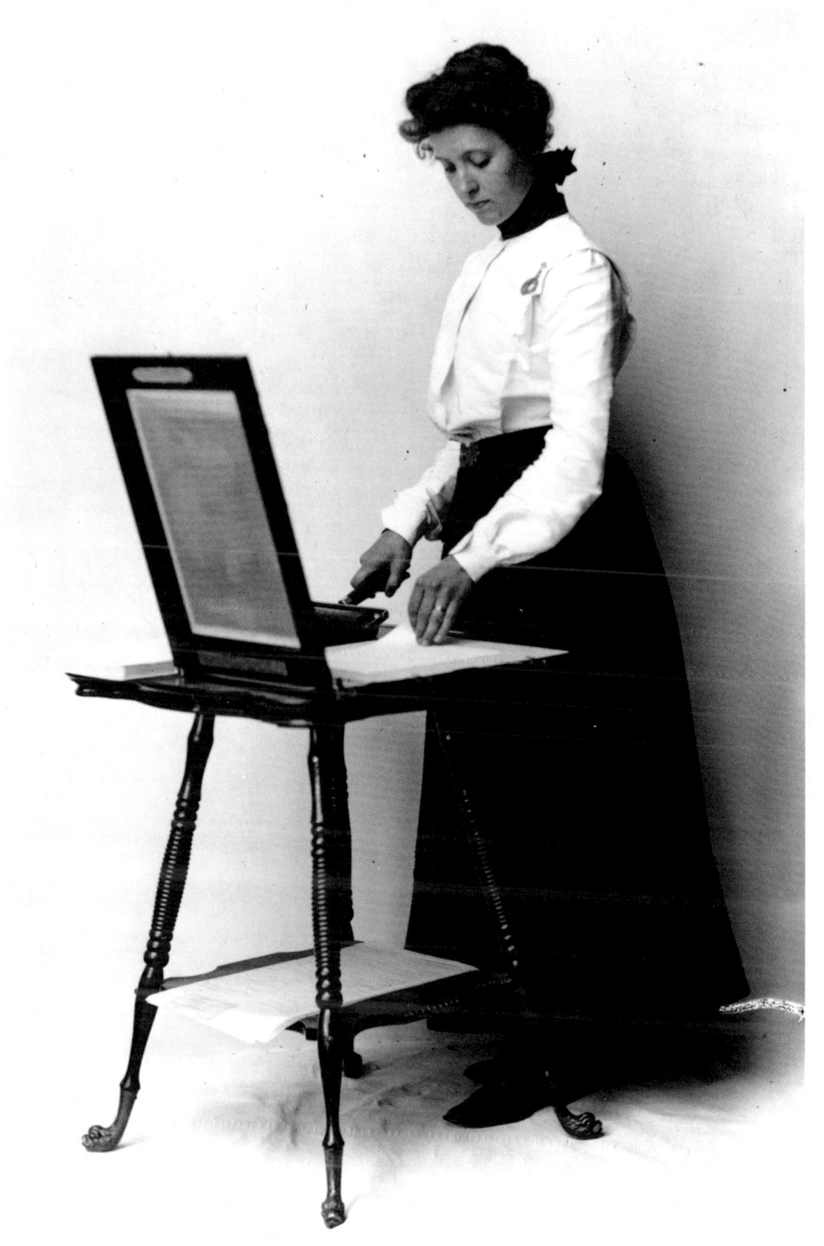

PLATE 69

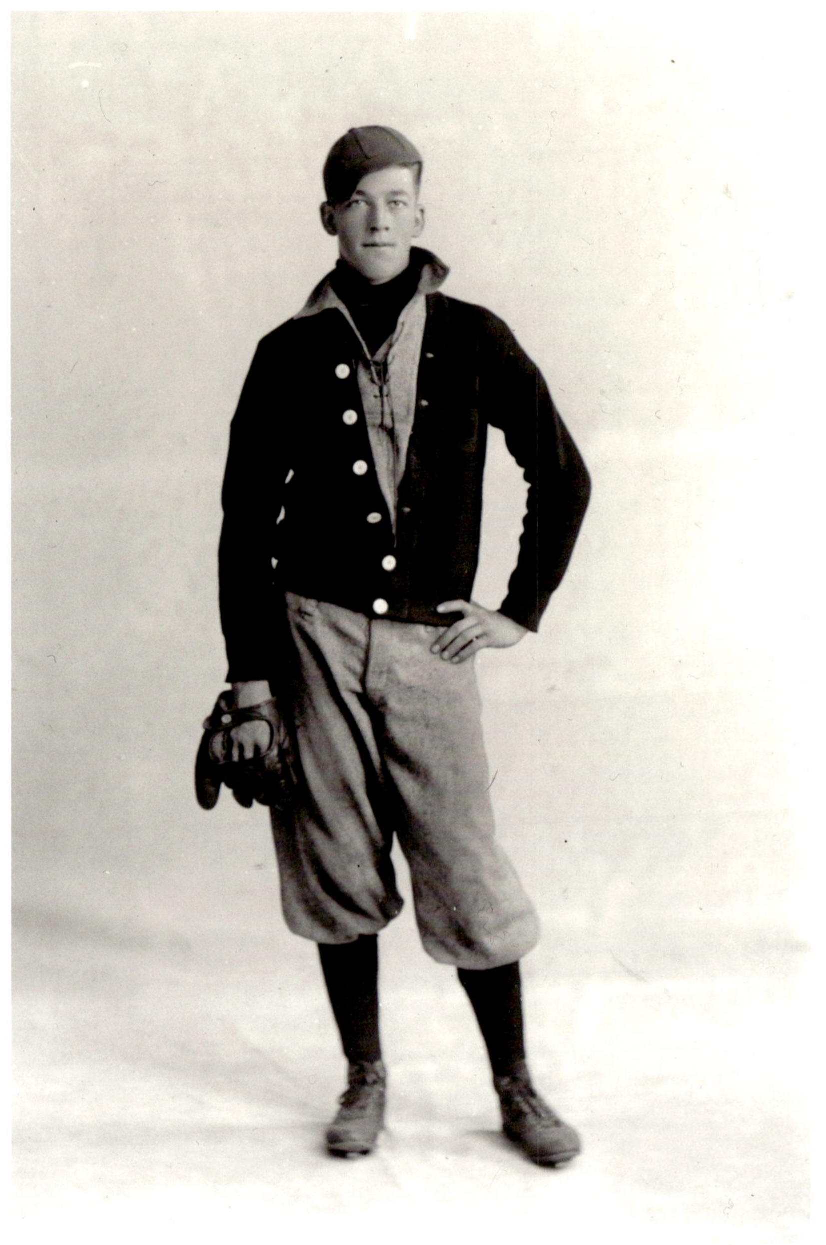

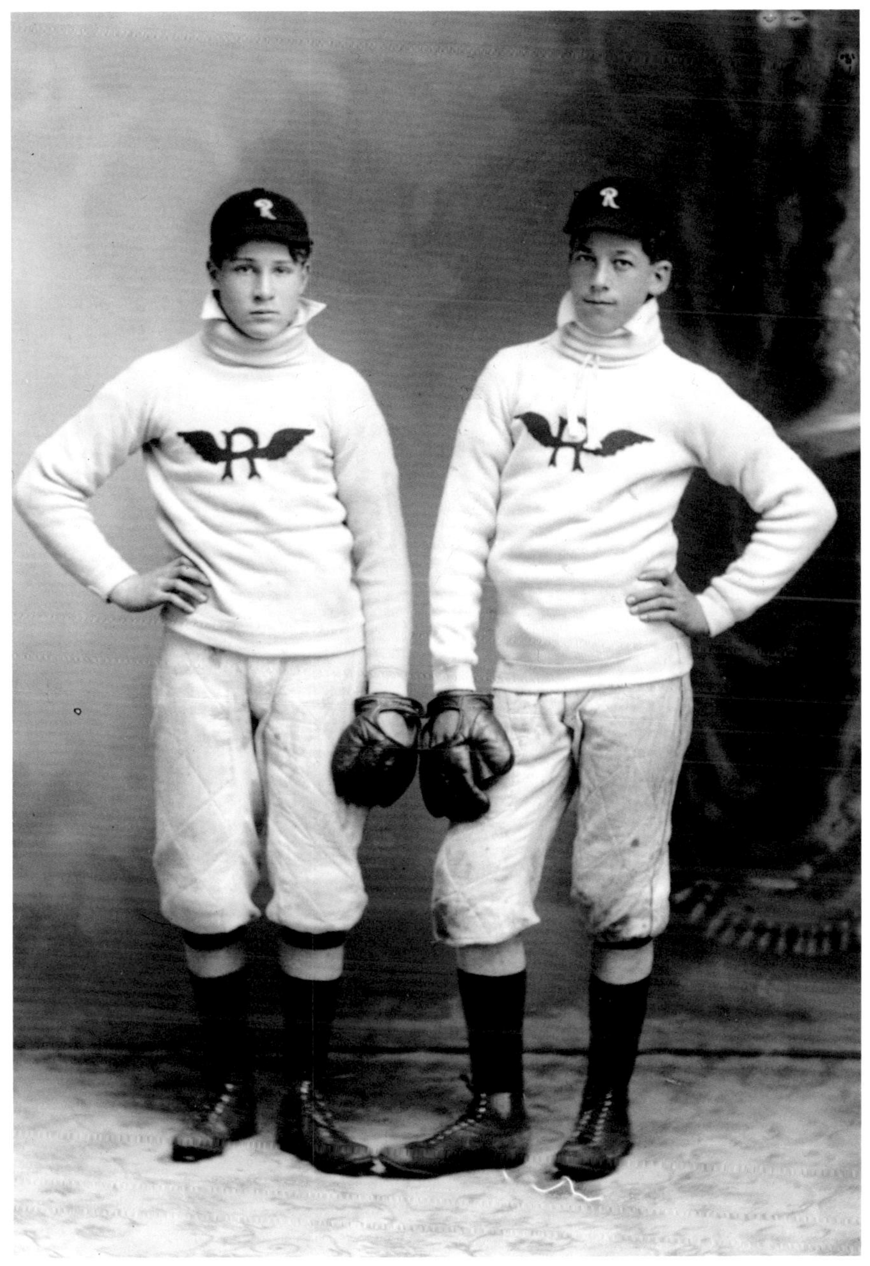

PLATE 71

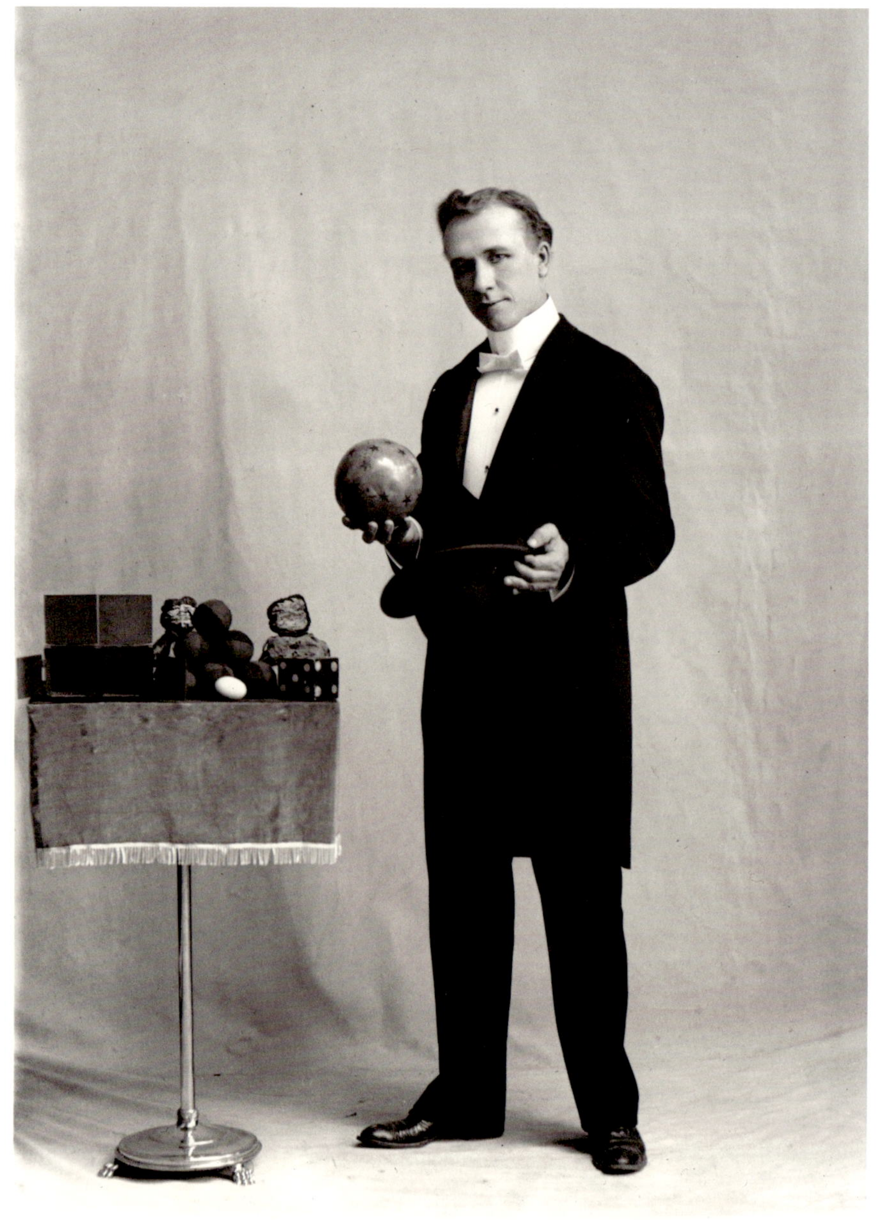

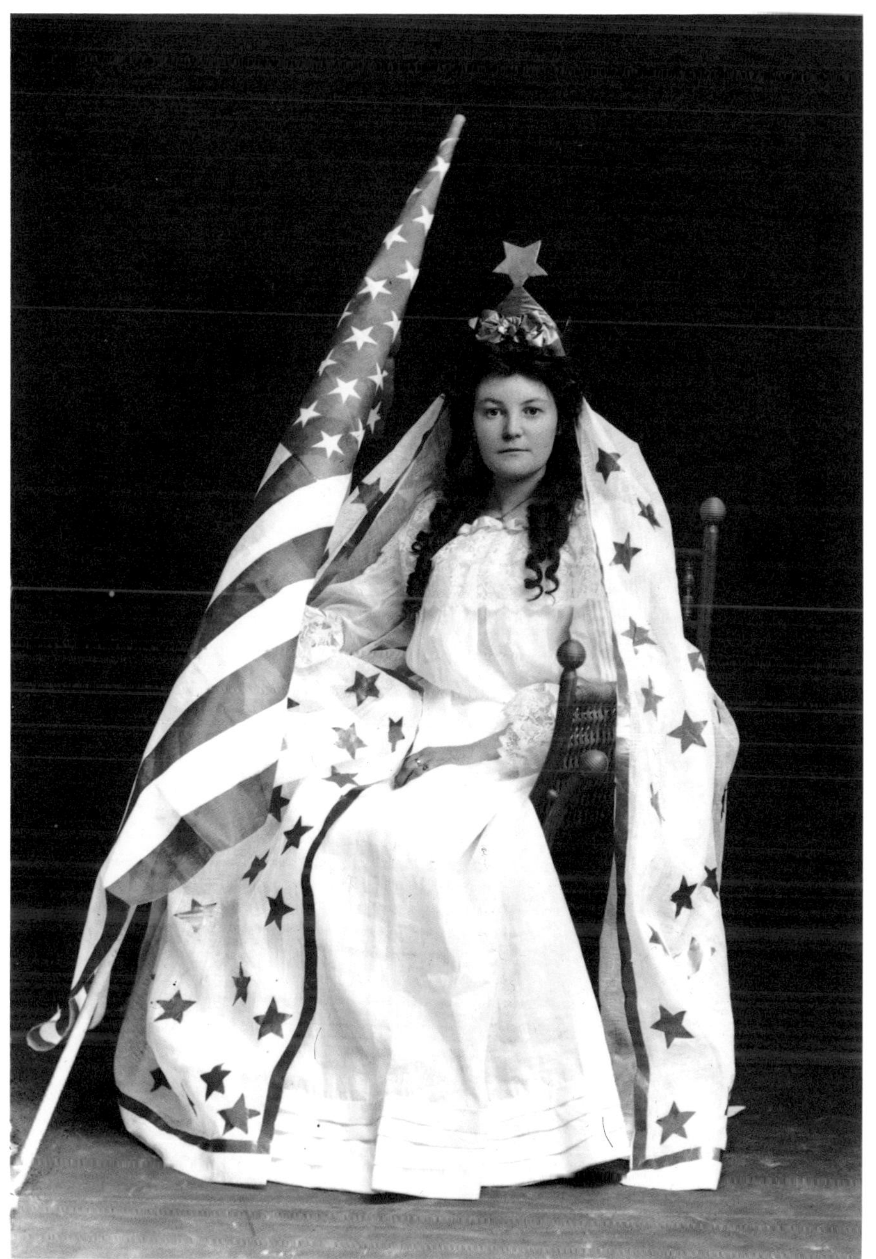

PLATE 73

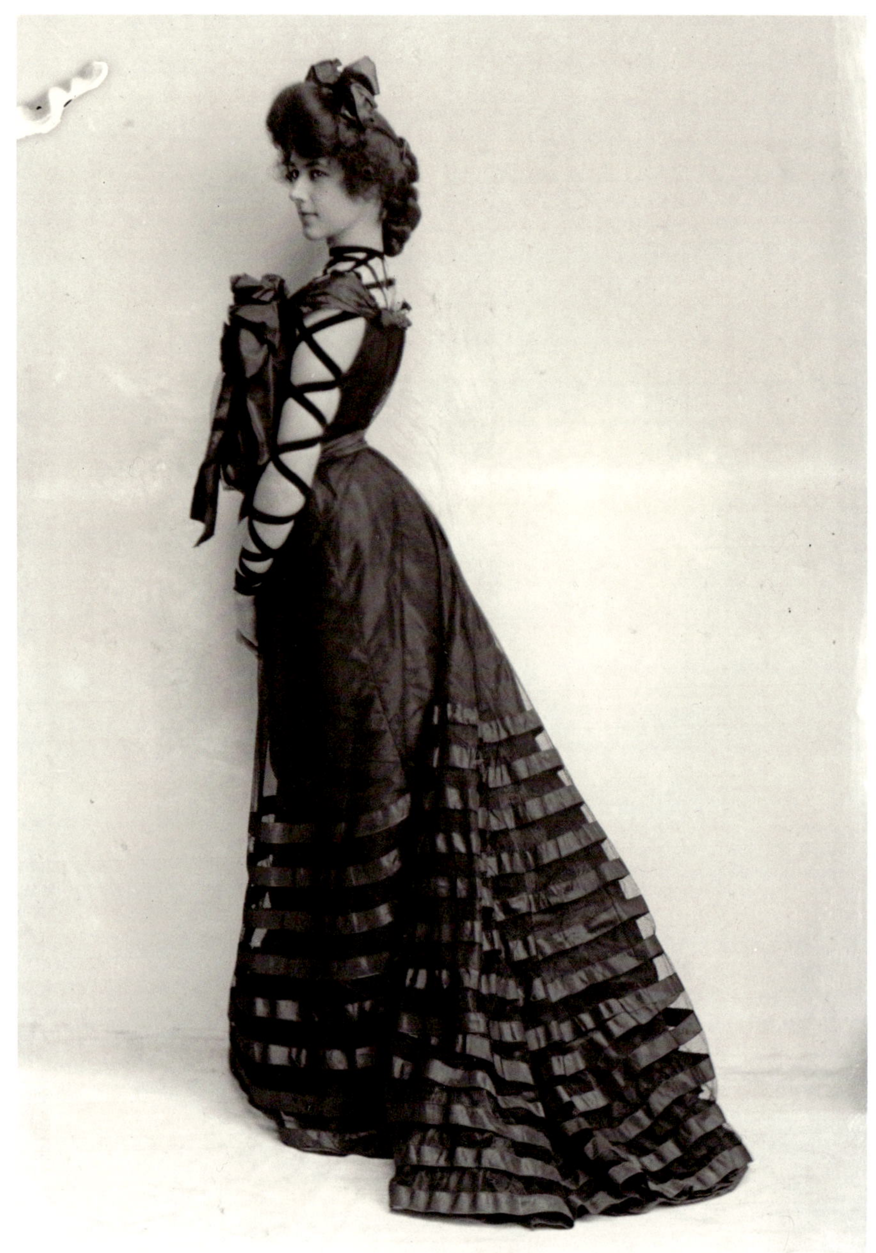

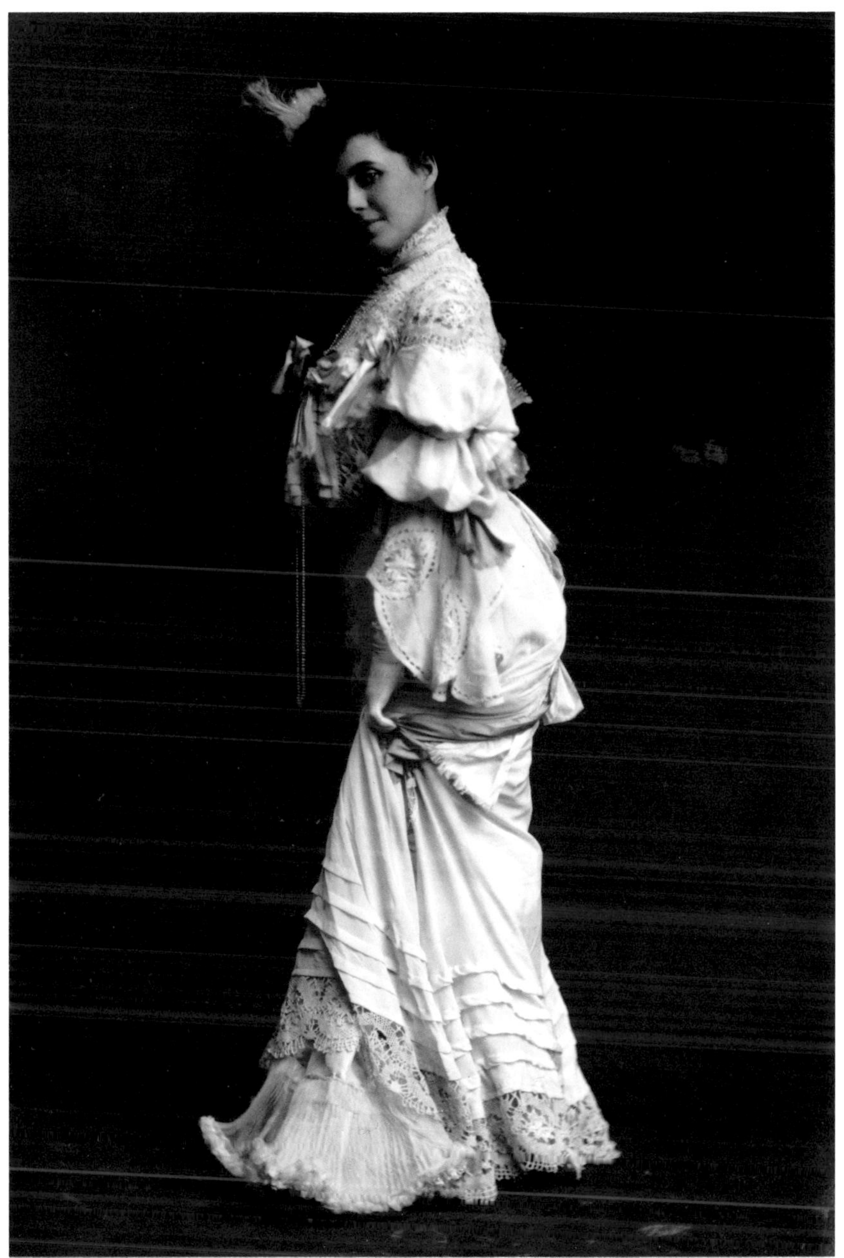

PLATE 75

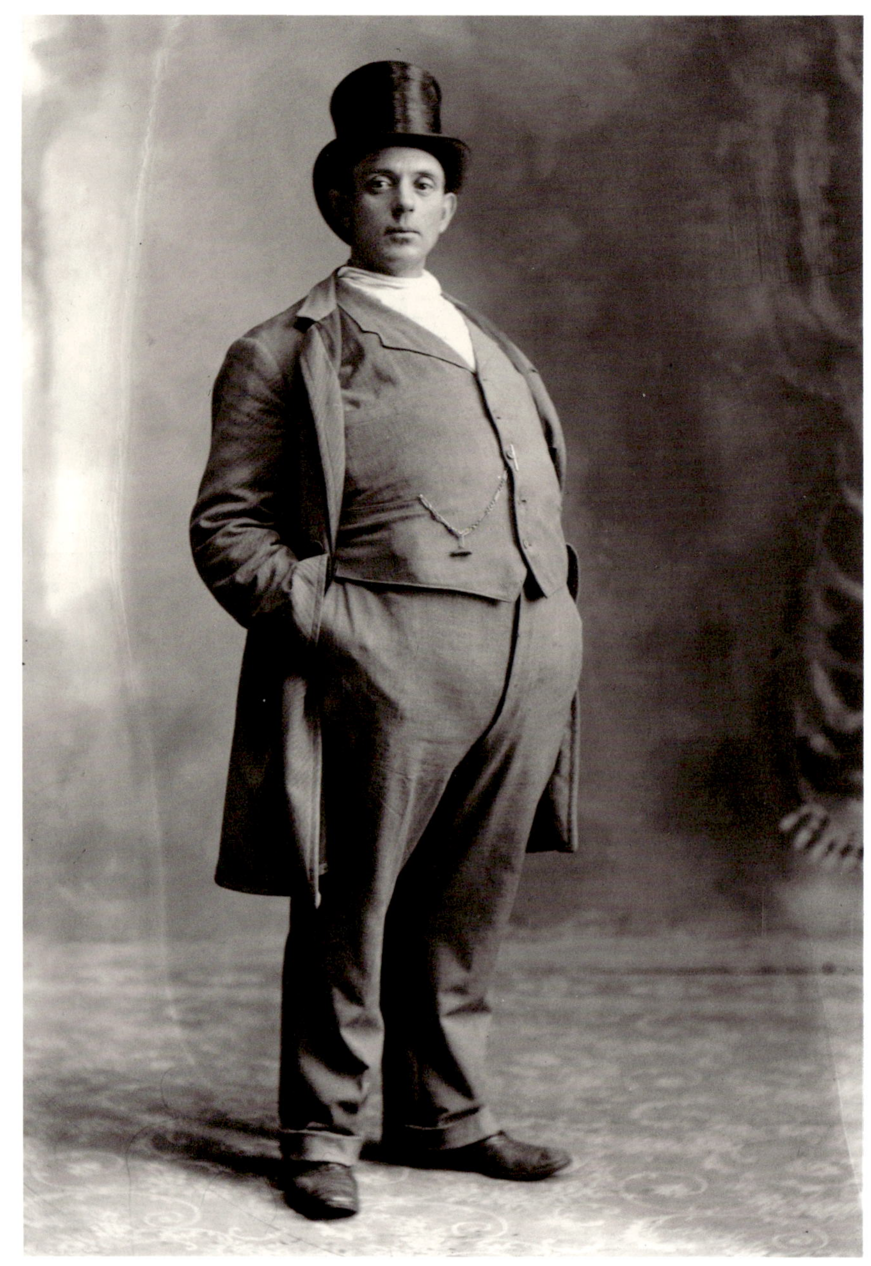

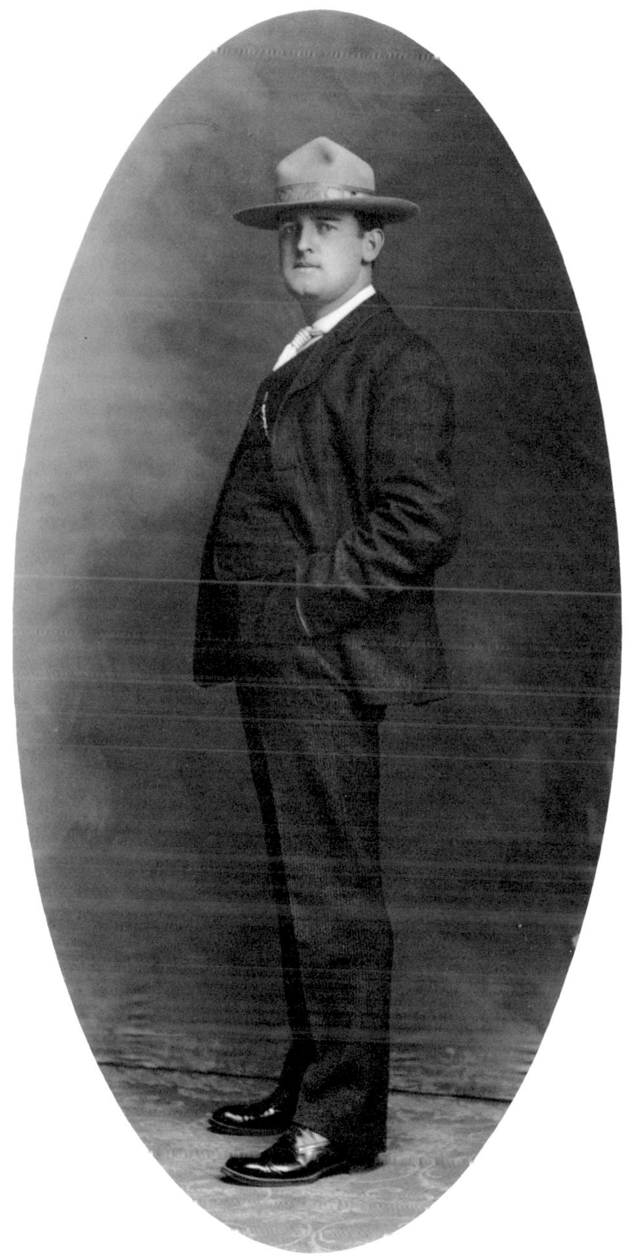

PLATE 77

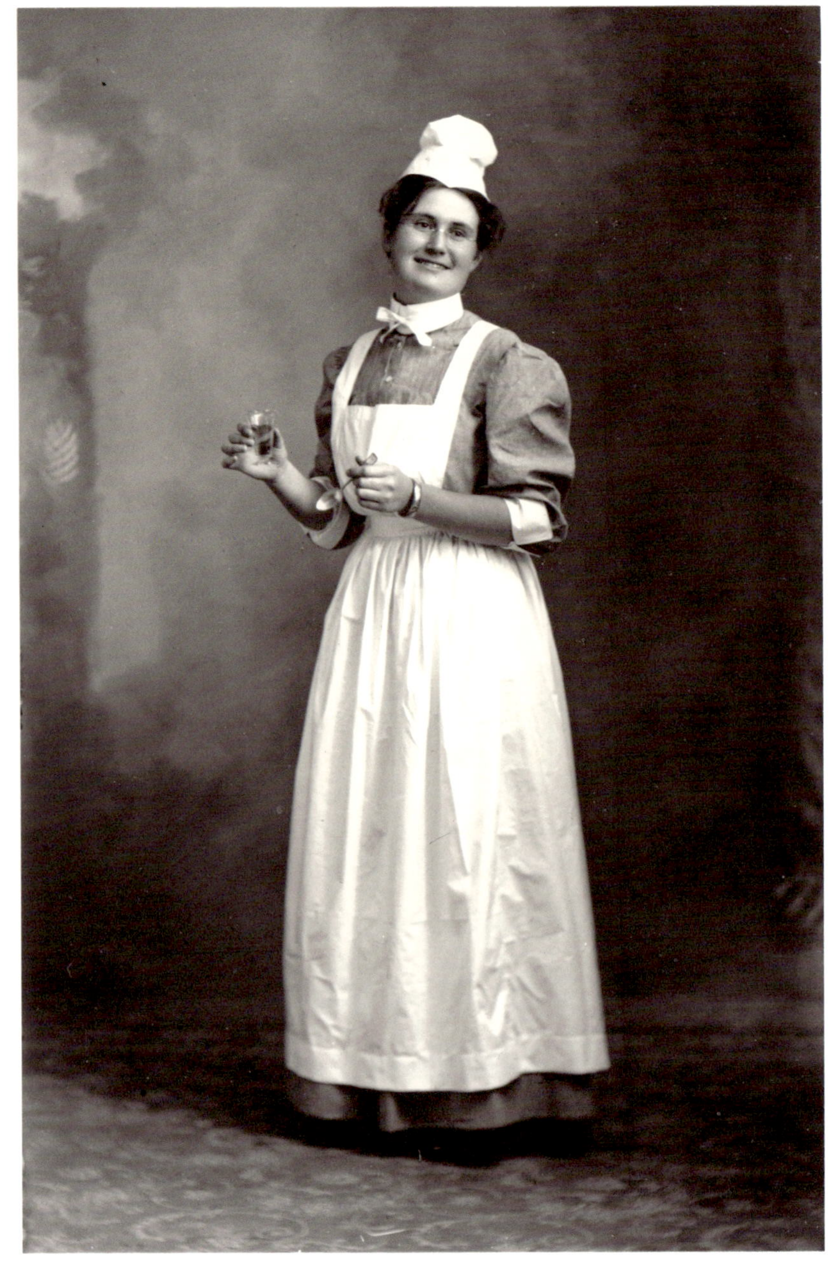

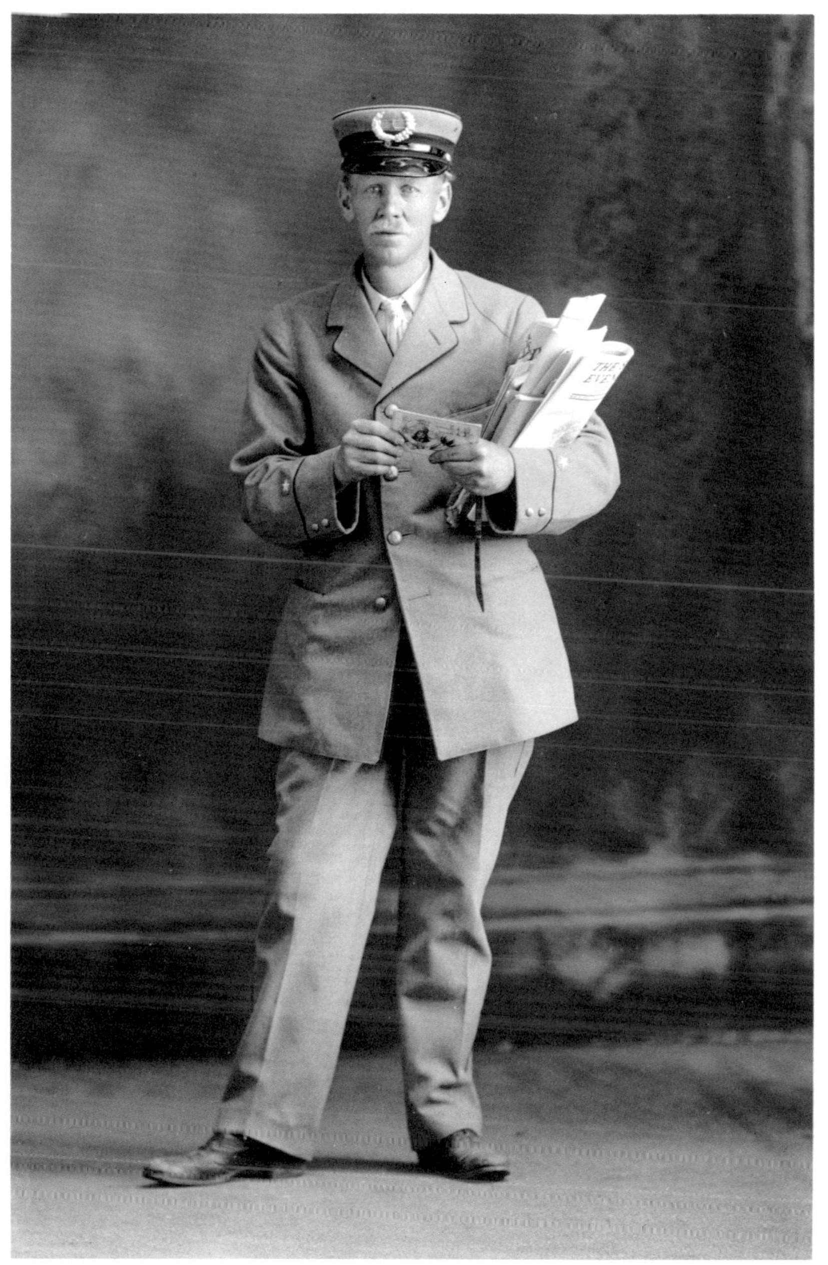

PLATE 79

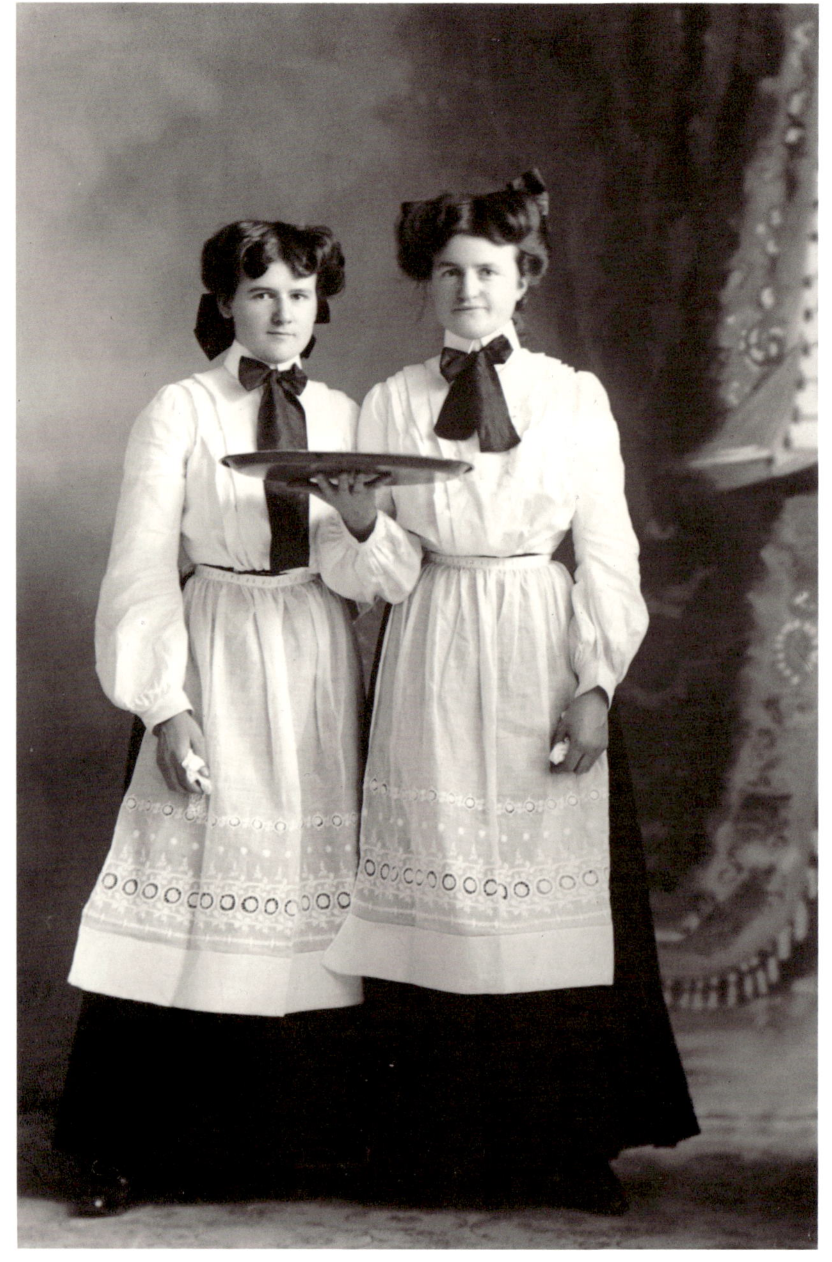

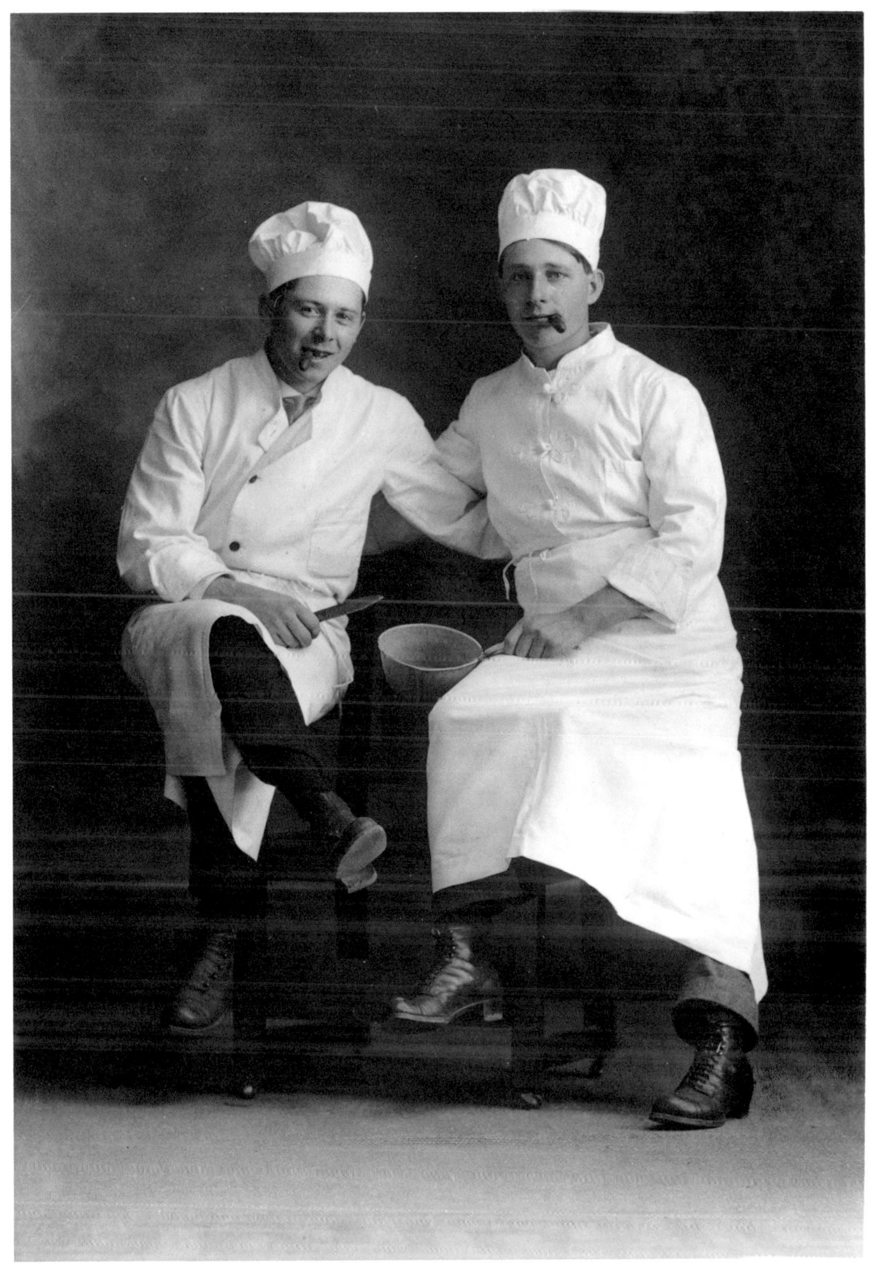

PLATE 81

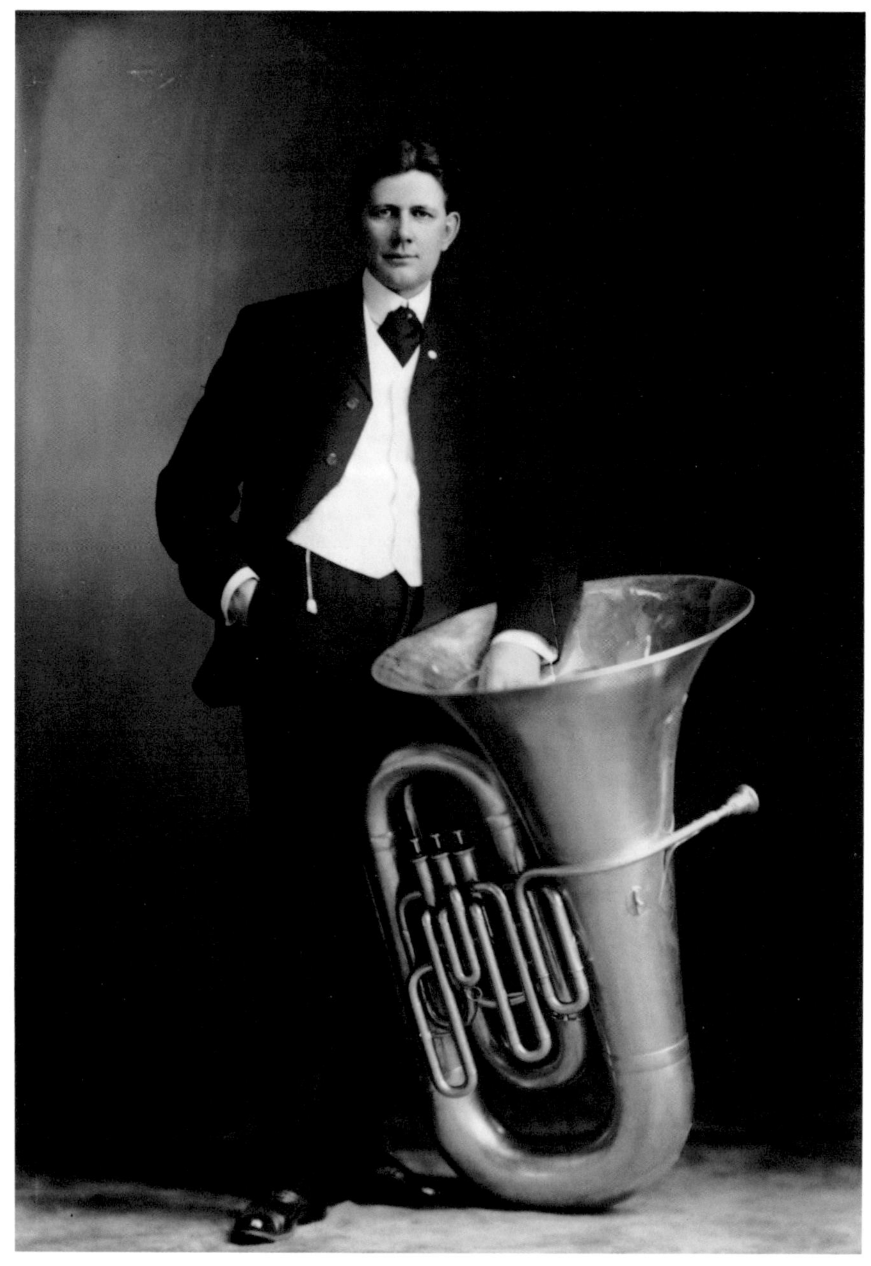

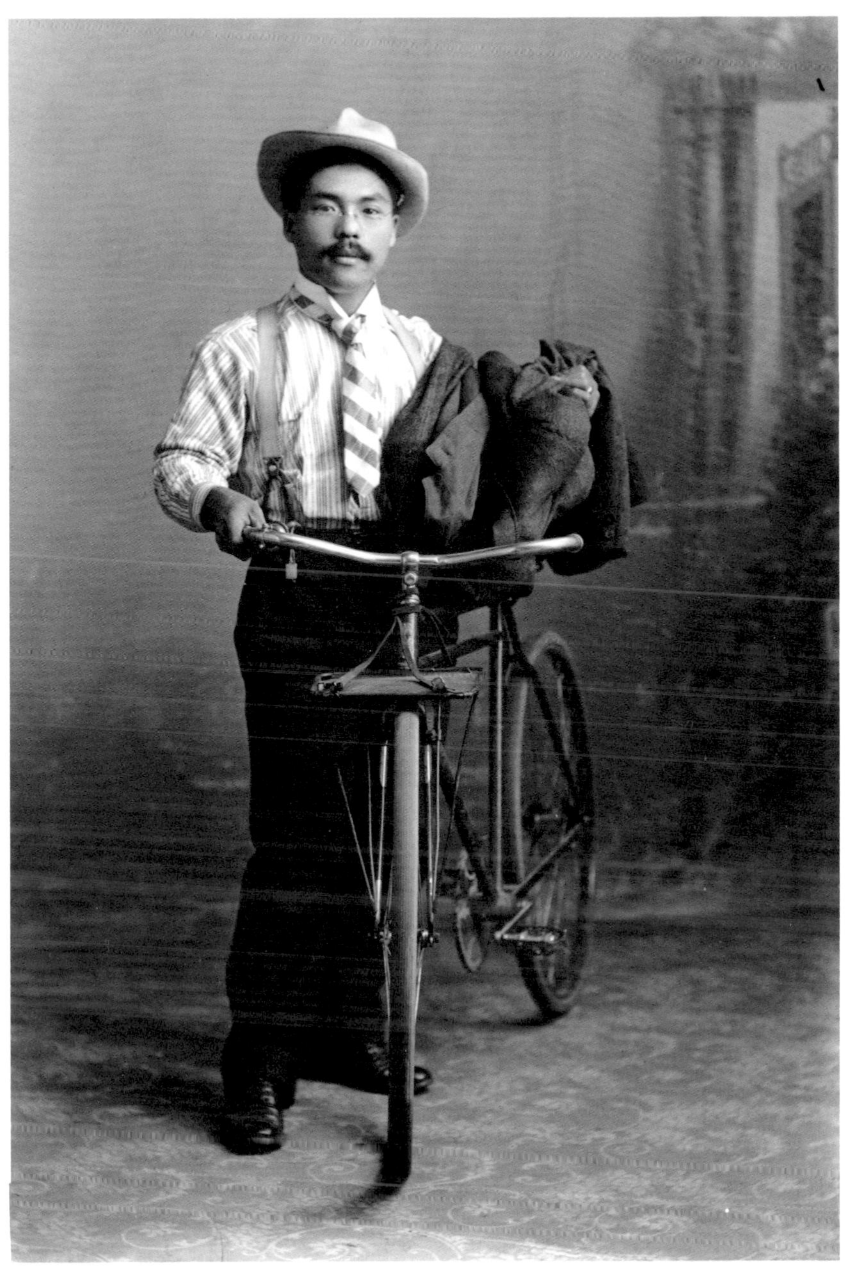

PLATE 83

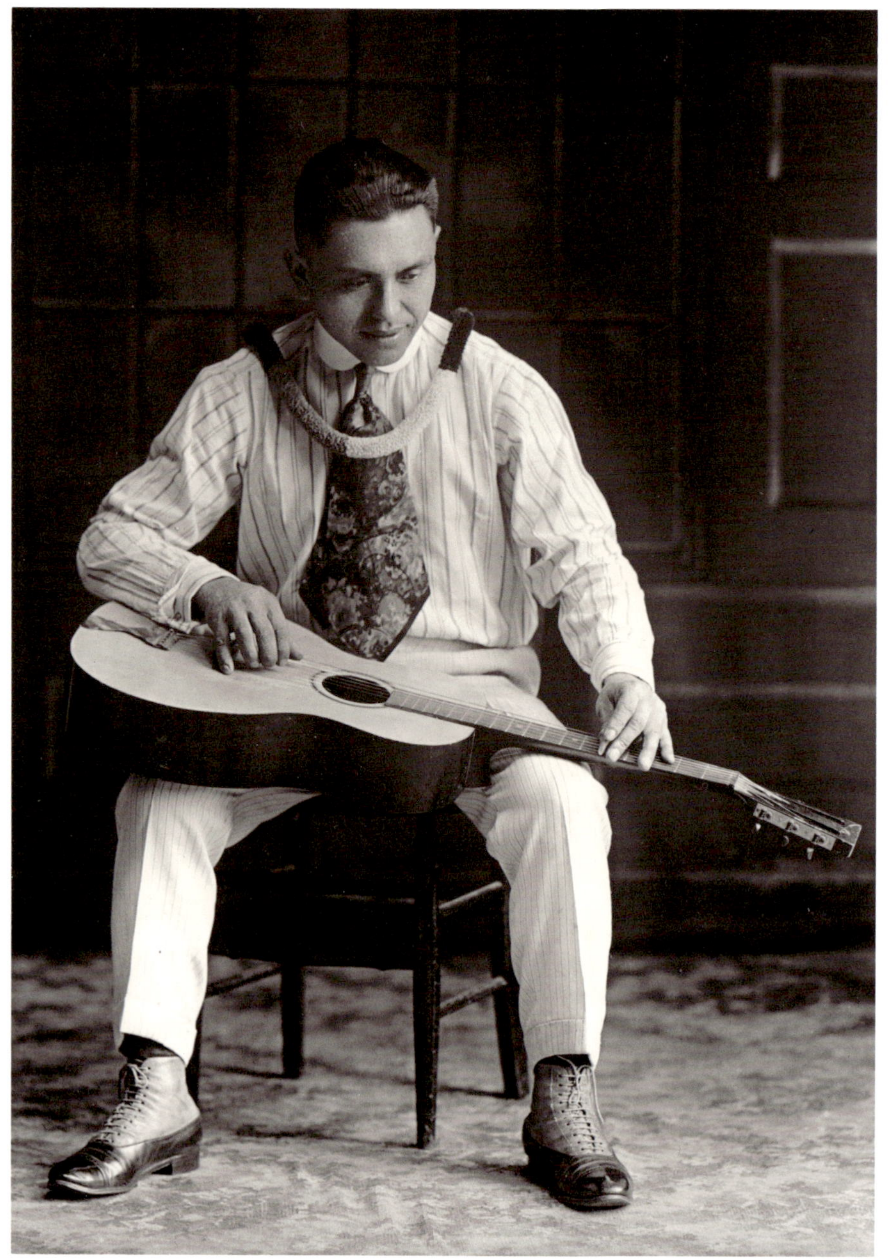

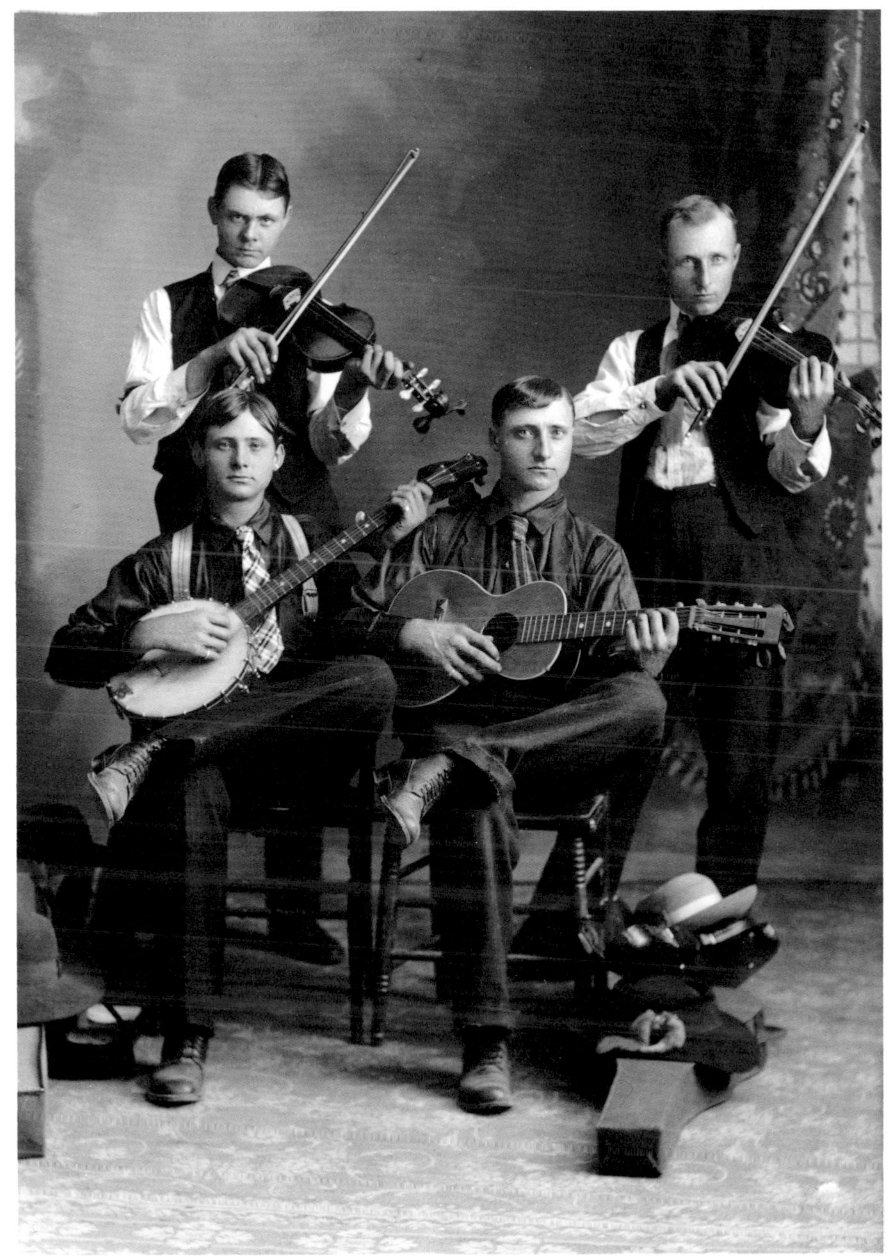

PLATE 85a

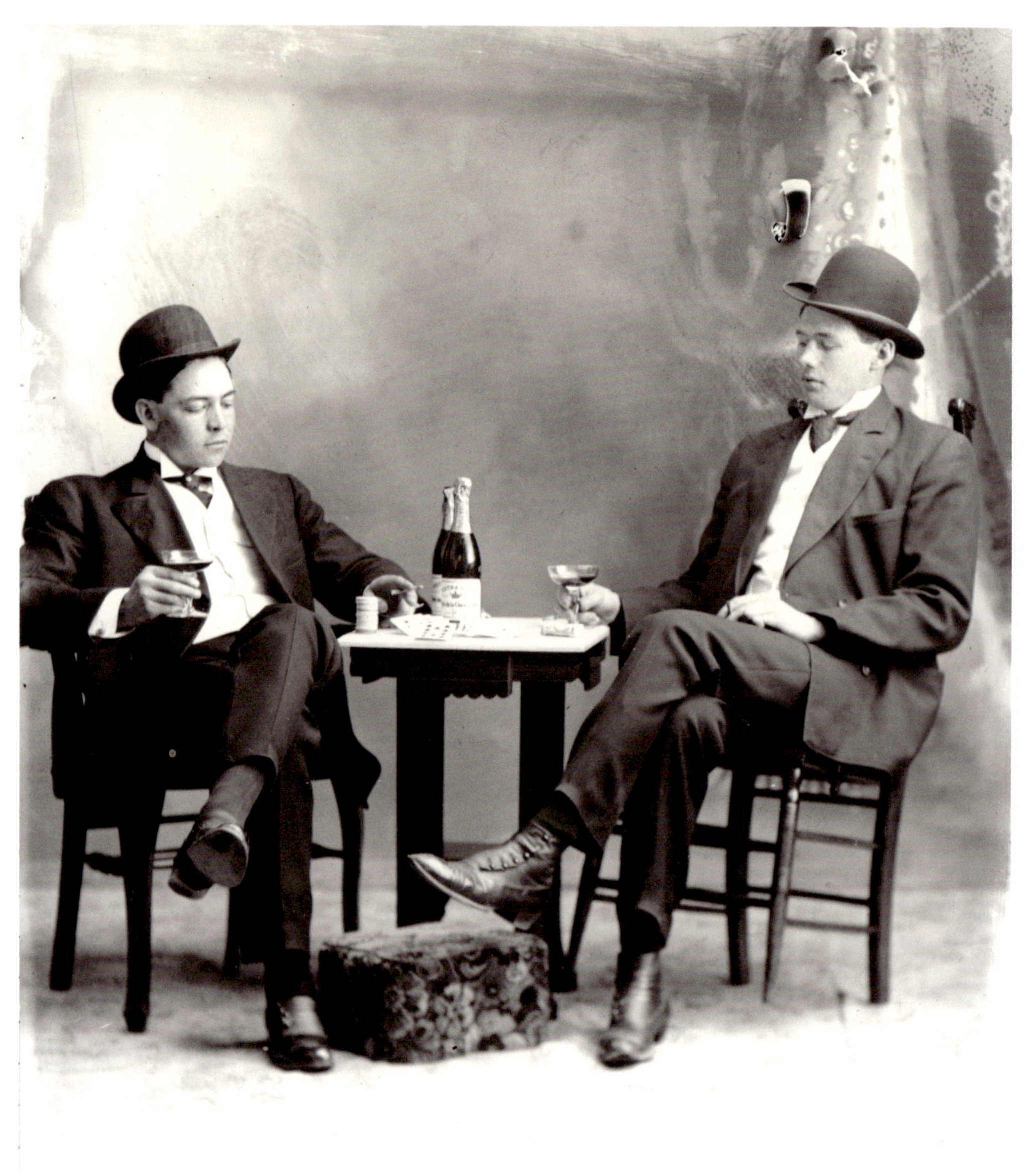

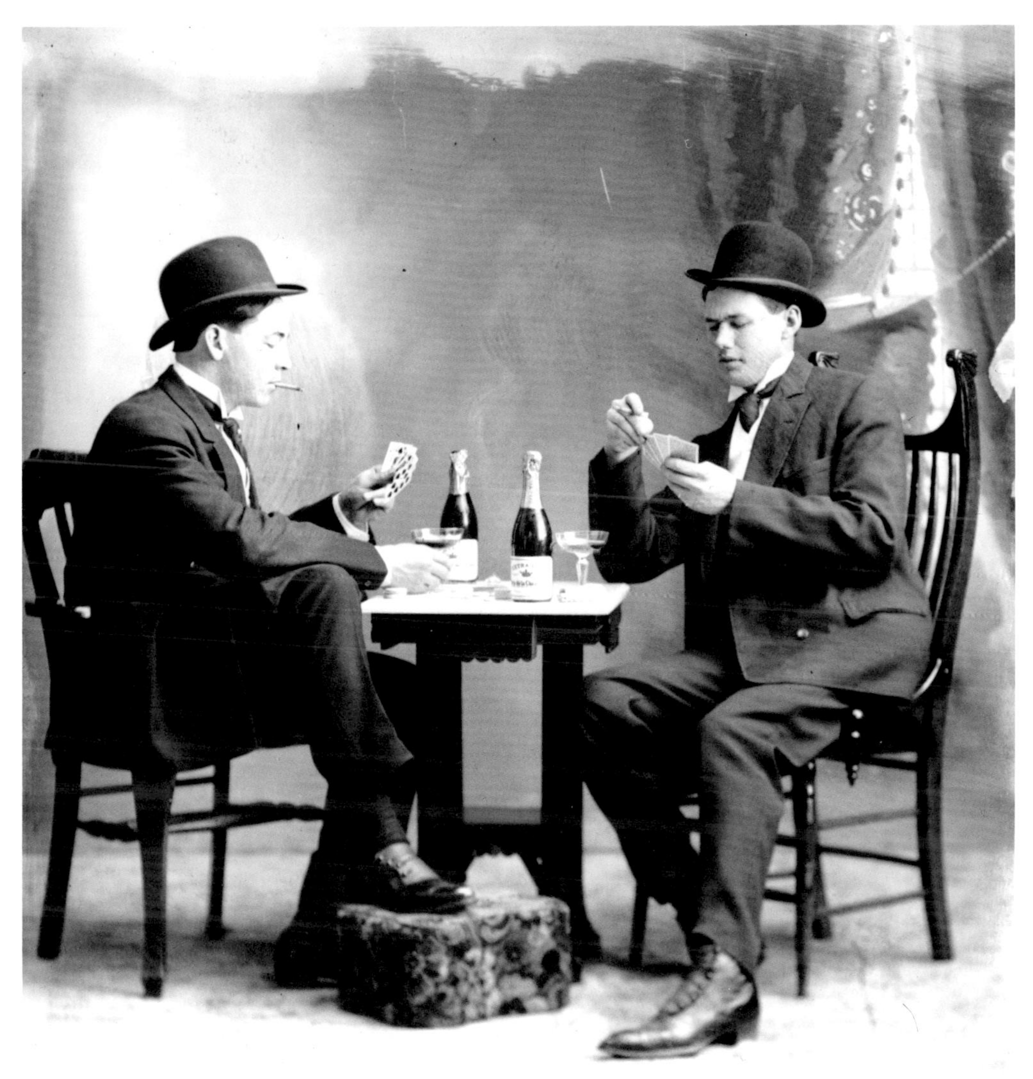

PLATE 85c

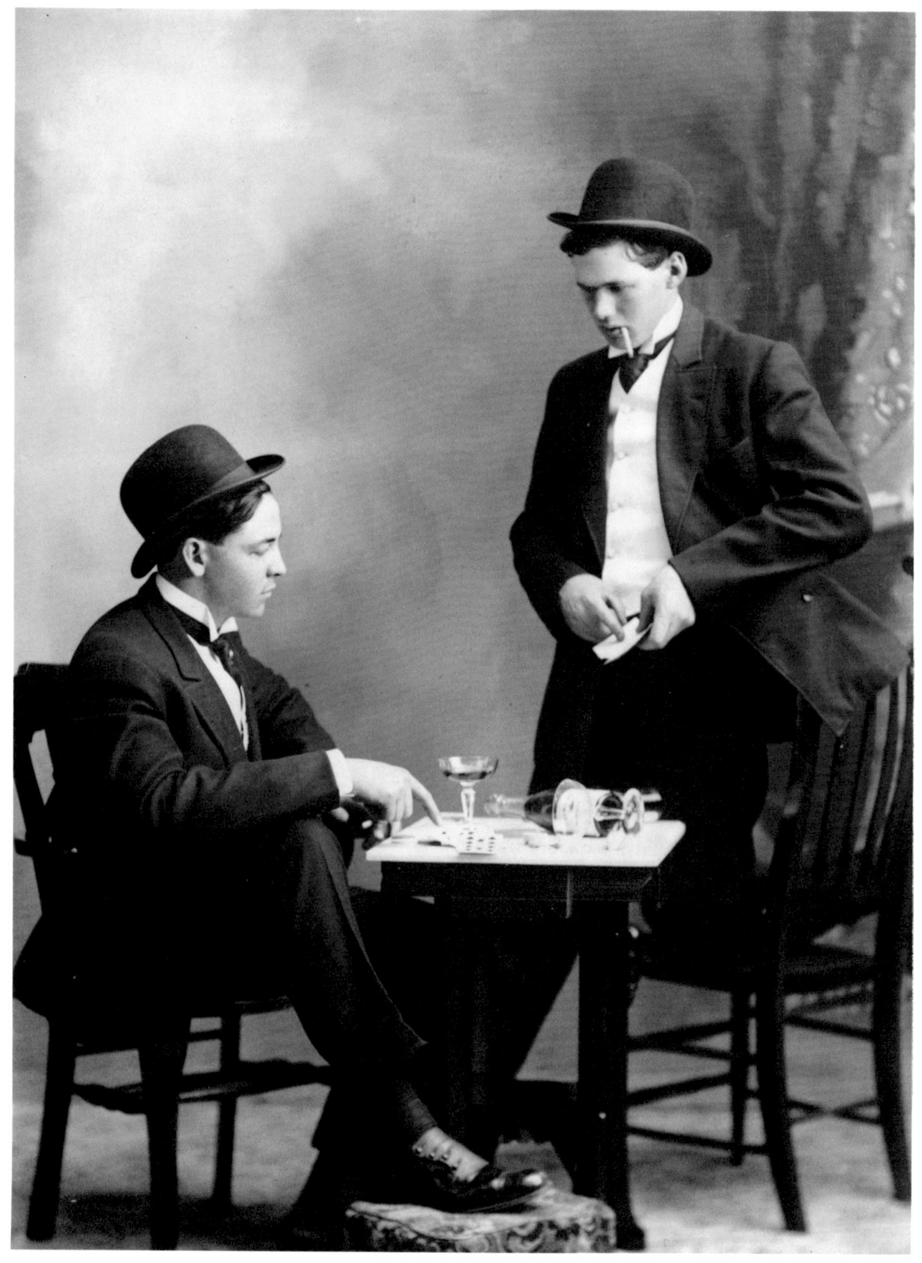

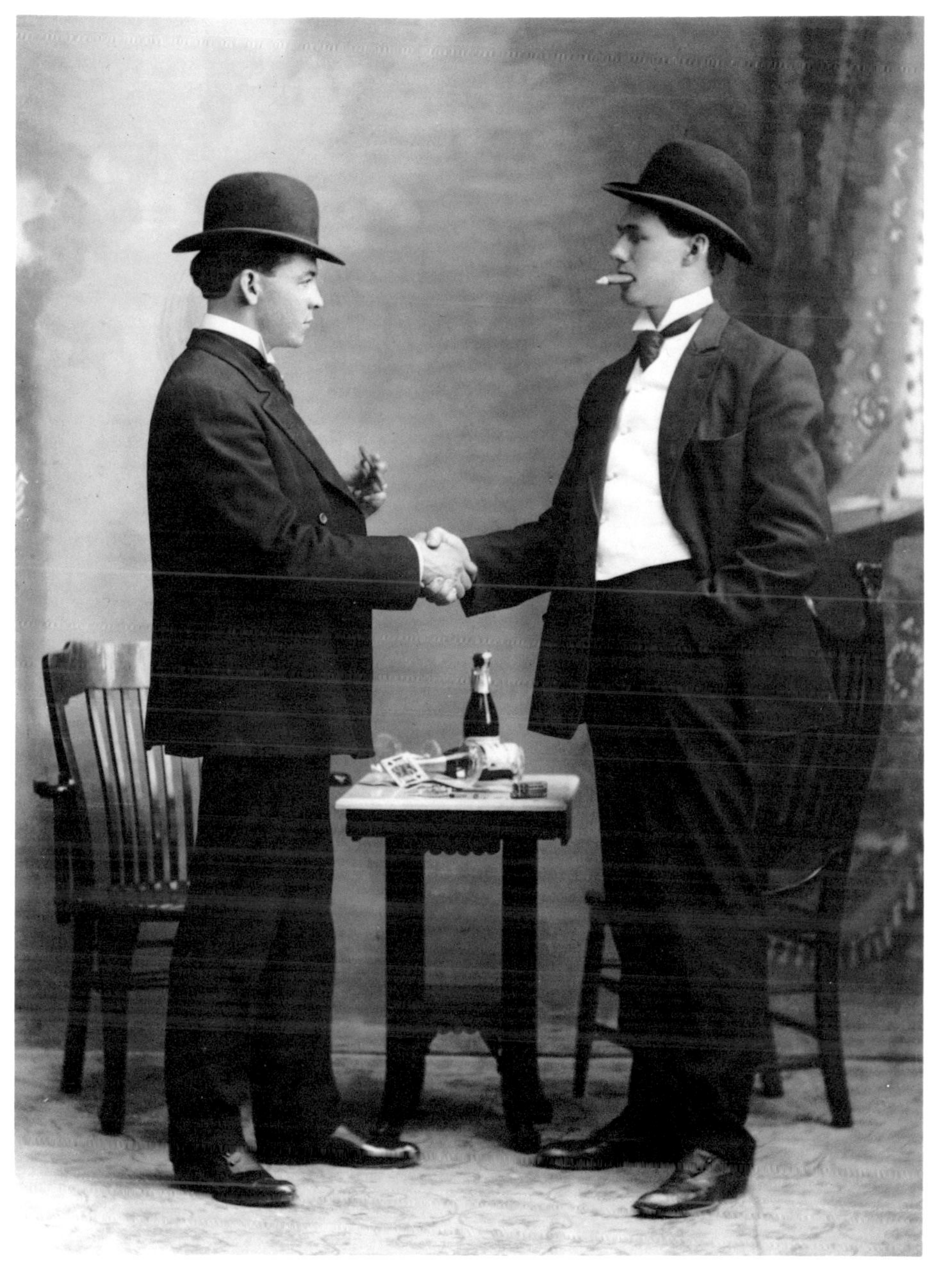

PLATE 86

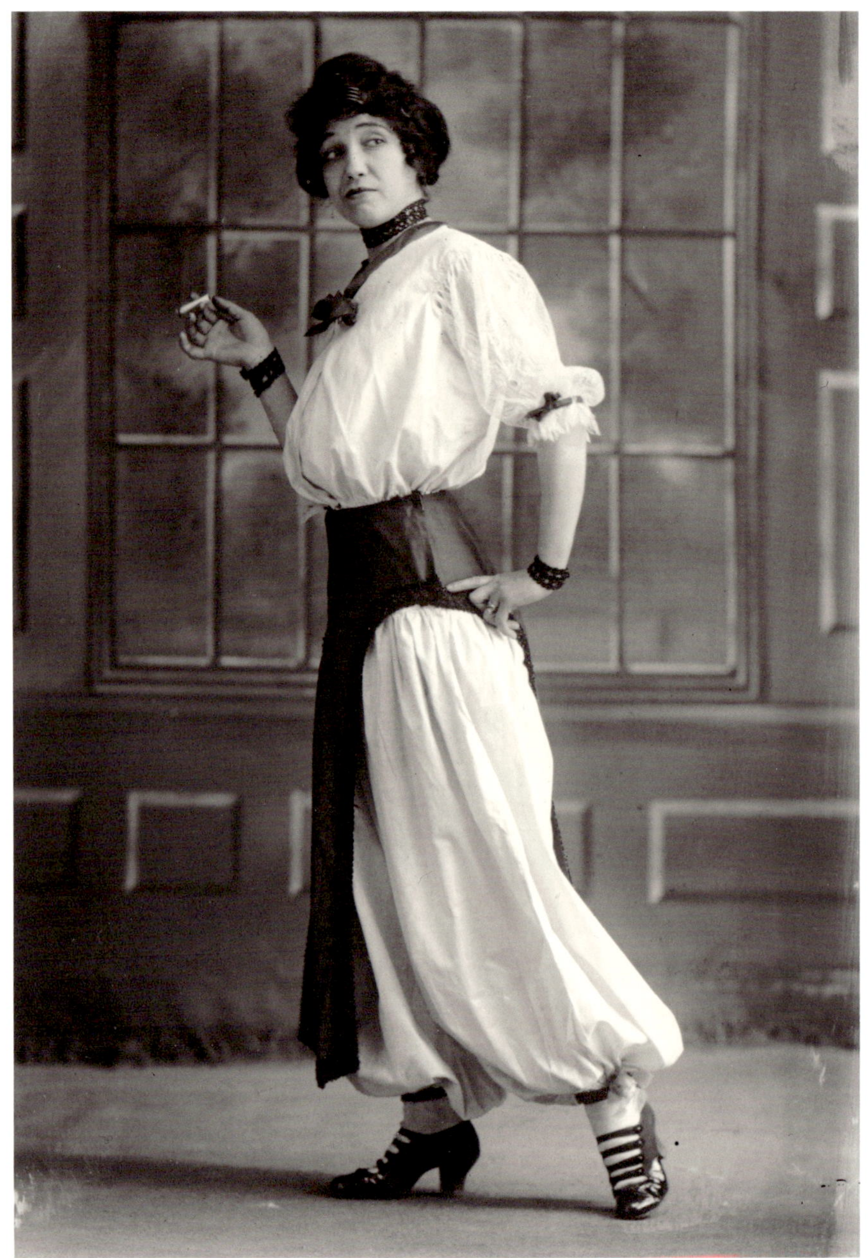

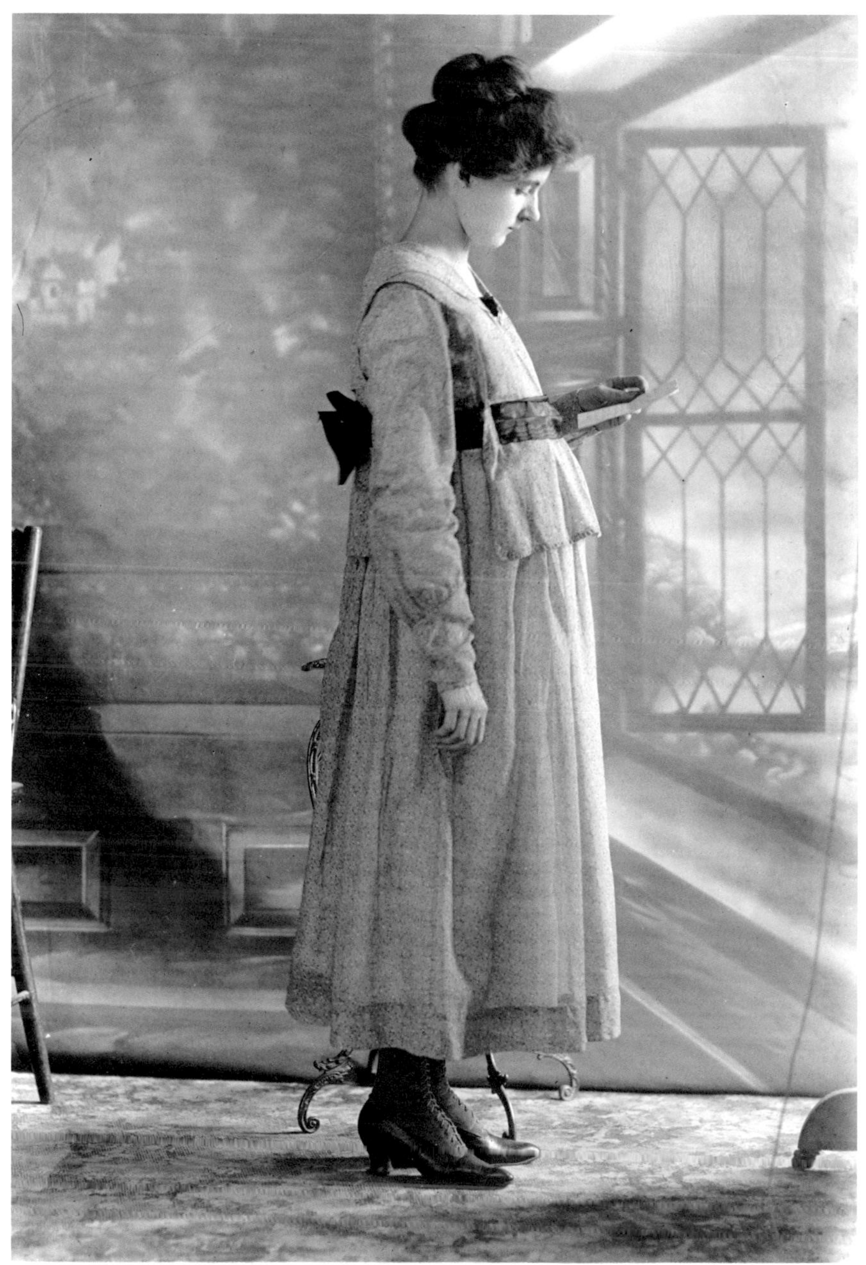

PLATE 88

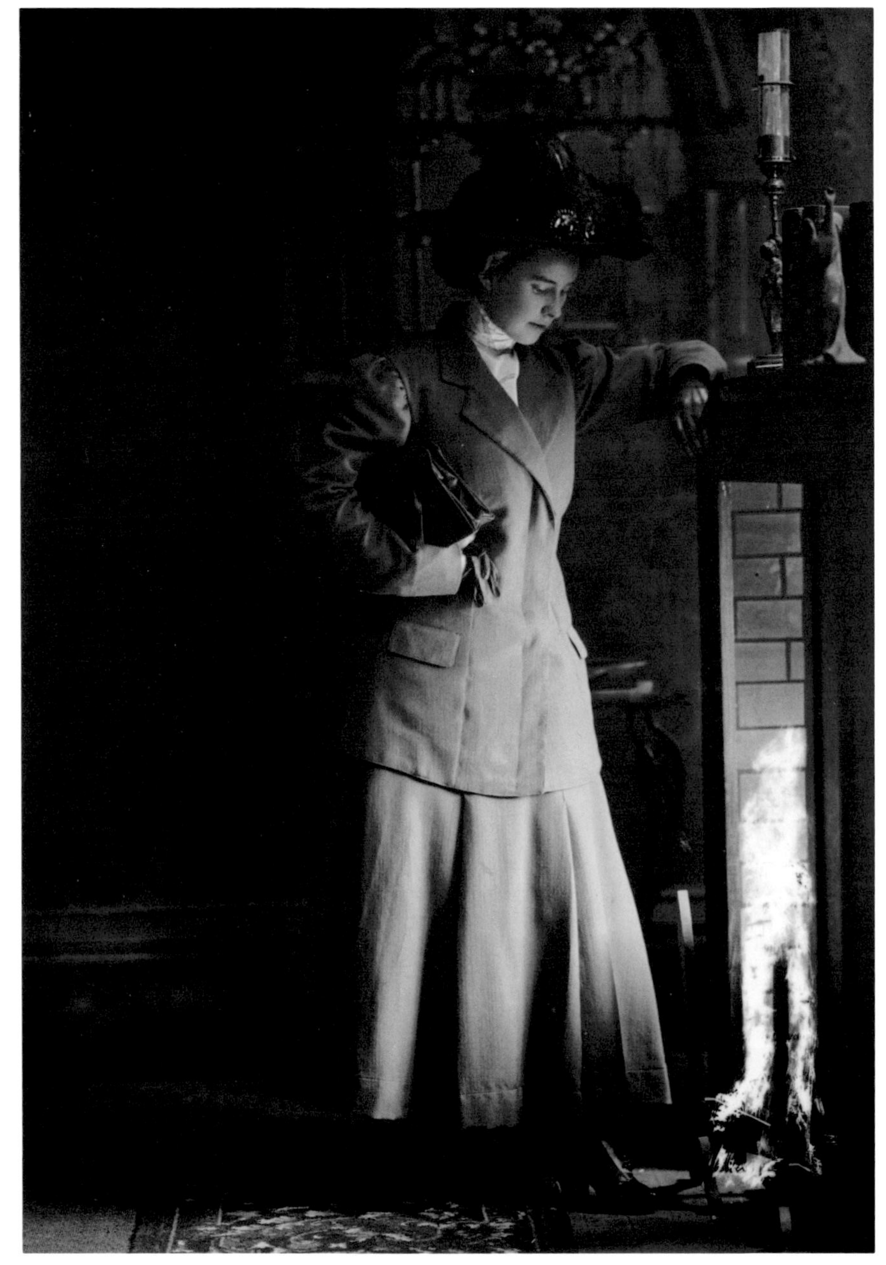

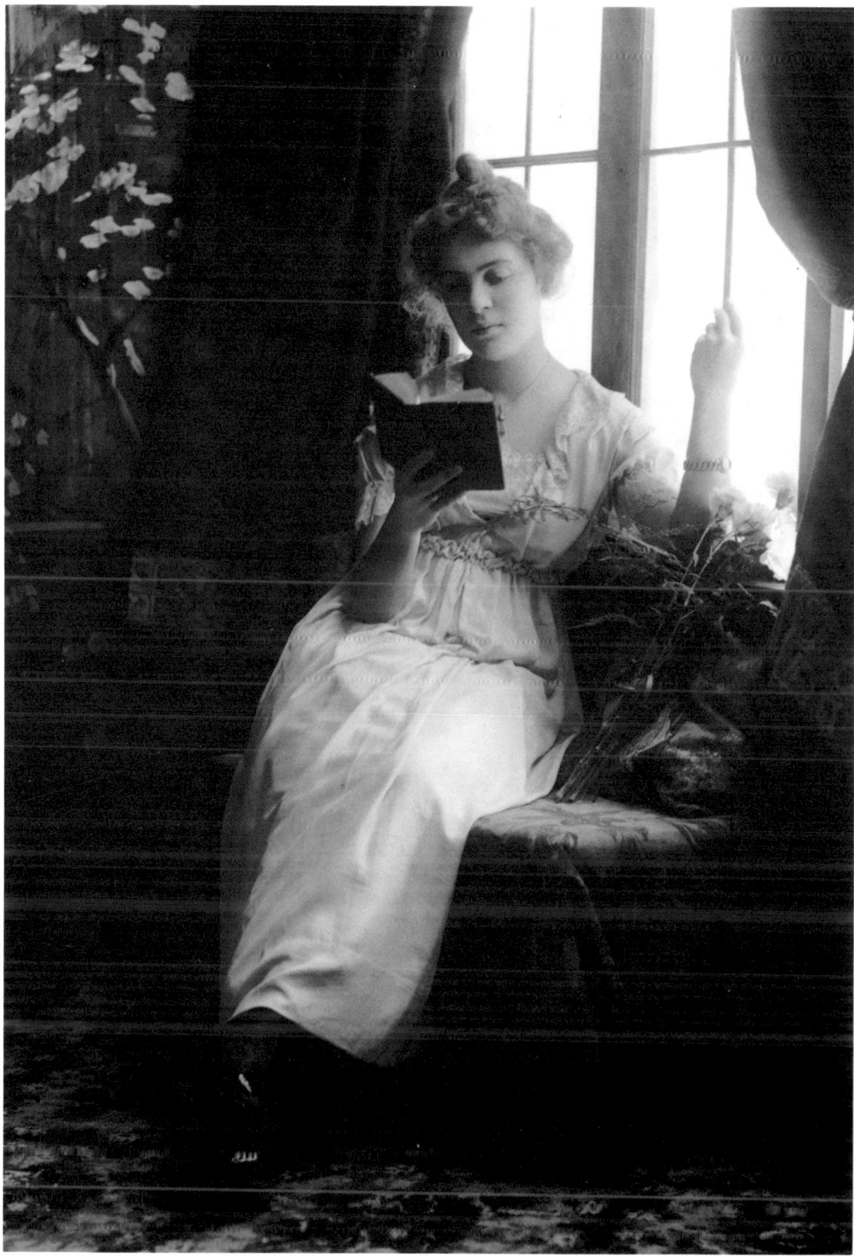

PLATE 90

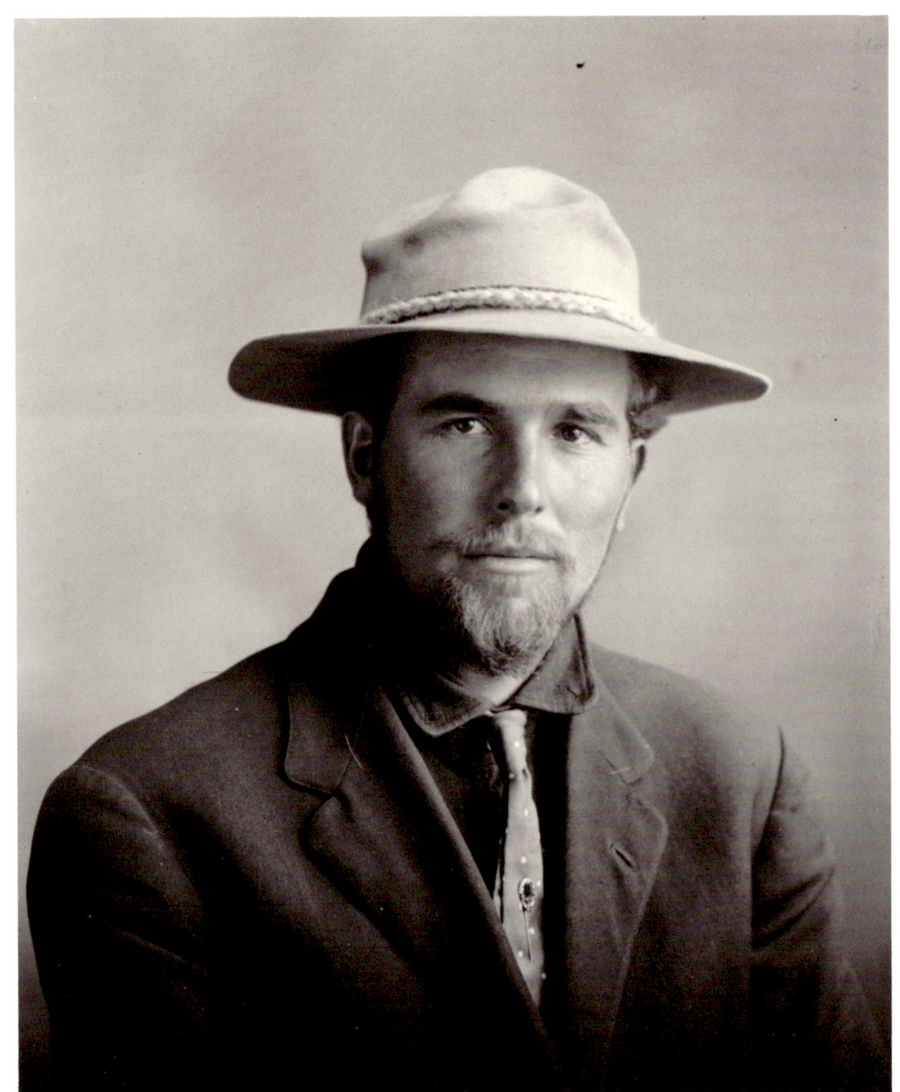

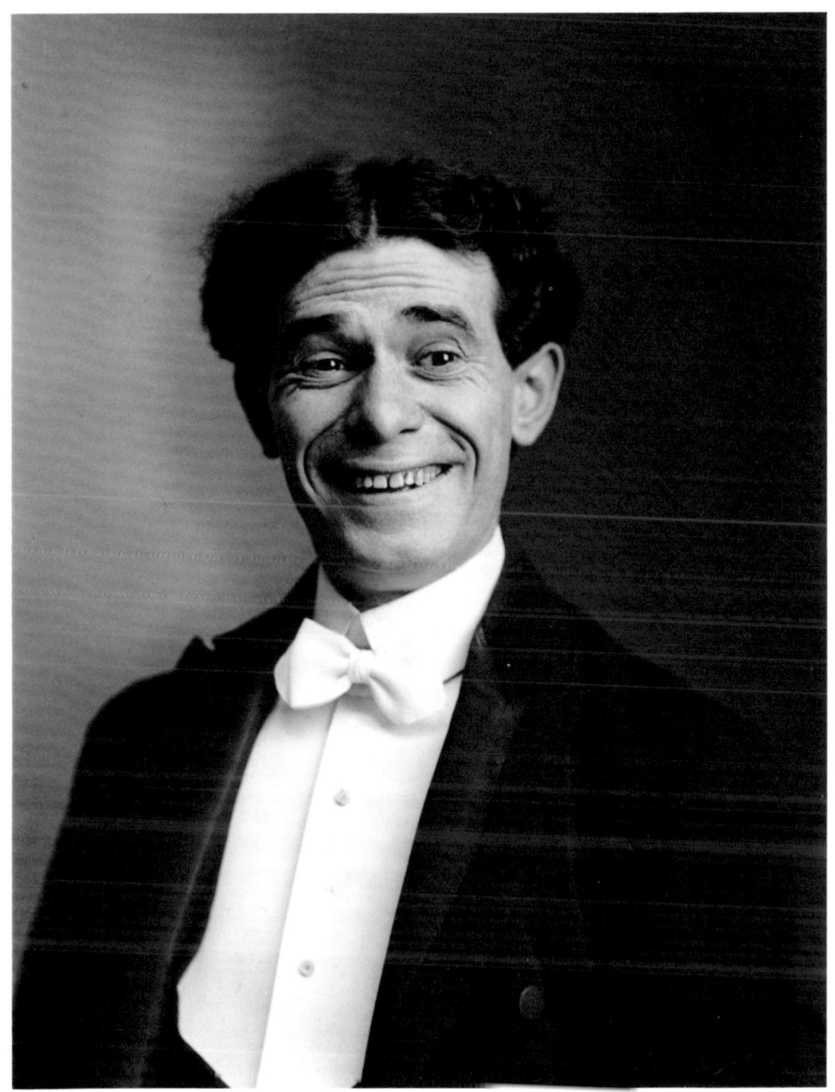

PLATE 92

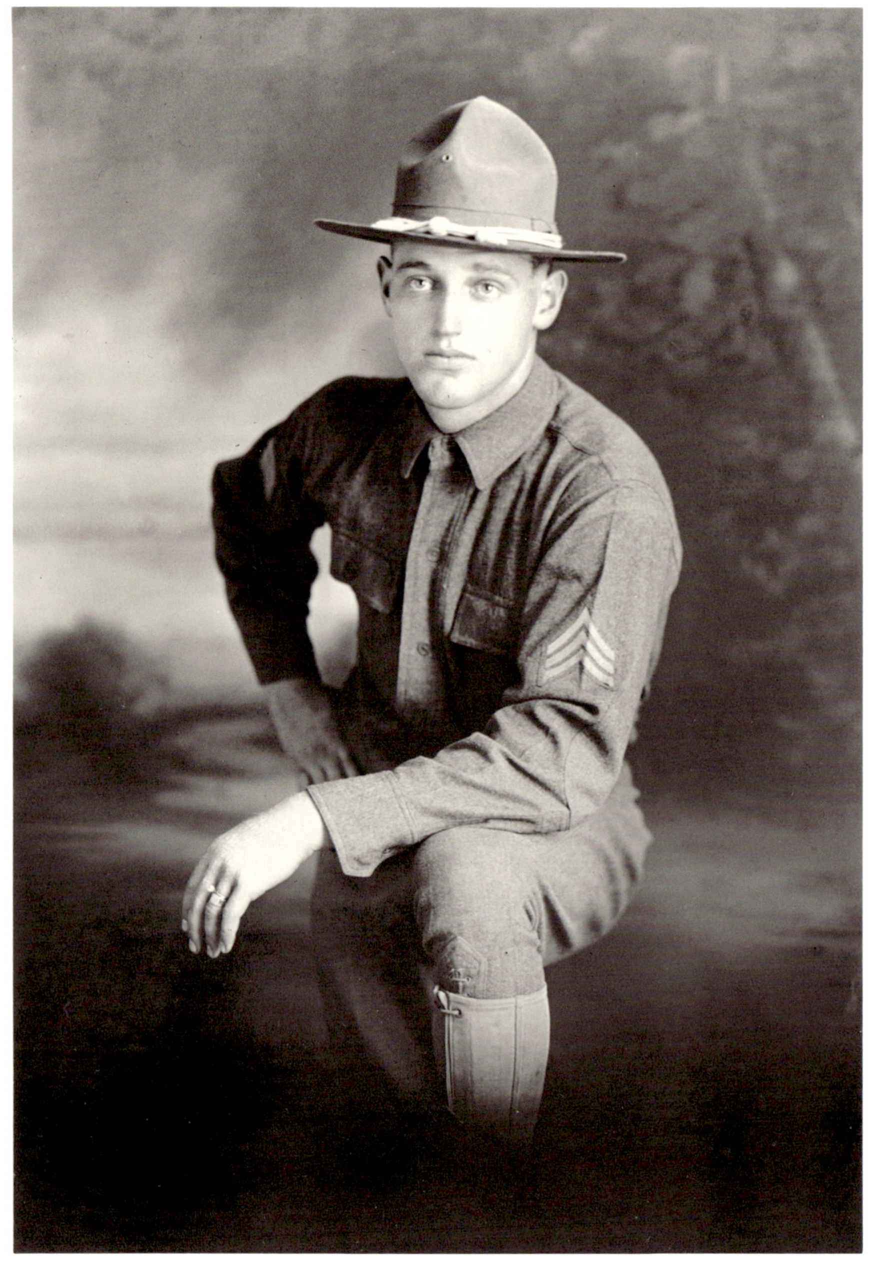

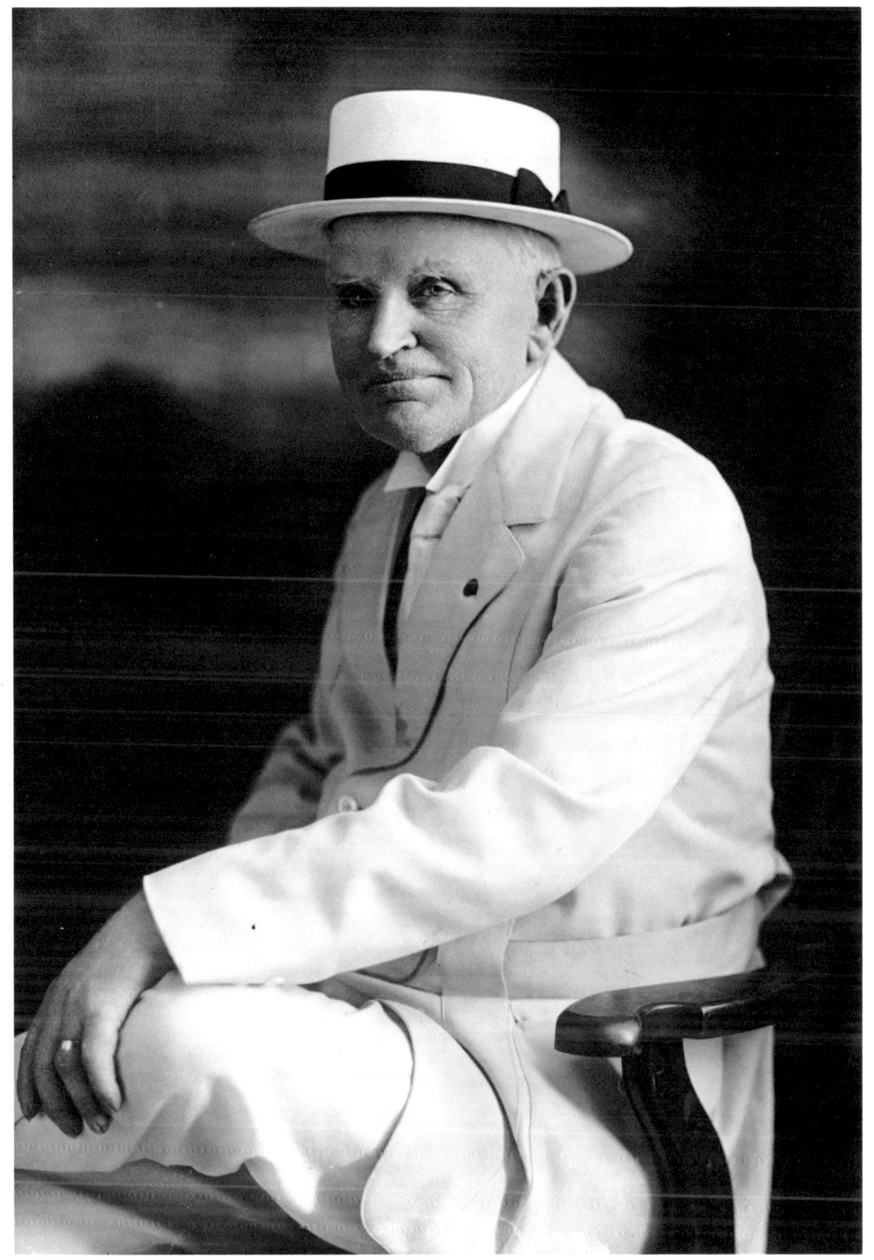

PLATE 94

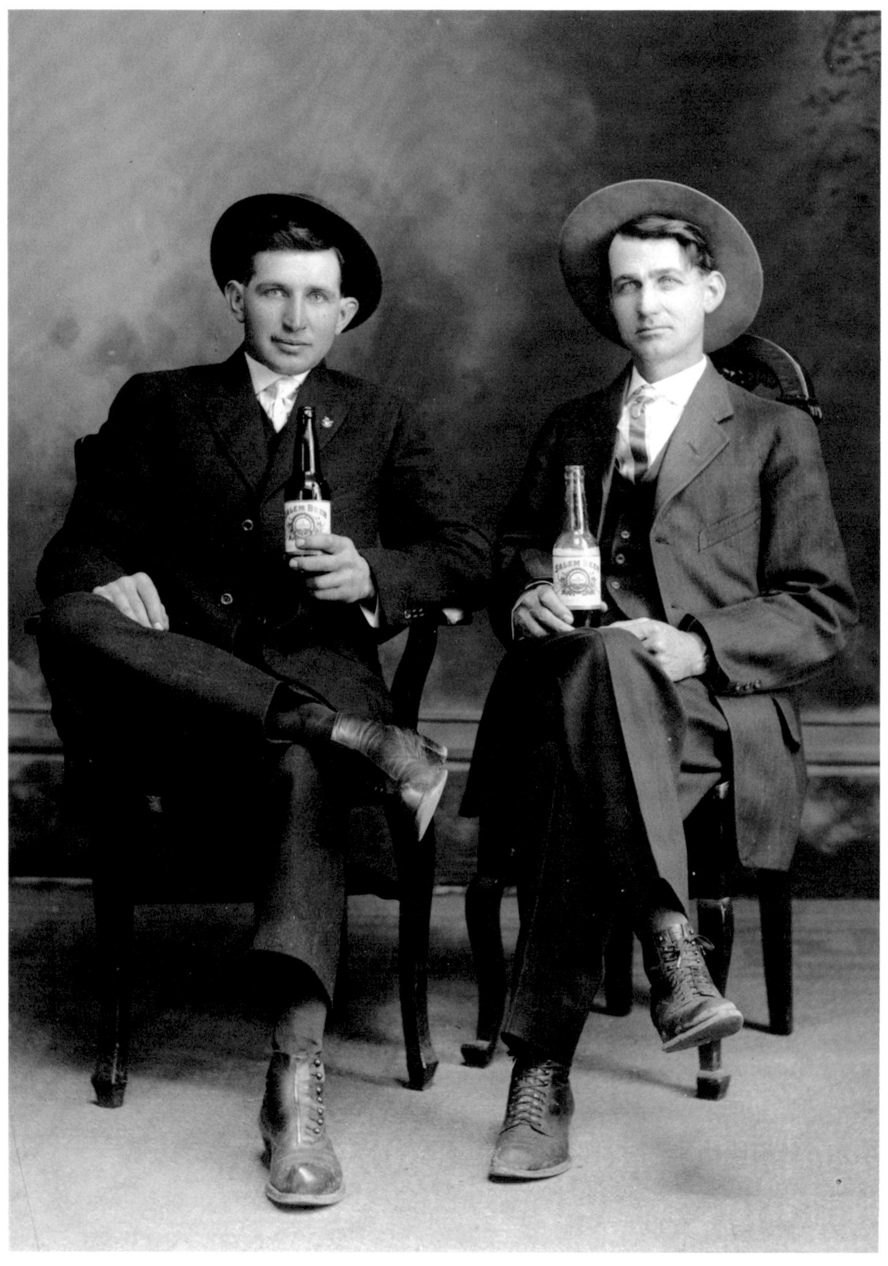

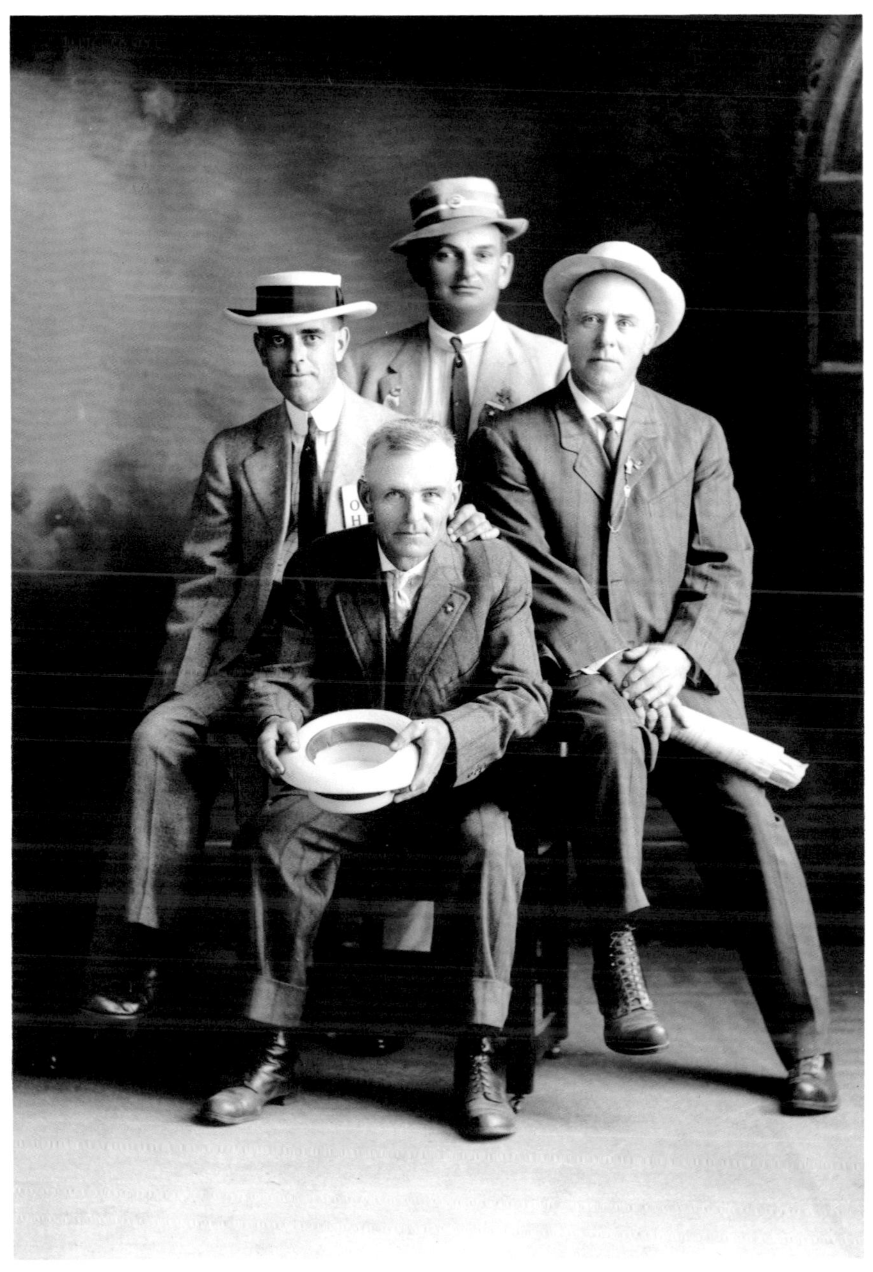

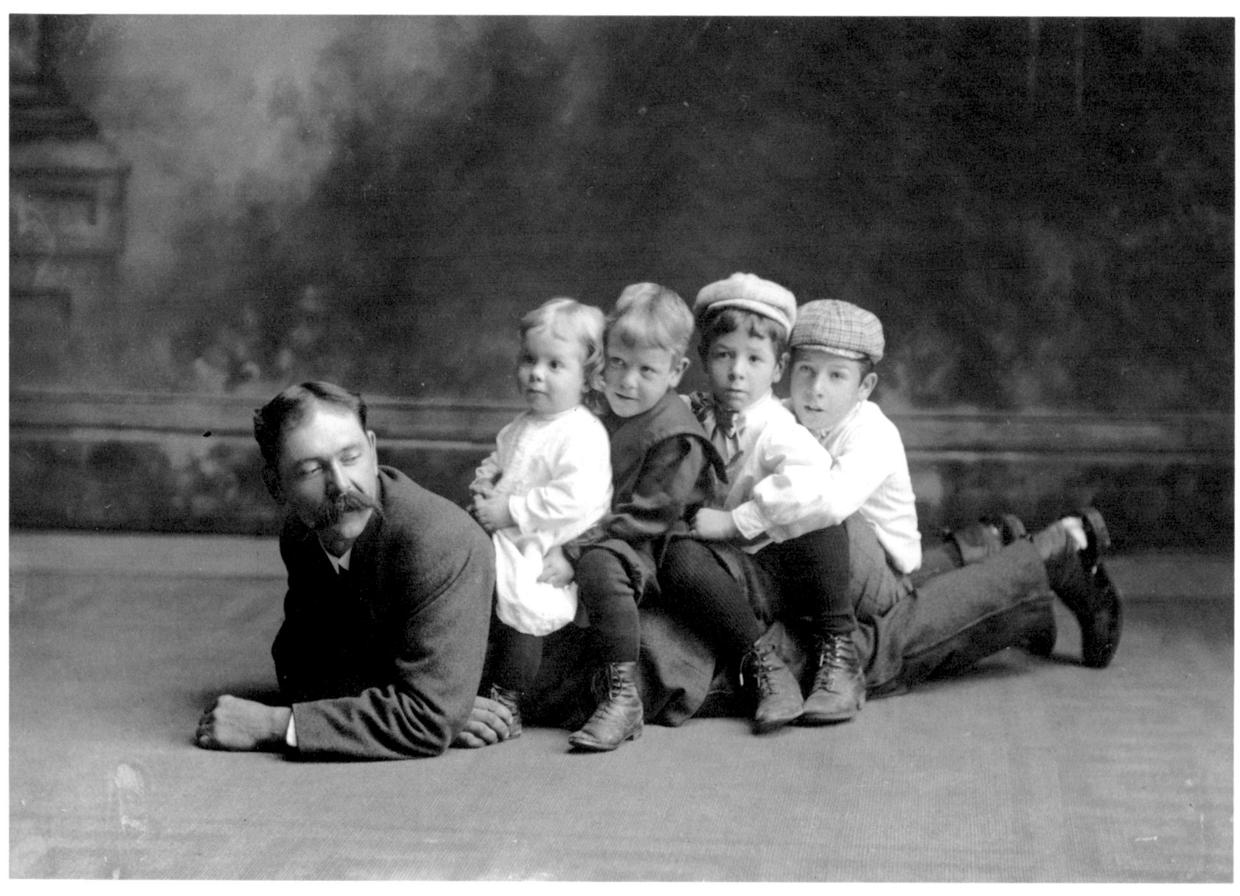

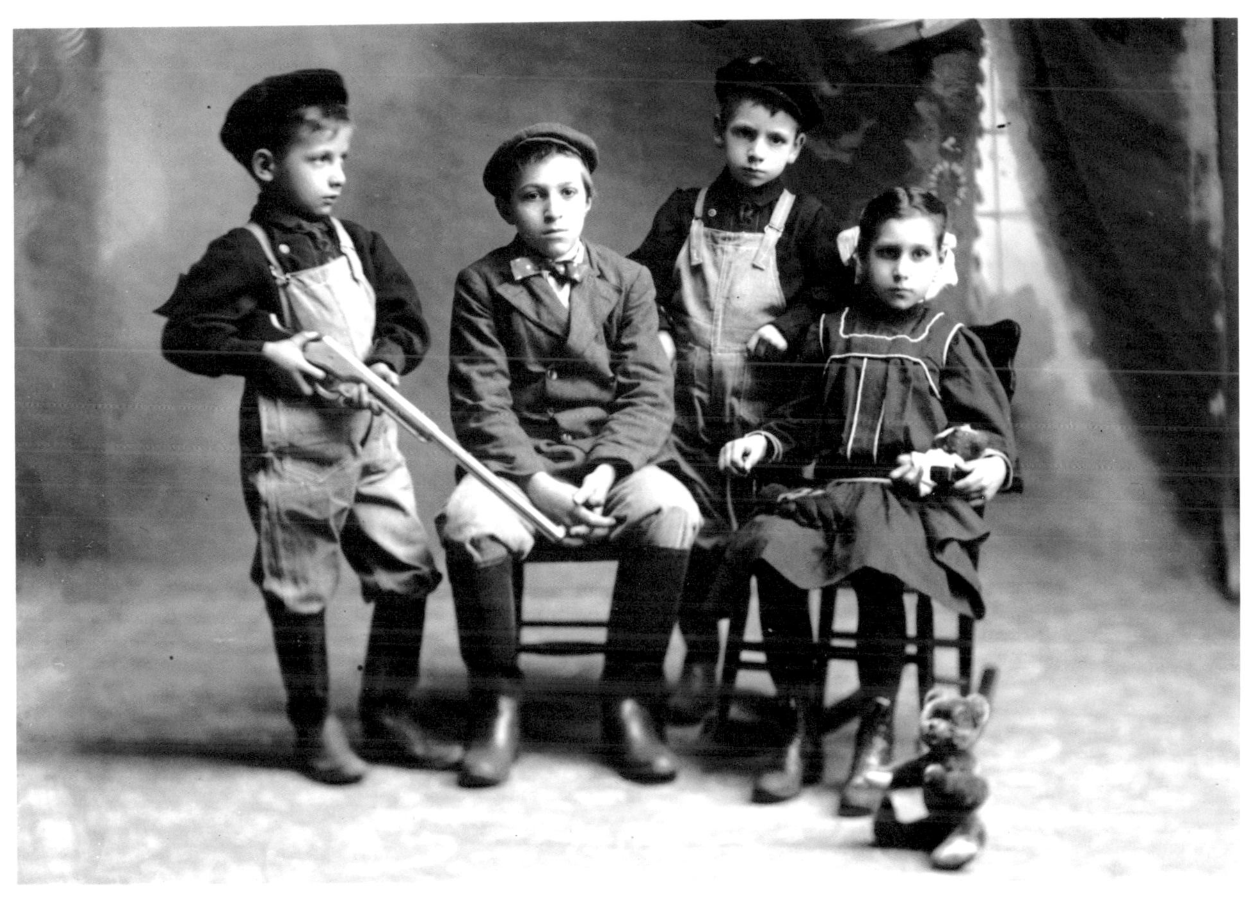

PLATE 98

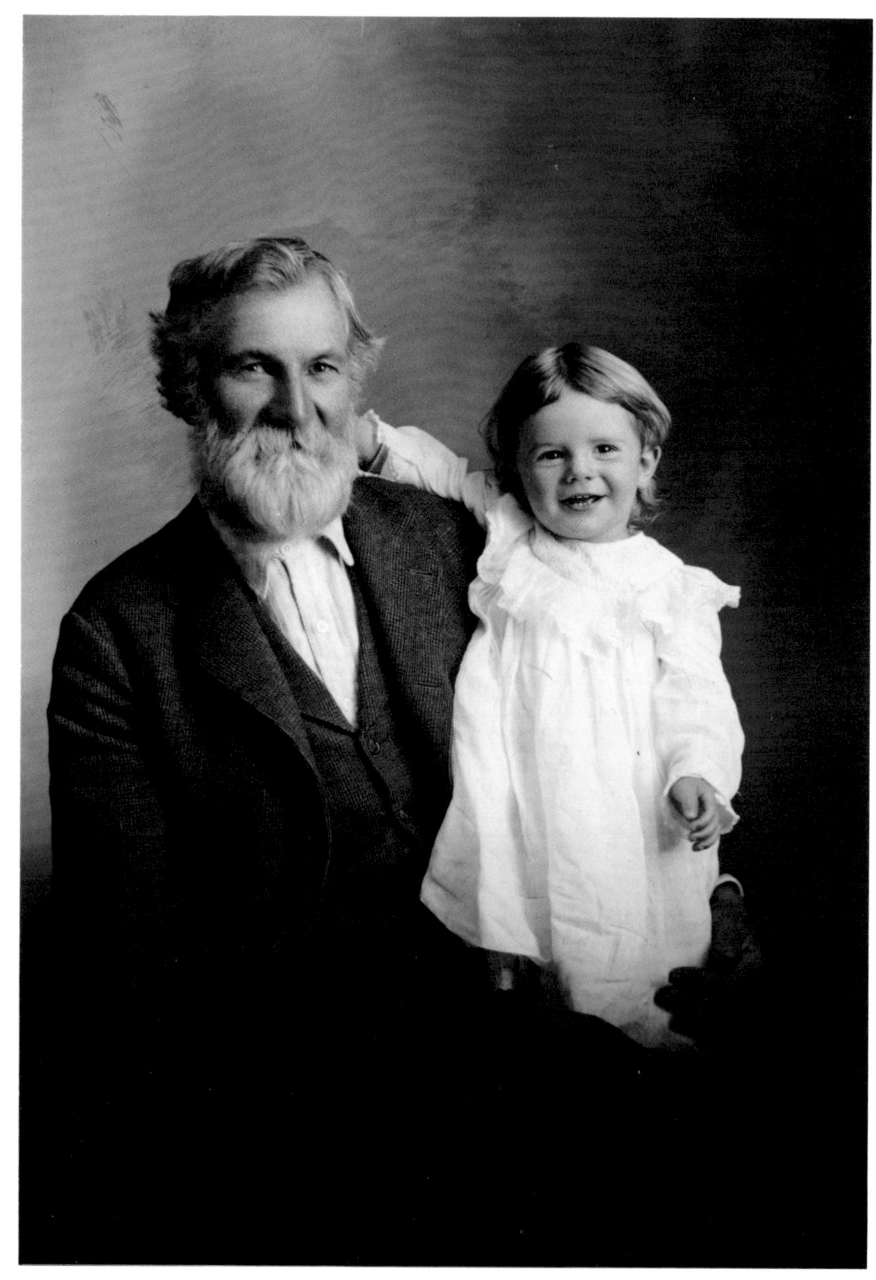

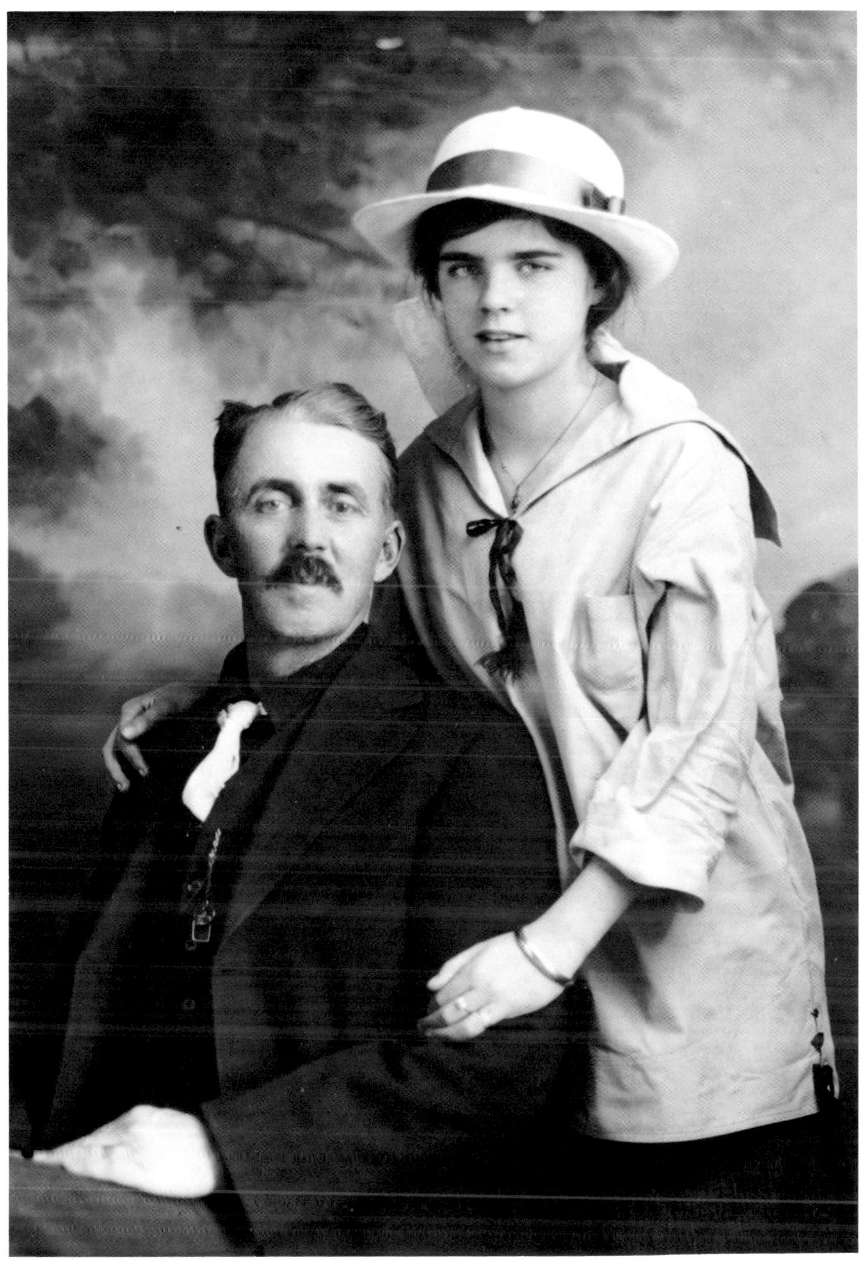

PLATE 100

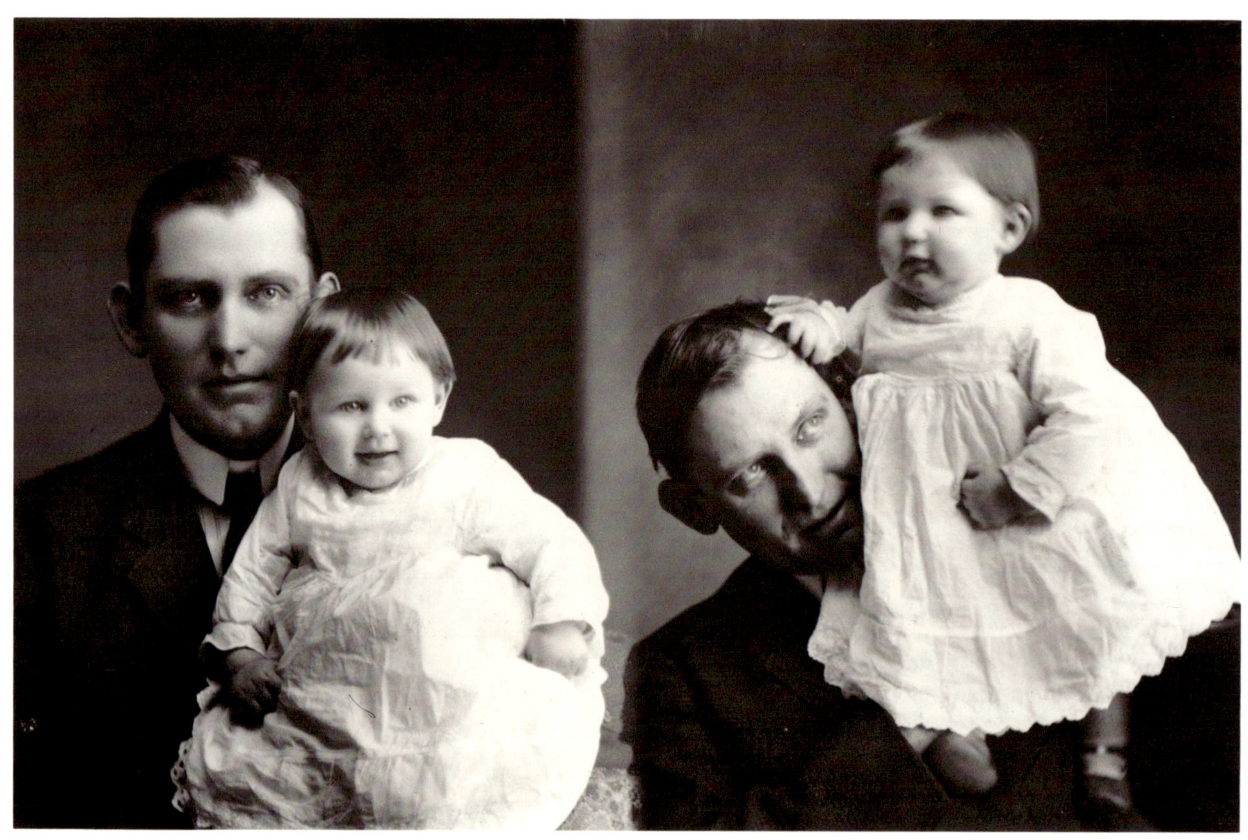

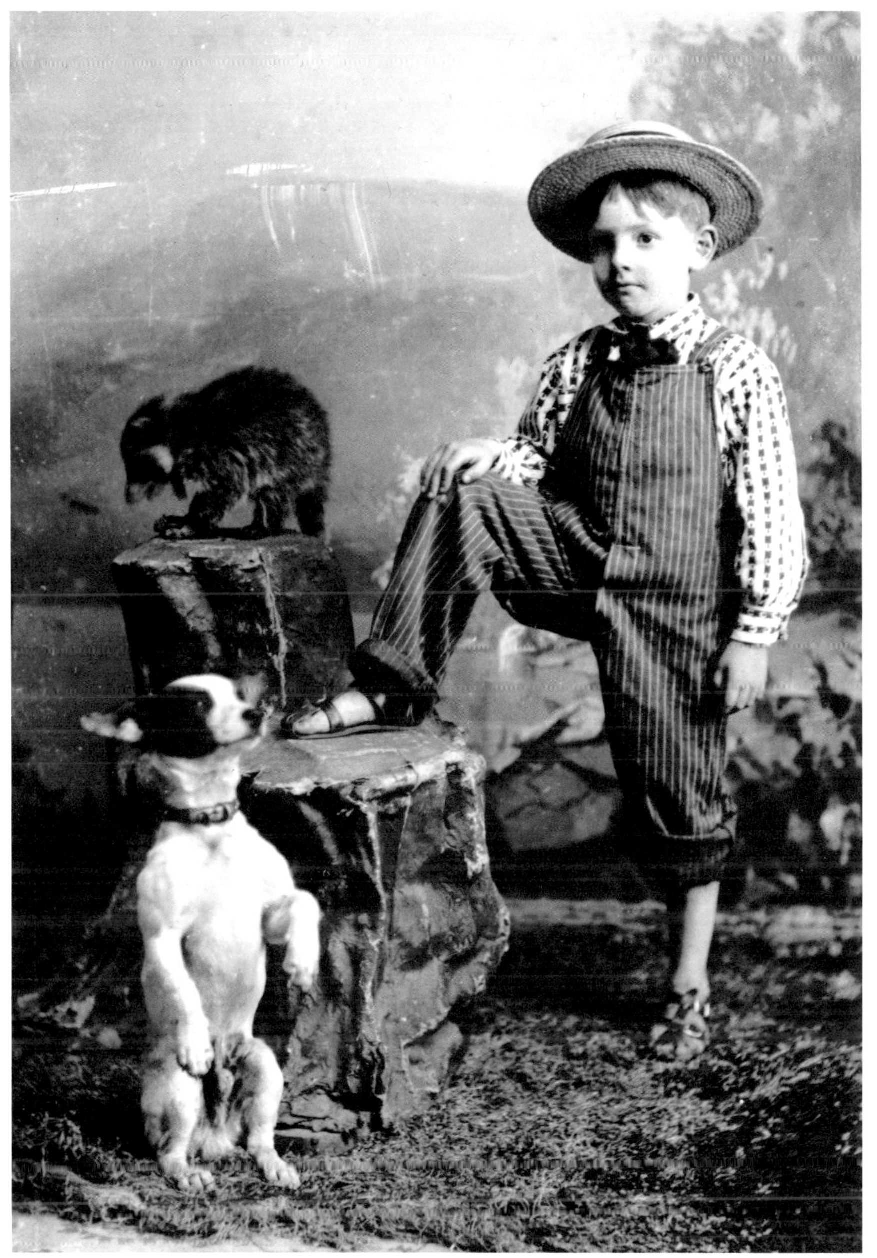

PLATE 102

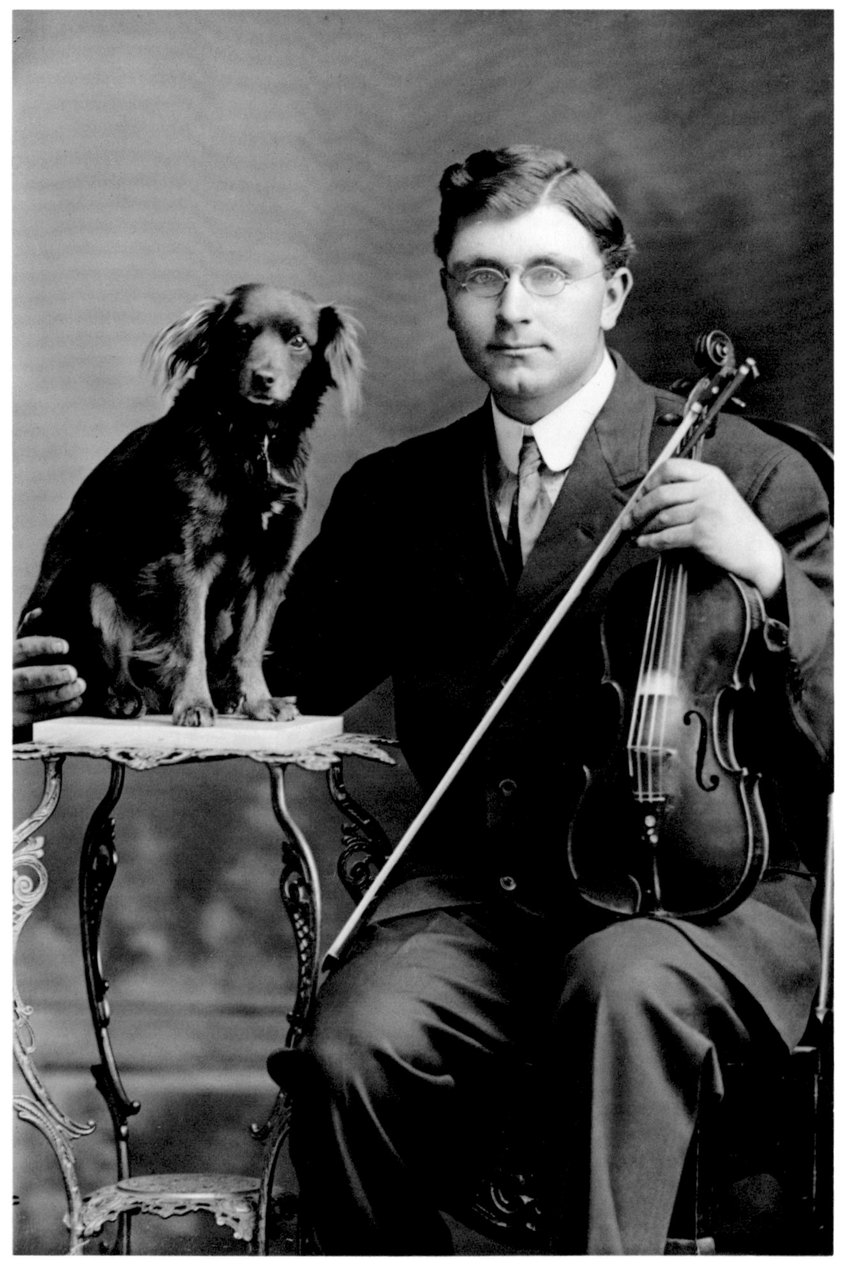

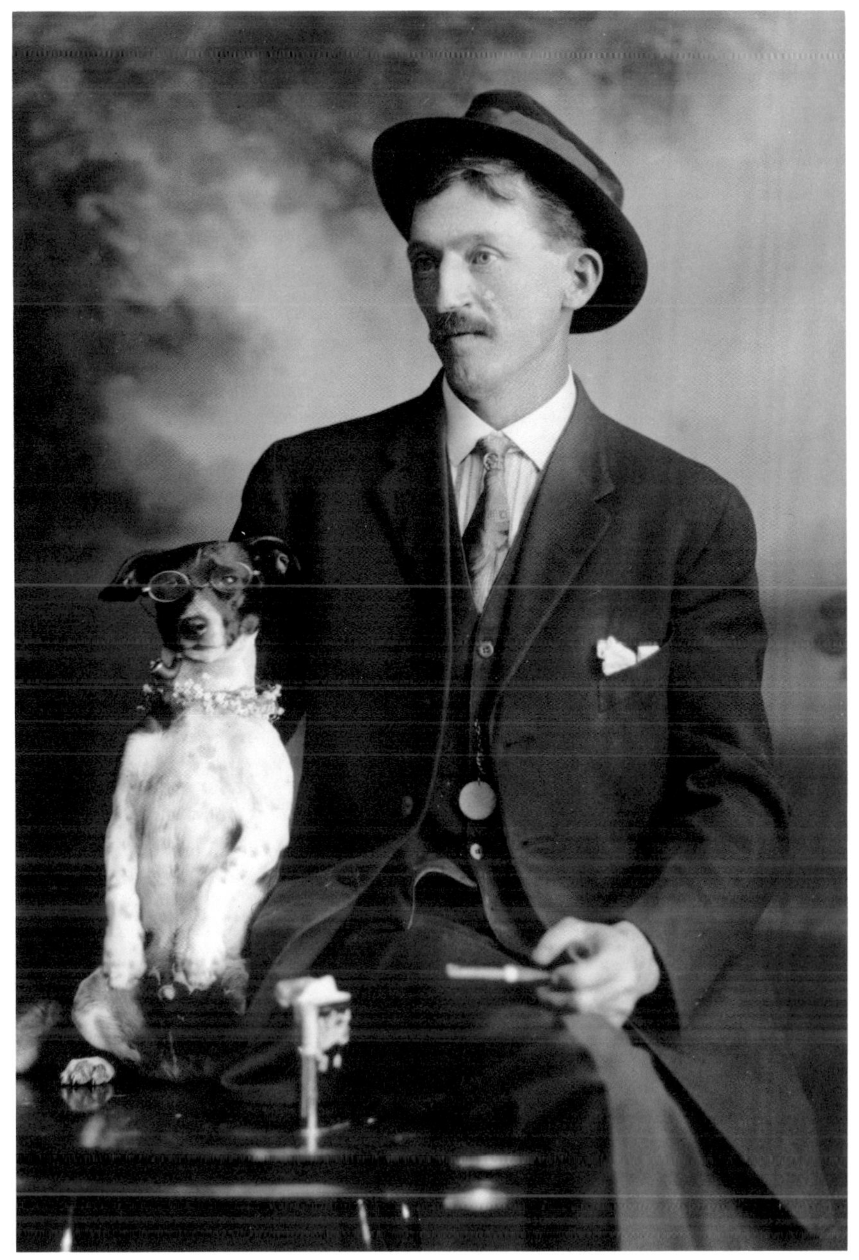

PLATE 104

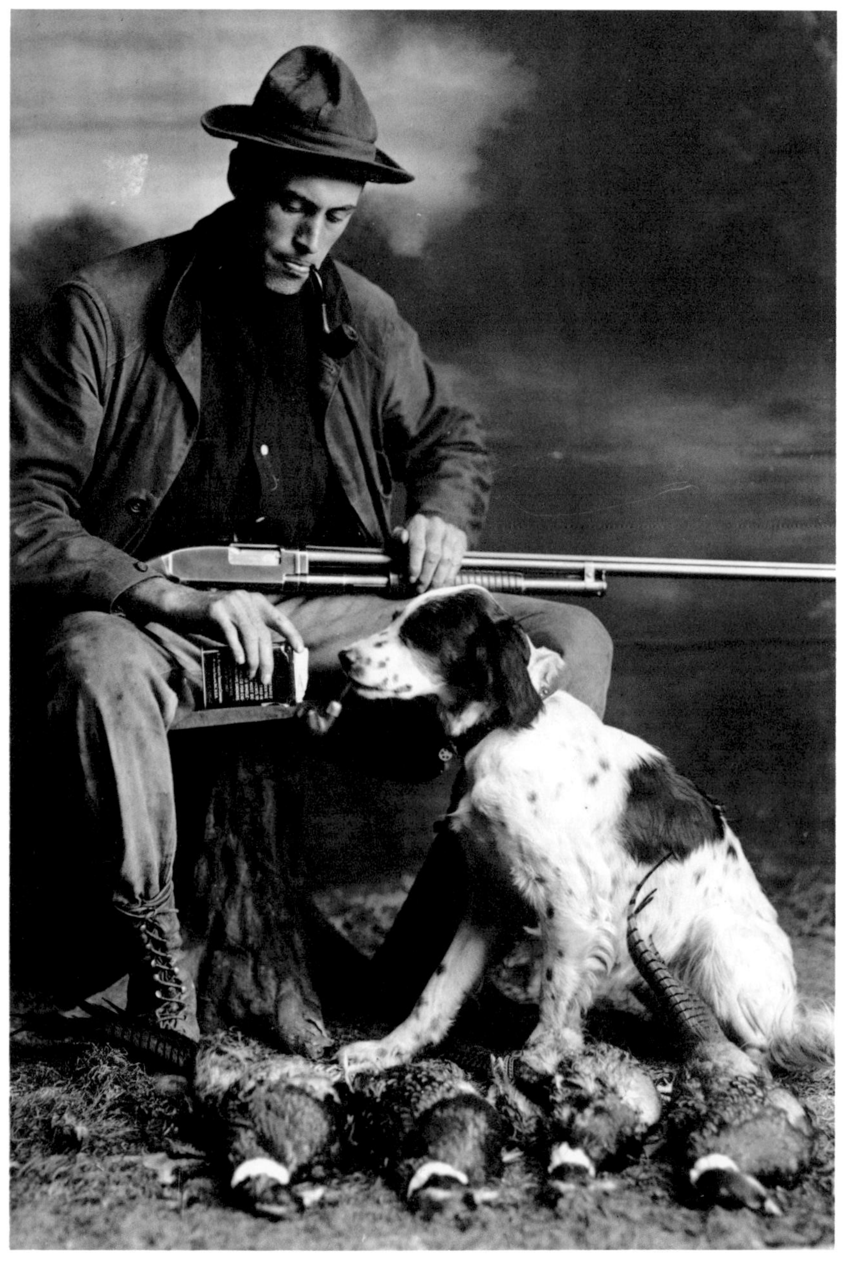

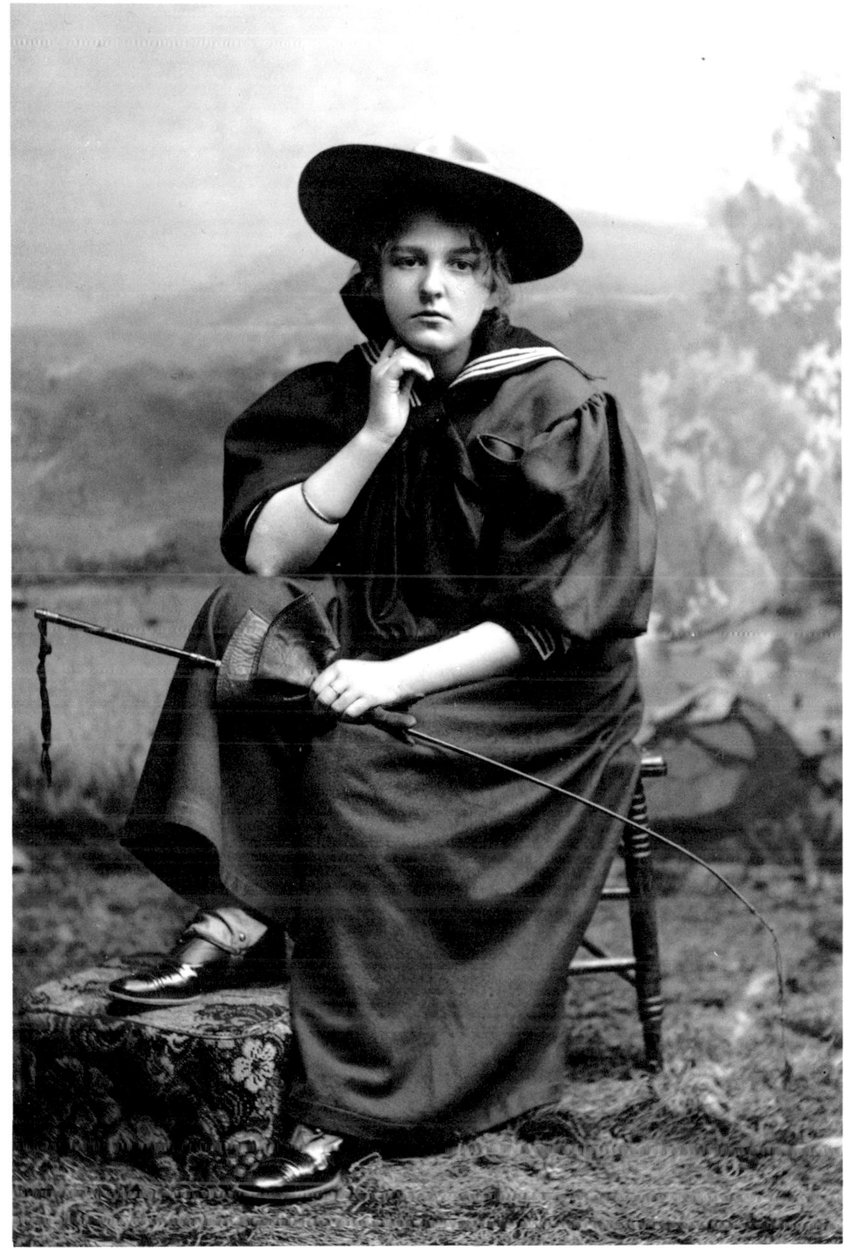

PLATE 106

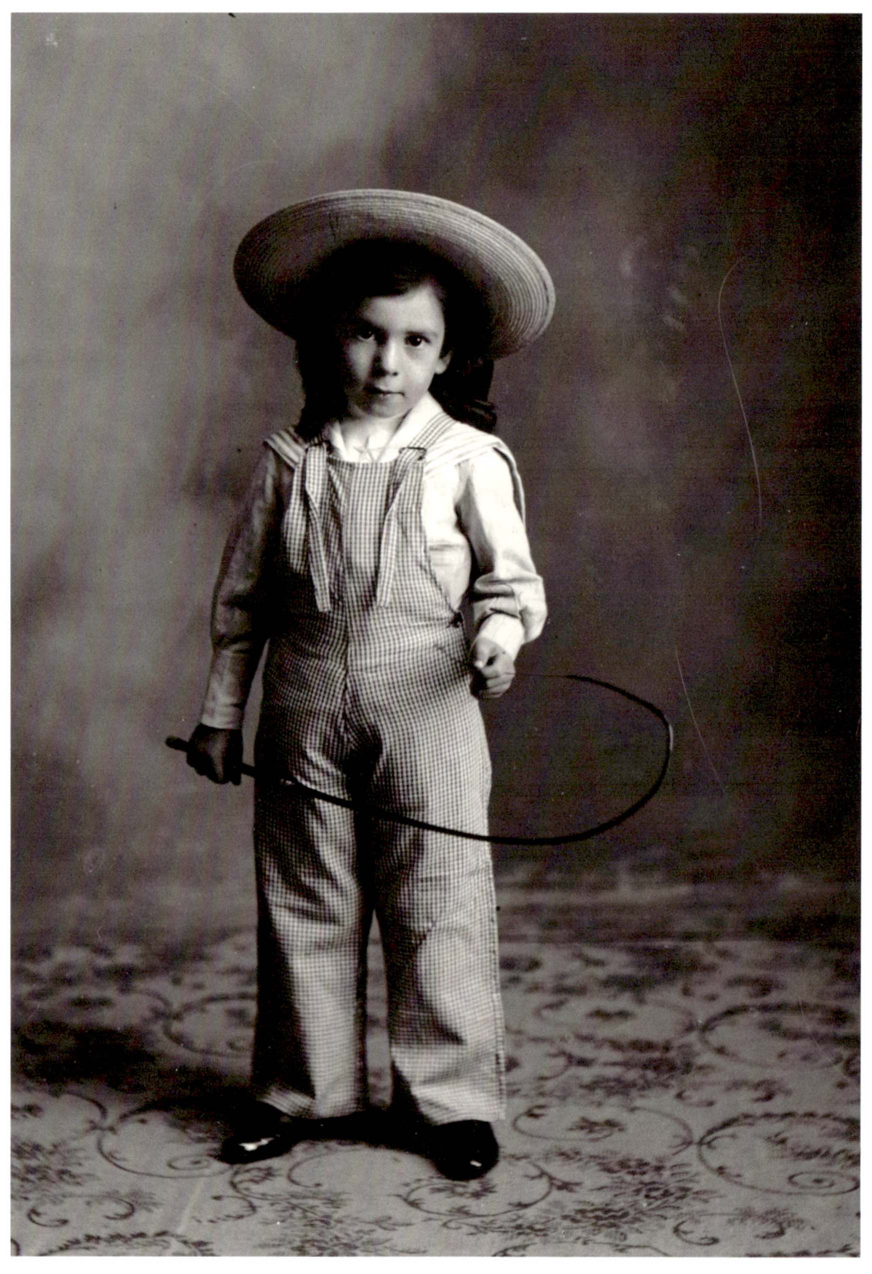

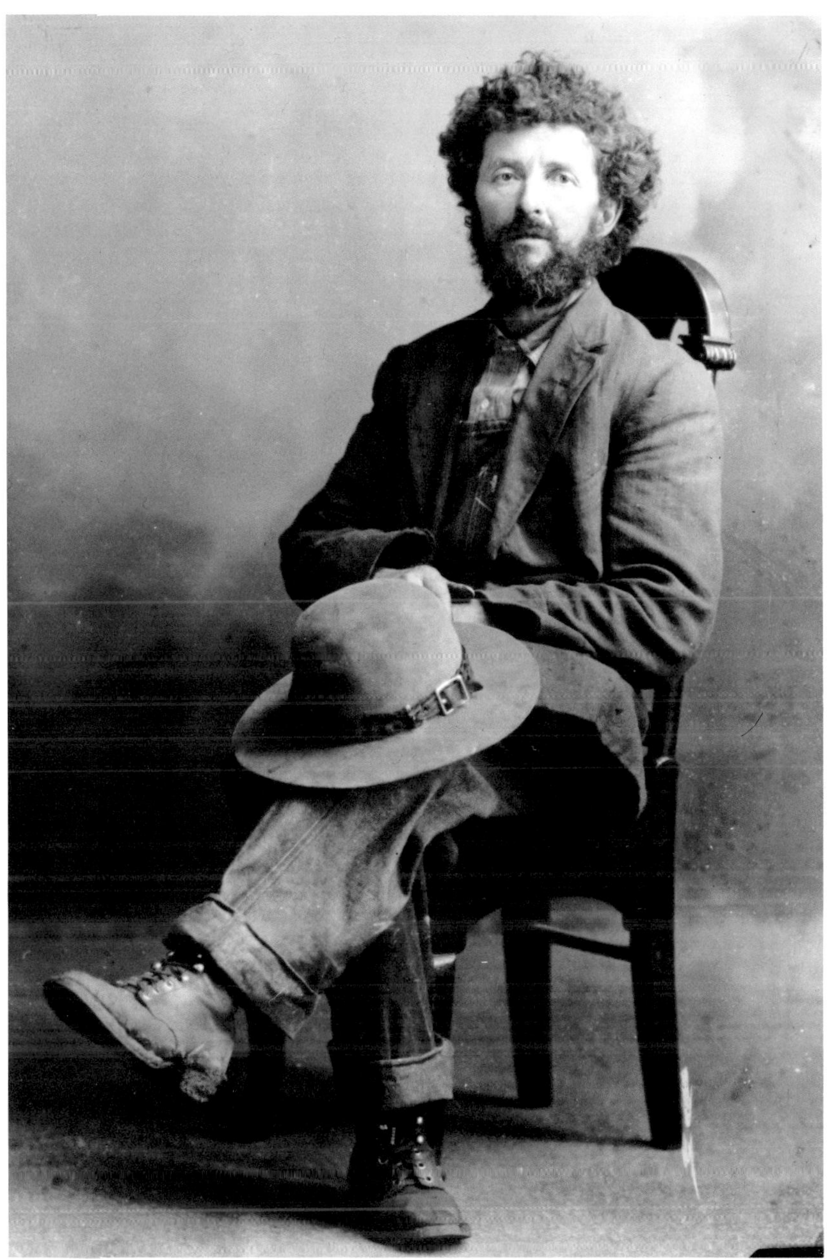

PLATE 108

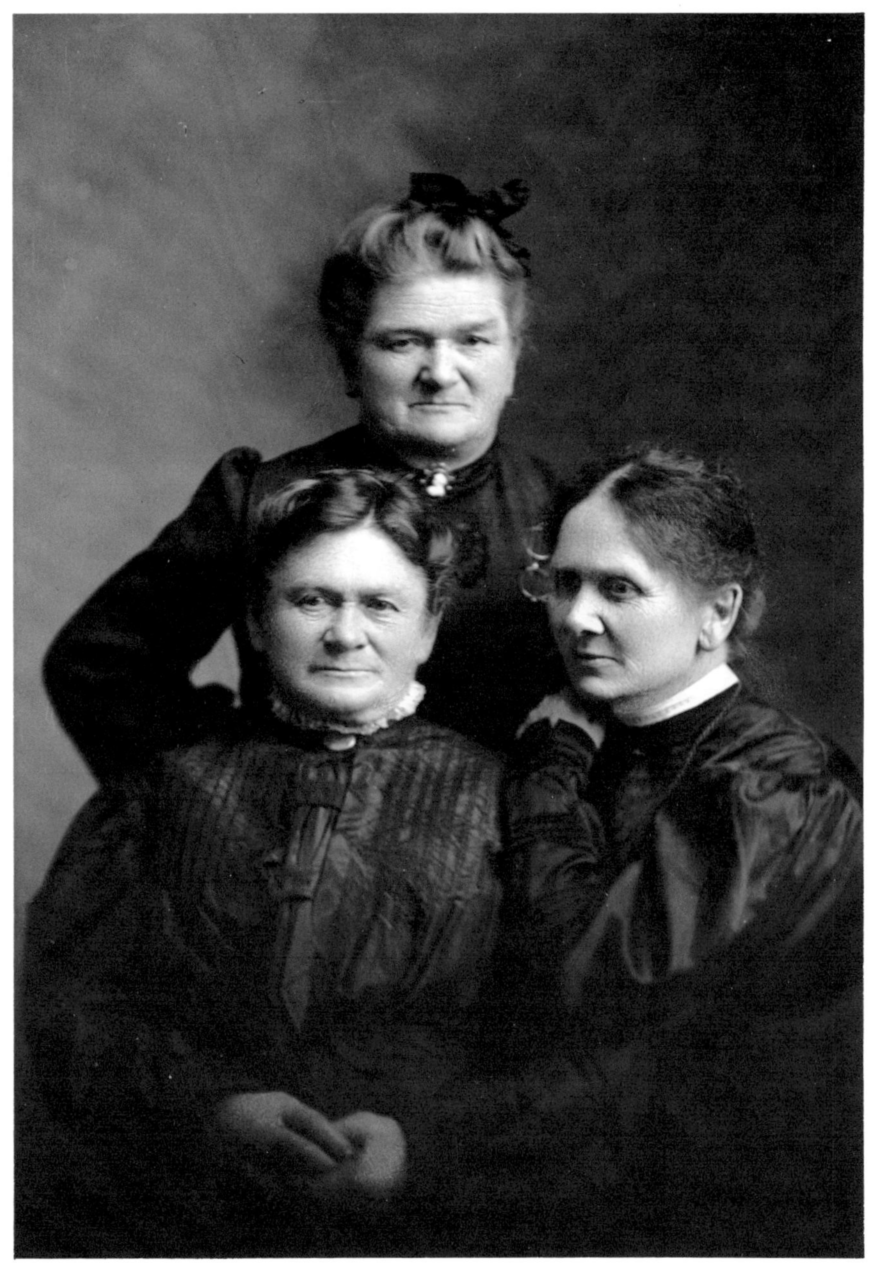

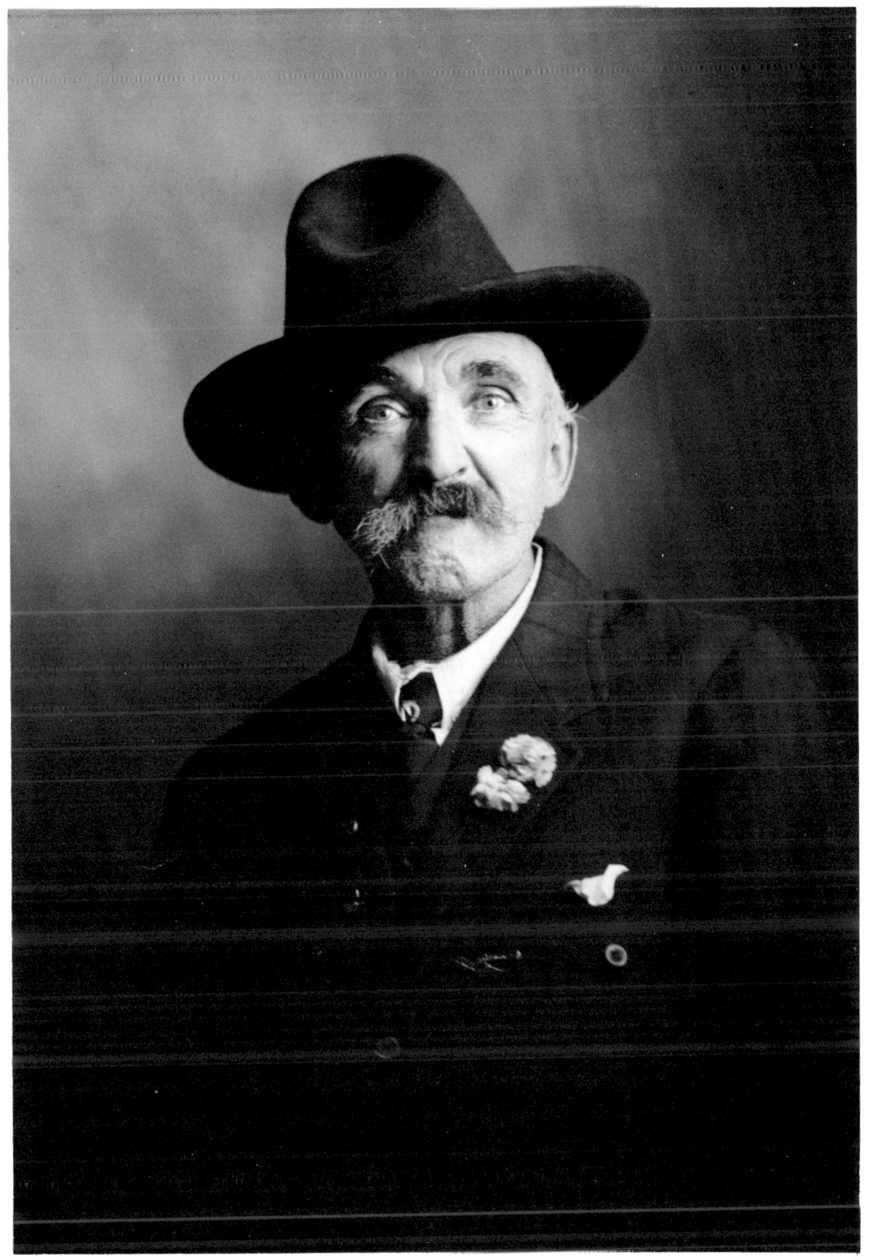

NOTES

The names and dates provided have been taken from Tom Cronise's studio registers that were received by the Oregon Historical Society with the negatives. This information has been supplemented by data from directories for Salem and Marion County to determine occupations and to verify spelling. Every effort has been made to supply exact dates. Because the registers list the name of the customer and not necessarily the name of the person photographed, certain assumptions regarding family relationships have been made, such as identifying young children as the offspring of the customer. All persons are from Salem unless otherwise noted.

Any assistance in positively identifying these portraits would be greatly appreciated.

The notes are listed by plate number.

1 Tong Hang
November, 1913

2 Miss F.M. Cerini (Oakland, California)
August 20, 1902

3 Paul H. Sroat, Capitol National Bank
March, 1903

4 Miss Anna Parker, binder, *Oregon Statesman*
August 17, 1902

5 Mrs. Ida M. Rollo
March, 1915

6 John Savage
October 15, 1903

7 Mr. and Mrs. E.M. Swafford
June 18, 1903

8 Mr. and Mrs. A.R. Rickard (Gervais, Oregon)
September, 1905

9 Mrs. Conrad Krebs
December 16, 1902

10 D. Armstrong
February, 1903

11 Child of Thomas C. Smith
December 11, 1903

12 John H. Albert, president Capitol National Bank
August 8, 1902

13 Representative Willis Kramer (Myrtle Creek, Oregon)
January, 1903

14 E.A. Devennis
October 6, 1903

15 Will Bachelor
October 13, 1902

16 May M. Cahpler, student, Willamette University (Salem, Oregon)
December 3, 1902

17 Lizette Fawk
1902
18 Pearl Hart, domestic and cook
September 28, 1903
19 Sons of Mr. and Mrs. Potter
June 1, 1902
20 Miss A. Mabel Branson, bookkeeper, Branson & Ragan, grocers, and Florence M. Laughead, student
July 12, 1902
21 Horace M. Sykes
March 25, 1905
22 Marie Thomason
December, 1915
23 W.G. Johnson
August 10, 1902
24 Nannelle Bloom, student and friend of Louise Cronise
January, 1911
25 Charles Chung
December 16, 1902
26 H. Martin Branson, Branson & Ragan, grocers
September 9, 1902
27 Daughter of Russell Catlin, Catlin & Linn, hops broker
November 22, 1902
28 Son of Claire Simeral (Macleay, Oregon)
June 28, 1902
29 William D. King, hostler, Gillian & Johnson, livery
July 12, 1902
30 Mrs. W.A. Carter (Gold Hill, Oregon)
June 12, 1902
31 W.H. Brown (residence unknown)
February, 1909
32 Emaline Shindler
December 14, 1902
33 I. Homer Van Winkle, assistant attorney general, state house, and child
October, 1911
34 G.H. Dodge and daughter
November 27, 1903
35 William H. Dalrymple, laborer, and family
September 22, 1908
36 Miss Leona Hirsch, daughter of Edward Hirsch, postmaster
August 7, 1902
37 Daughter of Edward J. Sauter, plasterer
August 31, 1903
38 Son of Robert Walsh, teacher, Willamette University
November 22, 1912
39 Hattie Grove (Chemawa, Oregon)
December 6, 1902
40 C. Douglas Jessup, hops broker
December 14, 1902
41 Mr. and Mrs. N.L. Taliafero (Natron, Oregon)
January, 1903
42 Hazel Riggs
September 13, 1903
43 Sam Chin (residence unknown)
July, 1906
44 Y. Takabatake
September, 1907
45 Luther S. Rowland, compositor, state printer, and family

August 15, 1903
46 T.J. Crabtree (Marion, Oregon) and friends
June 3, 1903
47 Harry Hiramatsu and friend
July 17, 1917
48 S. Wetmebi and friend
November, 1906
49 Officers of Woodsmen of the World
March, 1905
50 Harry Usui and friend
November, 1906
51 F.A. Moisan (Brooks, Oregon) and friend
July, 1910
52 Q. Granpe and friend (residences unknown)
June, 1912
53 W.O. Kendoll, clerk, R N. Morris, groceries and feed, and friend
September 3, 1913
54 Pricilla Lemon and friend (residences unknown)
January, 1914
55 Unidentified
November, 1914
56 Son of Thomas Ross (Chemawa, Oregon)
May 24, 1902
57 Daughter of Jack Ryan (residence unknown)
June 23, 1904
58 Son of Jacob H. Dunlap, starcher, Salem Steam Laundry
November 7, 1903
59 Son of Charlie Johns (residence unknown)
August, 1907
60 Child of S.E. Russell (Jefferson, Oregon)
March, 1903
61 Children of B. McGilchrist (Rosedale, Oregon)
May 21, 1903
62 Daughters of P.H. Magee (Turner, Oregon)
September 24, 1902
63 Wilbur Gordon Bennett (probably dressed as mascot for Cherry Fair)
July, 1912
64 Evelyn F. Reigelman, student, daughter of Jonathan G. (& Jennie) Reigelman, general blacksmith, carriage and wagon maker
December, 1913
65 J. Melvin Riggs, student, Willamette University
July 12, 1902
66 A.B. Hood (residence unknown)
February, 1915
67 Miss Zoe Stockton, daughter of James L. Stockton, dry goods
December 7, 1902
68 Unidentified student from Capitol Business College (Salem, Oregon)
July 11, 1902
69 William H. Perkins, student, Salem High School, son of William T. Perkins, chief clerk to state treasurer
May, 1908

70 Perkins and friend (residences unknown)
May, 1906

71 M.C. Meralo (residence unknown)
October, 1904

72 Mrs. J.J. Coyle (St. Paul, Oregon)
July, 1904

73 Emaline Shindler
March, 1903

74 Miss May McAdams
December 15, 1902

75 Charles W. Ranck, porter, Stanton & Schultz, barbers
December 26, 1908

76 Frederick R. Waters, clerk, G.E. Waters, wholesale and retail cigars, tobacco and smoker's articles
September 13, 1903

77 Mrs. Kate Hart (widow of John S.), nurse (residence unknown)
November 13, 1908

78 George E. Hatch, letter carrier, post office
May, 1912

79 Laura Koerner and friend (residences unknown)
February, 1905

80 James E. Ramey, attendant, Insane Asylum, and friend
June, 1912

81 J. Steelhammer, attendant, Insane Asylum
December 12, 1904

82 Mr. Watanabe
June 15, 1908

83 Tom Phillips (Chemawa, Oregon)
March 2, 1918

84 W.M. Derrick and friends
October 7, 1907

85 (a-d) Philip C. Patrick, bookkeeper, A.M. Patrick & Co., building materials, and friend
March, 1906

86 Unidentified
n.d.

87 Mrs. Church, wife of Gale W. Church, Carman Salem Street Railway
April 13, 1918

88 Cora Gilbert
December 16, 1910

89 Verna R. Cooder, clerk, F.W. Woolworth Co.
November, 1915

90 A.E. Pelker
April 1, 1913

91 Charles LeWitt (residence unknown)
September 12, 1904

92 Paul C. Maurer, son of Kate J. & John, proprietors, Pioneer Repair Shop and Garage
July 14, 1917

93 James L. Stockton, J.L. Stockton, dry goods, clothing, etcetera
August 4, 1917

94 George W. Wood (Turner, Oregon), Holt R. Miles and L.C. & G.W. Wood Brothers, livery, and friend
September, 1912

95 W. Scott Sawyer, proprietor Silverton Steam Laundry, and friend
July 12, 1912

96 Artemus Everett Bradley, electrician, with his children
September 8, 1911

97 Children of J.A. McLean
December, 1907

98 A.M. Holmes and child of Mrs. W.I. Lacey (Rickreall, Oregon)
July 26, 1904

99 S.W. Bradley and daughter
March, 1916

100 Mr. Brown and child (residence unknown)
February, 1906

101 Son of Mrs. Nealand (residence unknown)
July 18, 1905

102 Edgar B. Daugherty, laborer, Salem Sewer Pipe Co.
April, 1910

103 Oscar Bridges
May, 1916

104 A.J. Sweeney (residence unknown)
November 1, 1918

105 Louise Thompson, daughter of Sherman W. Thompson, jeweler
March, 1906

106 Child of Mr. and Mrs. Frances E. Shafer, harness dealer
August 22, 1904

107 Lee Cron, laborer
March, 1915

108 Mrs. Pugh, Mrs. Usafyes and her sister (residences unknown)
December 29, 1906

109 James R. Pierce, helper, Hotel Marion (Salem, Oregon)
November, 1913

COLOPHON

In *The Art Perfected* every effort has been made to reproduce with as much fidelity as possible the images made from the original glass plates in the Cronise Collection. To that end, the illustrations have been printed as 300-line duotones, the first color black, and the second a gray (modified by rubine red). Each illustration has been spot varnished to enhance the image. The text stock is 100# Optimum dull offset, and the binding is coated-oneside 80# Optimum dull cover stock. The pages are sewn for added quality.

The Art Perfected was typeset by Harrison Typesetting, Inc., in Compugraphic 12 on 15 point Kennerley, a typeface introduced in 1911 by one of America's premier designers Frederic W. Goudy. It is a Venetian typeface, akin to the early romans cast in Venice about 1500. It is noted for its capital G's spur and the high crossbar on the capital H. The companion italic face has a strong calligraphic quality. *The Art Perfected* was printed by Durham & Downey.

The Art Perfected was designed by Bruce T. Hamilton